THE EURO CRISIS
IN THE MEDIA

The Reuters Institute for the Study of Journalism at the University of Oxford aims to serve as the leading international forum for a productive engagement between scholars from a wide range of disciplines and practitioners of journalism. As part of this mission, we publish work by academics, journalists, and media industry professionals focusing on some of the most important issues facing journalism around the world today.

All our books are reviewed by both our Editorial Committee and expert readers.

EDITORIAL COMMITTEE

The Reuters Institute would like to acknowledge the assistance of Max Hanska-Ahy and Katrin Voltmer as editorial advisers on behalf of the Institute.

This publication arises from research funded by the John Fell Oxford University Press (OUP) Research Fund.

THE EURO CRISIS
IN THE MEDIA

JOURNALISTIC COVERAGE OF ECONOMIC
CRISIS AND EUROPEAN INSTITUTIONS

Edited by ROBERT G. PICARD

REUTERS
INSTITUTE for the
STUDY of
UNIVERSITY OF
OXFORD JOURNALISM

I.B. TAURIS
LONDON · NEW YORK

Published by I.B.Tauris & Co. Ltd in association with
the Reuters Institute for the Study of Journalism, University of Oxford

Published in 2015 by
I.B.Tauris & Co. Ltd
London • New York
www.ibtauris.com

0 6 JUN 2017

ISBN: 978 1 78453 059 4 (HB)
ISBN: 978 1 78453 060 0 (PB)
eISBN: 978 0 85772 905 7

A full CIP record for this book is available from the British Library
A full CIP record is available from the Library of Congress

Library of Congress Catalog Card Number: available

Typeset by Riverside Publishing Solutions, Salisbury SP4 6NQ
Printed and bound in Great Britain by TJ International Ltd. Padstow, PL28 8RW

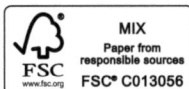

MIX
Paper from
responsible sources
FSC
www.fsc.org   FSC® C013056

Contents

Tables and Figures

Tables

Figures

Contributors

Ángel Arrese is Associate Professor of Economic and Business Journalism, and Director of the PhD Programme on Public Communication at the School of Communication, University of Navarra, Spain. He is author of *La identidad de The Economist* [The Economist's Identity] (1994), *Prensa Económica* [Economic and Financial Press] (2002), and *¿Interesa la economía? Economía, medios y ciudadanía* [Is Economics Interesting? The Economy, Media, and Citizens] (2011).

Giovanni Barbieri is Assistant Professor of Political Sociology at the University of Perugia, where he teaches Sociology of Globalisation. Recent publications include: *L'uomo comunitario nella società globalizzata* [The Communitarian Man and Globalised Society] (2010) and 'The Northern League in the "Red Belt" of Italy', *Bulletin of Italian Politics*, 4(2) (2012): 277–94.

Donatella Campus is Associate Professor of Political Science at the University of Bologna, where she teaches Political Science and Political Communication. She is the author of *Antipolitics in Power* (2010) and *Women Political Leaders and the Media* (2013).

Leen d'Haenens is Professor of Communication Science at the Institute for Media Studies at the University of Leuven, where she teaches Western media policy, media and diversity, and analysis of media texts. Her research interests include digital media and youth, news media, media and ethnic minorities, and Western media policy and governance mechanisms.

Timo Harjuniemi is a doctoral student of Media and Communication Studies at the University of Helsinki. His dissertation studies the media representations of the euro crisis.

Juha Herkman is Academy Research Fellow of Media and Communication Studies at the University of Helsinki. He is the author of seven monographs. His recent publications have appeared in *Media, Culture and Society, Javnost – The Public,* and *Convergence: The International Journal of Research into New Media Technologies.*

Nicolas Hubé is Associate Professor of Political Science at the University Paris 1 Panthéon-Sorbonne and a visiting professor at the Europa Universität Viadrina (Francfort/Oder, Germany). He teaches European Studies, political sociology, and comparative political communication. He is the co-author of *Perceptions of Europe: A Comparative Sociology of European Attitudes* (2011) and *'Design is Content': On Tabloizidation of the French Quality Newspaper Journalism* (2014).

Willem Joris is a PhD student at the Institute for Media Studies at the University of Leuven. His current research interests include news framing analysis, media policy, and public management.

Hans Mathias Kepplinger is Professor (Em.) of Communications Research at the Johannes Gutenberg University of Mainz. He has been a research fellow at the University of California, Berkeley and Harvard University, guest professor at several universities, among them Munich, Tunis, Zurich, and Lugano. His research interests include the relationship between media performance and performance of political systems.

Christina Köhler is a research assistant at the Department of Communication at the Johannes Gutenberg University of Mainz and is pursuing her doctoral degree in Communications Studies. Her research activities focus on issues in the context of political and economic communication as well as information processing during media exposure.

Paolo Mancini is Professor at the Department of Political Science, University of Perugia. His research focuses mostly on political communication in a comparative dimension. Mancini's major publications include *Comparing Media Systems: Three Models of Media and Politics* (with Dan Hallin), which won the 2005 Goldsmith Book Award from Harvard University, the 2005 Diamond Anniversary Book Award of the National Communication Association, and the 2006 Outstanding Book Award of the International Communication Association.

Marco Mazzoni is Associate Professor at the Department of Political Science, University of Perugia. His research interests include popularisation of politics and the effects of mass media. His recent work appears in *Journalism, European Journal of Communication, International Journal of Cultural Studies,* and *Perspectives on European Politics and Society.*

Heinz-Werner Nienstedt is Professor for Media Management in the Department of Communication at the Johannes Gutenberg University of Mainz. He studied Economics and received his PhD in Econometrics. For 20 years he held leading positions in international media companies. His main research is in the field of media markets and marketing.

Robert G. Picard is North American Representative for the Reuters Institute, University of Oxford. He was previously Director of Research at the Institute and directed the project that undertook the research for this book. He is Hamrin Professor of Media Economics at Jönköping International Business School, Sweden. He is the author and editor of 28 books and has been editor of the *Journal of Media Business Studies* and the *Journal of Media Economics.*

Senja Post is a post-doc researcher at the University of Zurich. In 2012, she completed her PhD at the Johannes Gutenberg University of Mainz with a dissertation on journalists' and scientists' criteria of truth. In 2007, she completed her master's degree in Mainz with a thesis on German climate change communication.

Liina Puustinen is a researcher in Media Studies at the University of Helsinki. Her research interest areas include consumer culture, advertising, and media audiences. She has also published on audiences' trust in the media, and she is currently working on representations of economy in the media.

Oliver Quiring is Professor for Communication Science at the Department of Communication, Johannes Gutenberg University of Mainz. His research interests include economic reporting, digital media and social communication.

Susana Salgado is Research Fellow and Professor of Political Communication at the Institute of Social Sciences, University of Lisbon.

Previously, she also worked at the Reuters Institute for the Study of Journalism, University of Oxford. Her most recent publications include the books *The Internet and Democracy Building in Lusophone African Countries* (2014) and *Presidential Candidates: Construction of Images and Discourses in the Media* (2010, in Portuguese).

Lennart Schneider received his Bachelor in Communication Studies and now attends the master's programme 'Media Management' at the Johannes Gutenberg University of Mainz, where he also works as a student research assistant at the Department of Communication.

Katarzyna Sobieraj is a doctoral researcher at the University of Wrocław, Poland. Her research interests include media discourse, political communication, political campaigns, EU policy, and foreign affairs. She currently lives in Brussels and works as an assistant in the European Parliament.

Alfonso Vara is Head of the Media Management Department at the School of Communication, University of Navarra (Spain), where he teaches as Assistant Professor of Economics, Financial Journalism, and Media Management. He is the author or co-editor of several books and papers, including among others *Fundamentos de periodismo económico* [Fundamentals of Economic Journalism] (2011) and *Economía básica para comunicadores* [Economics for Journalists] (2013).

1

Understanding the Crisis

Robert G. Picard

The euro crisis produced the most significant challenge to European integration in 60 years by testing the structures and powers of the European Union and the eurozone and by threatening the common currency. Although the crisis is identified by a singular term, it was actually a group of interrelated economic crises that exacerbated fundamental differences in the EU and called into question its governance and common identity. The financial and political emergency was shaped by financial problems in the banking sector, national fiscal policies, and sovereign debt incurred by eurozone nations. Although those short- and mid-term challenges have now been partially addressed, the European and the global economies are still enduring the longer-term effects of the events and political divisiveness created by the crisis. These were evident in the 2014 elections to the European Parliament in which opponents to a strong EU garnered notable support and gained significant voices in the Parliament.

European news coverage since the emergence of the crisis in 2008 has played a central role in shaping public perceptions of the crisis and public reactions to the responses of policy makers. It has created highly mediated portrayals of Europe, European institutions, EU members and the euro, and Europeanness itself. The lenses provided by news organisations across Europe affected public understanding of the developments, their causes, the responsibilities for addressing the crisis, and the roles and effectiveness of European institutions, and these portrayals have significant implications for European identity and integration.

Coverage of Europe and its institutions has been criticised as highly limited, elite oriented, and subordinate to national institutions and politics (Lloyd and Marconi, 2014; Meyer, 2005; Trenz, 2004). Assessing European news coverage presents particular challenges because European-wide news media effectively do not exist and coverage of European institutions and issues is refracted through the prisms of national media or English-language business papers and specialist journals that are read across borders. Europeans are thus provided with national frames from which news is constructed and perceived (Bryant and Oliver, 2008; Kopper, 2007; Scheufele and Tewksbury, 2007; Weaver, 2007). These national frames tend to emphasise domestic interests and address common European interests as secondary.

In doing so, news media rely on national leaders, symbols, and places in order to give an often inattentive audience some connection to the stories told. If it is true that all politics is local, so are all news media. Consequently, previous research has shown most coverage of Europe is routed through the perspectives of political and economic institutions of individual European member states (Adam, 2007; Gattermann, 2013; Machill et al., 2006; Trenz, 2004). The means and extent to which this coverage takes place is influenced by the national culture of journalism, so some media will do more than others in covering the EU and its institutions as a centre of power. There is some evidence that news has been somewhat more Europeanised in some media than in the past (Meyer, 2005; Peter et al., 2003).

The adequacy of the accounts news enterprises provide on major matters concerning citizens of Europe, how they attempt to make these interesting to a broad range of people, and how varied are the views on issues of the day, is crucial. The grand, enduring themes they convey about the EU and the European states are fundamental to understanding the development of the EU in the minds of its member states and citizens.

The analyses in this book address the challenges posed by news coverage of the euro crisis. They explore how the European press addressed those issues, and the implications of that coverage for understanding Europe, its institutions and relations within the EU between 2010 and 2012, and its future development. That period of time was selected for the analysis because it marked a period of intense European scrutiny, action, and discussion of the crisis that informed previous and subsequent policy.

The scope and scale of the crisis produced opportunities for it to be framed and interpreted in multiple ways across Europe and for those descriptions to compete for attention and acceptance by the public and policy makers. Multiple factors influenced that coverage, yet little comparative work has been undertaken to understand their influence on the press in different countries and ultimately the views of the crisis presented to the citizens of member states and Europe as a whole. Political and communication theory indicate that news coverage is shaped by opinions of domestic and international elites, leading news providers, and variations in national media systems and journalistic cultures. Such differences would be expected to produce differences in information and understanding of the crisis and perspectives on potential responses to the crisis across Europe. This book explores those factors and what the coverage tells us about perceptions of Europe and European institutions and the range, limits, and spheres of European political debate. It also addresses the adequacy of existing explanations for understanding the influences of media on public opinion and political action when multiple sovereign states and multinational governance are involved.

The central questions are how debates take place and are framed in the press and the extent to which domestic and European debate takes place.

What is the crisis about?

Before addressing the coverage, it is important that the context of the euro crisis be fully understood. The causes are complex, involving multiple European and national economic and political factors related to fiscal and monetary policies and structural abilities to influence those policies (Noord and Székely, 2011). Weakened banks and flawed banking systems, national sovereign debt and budgetary challenges, loss of confidence in government policy, and an emphasis on national rather than European political interests have all been shown to contribute to its development and response (Authers, 2012; Bastasin, 2012; Beblevý et al., 2011; Lapavitsas, 2012).

The proximate issues changed as the crisis unfolded and developed over time. In its initial stages, European banks and financial institutions suffered from the effects of generous domestic lending policies and then from the subprime mortgage crisis in the US because many had invested in derivatives of those mortgages. Local housing bubbles in countries such as Ireland or Spain only made the situation worse. This destabilised banks, leading to bank failures and weaknesses and – despite state support for banks and nationalisation of weak banks – credit became harder to obtain, leading to a decline in production and consumption that pushed Europe into a recession. The national economies of a number of southern European countries soon became the focus of the crisis because the recession reduced governmental income and they lost the ability to service sovereign debt that had grown because they had fiscal policies that spent public funds well in excess of state revenues. Sovereign debt is money borrowed by countries, often to pay for construction of infrastructures and public buildings, but also to pay for government costs when tax revenues do not provide sufficient income. Southern European states had essentially expended all their abilities to borrow funds and could not maintain their existing budgets and debt structure.

States can use monetary policies to ameliorate the effects of such debt and revenue challenges by devaluing their currencies. This was not possible during the crisis because Greece, Italy, and Spain – the three largest countries with sovereign debt issues – had all adopted the euro. As they could not control monetary policy for the euro because it was used in 18 eurozone countries, the nations with sovereign debt issues were denied a traditional mechanism through which a state can influence its economy. The problems of the countries with sovereign debt issues did not remain in those countries, but spilled over to the entire eurozone, reducing global confidence in the euro currency, decreasing its exchange value, and pushing the economic effects onto other countries that used the euro but whose fiscal policies were more conservative.

Fundamental questions about the nature of the crisis existed during the crisis and remain salient today. It was debated whether the crisis was driven by externally economic and financial causes, national policies, the currency, structural conditions of the EU, or other factors. Even the beginning point of the crisis remains obscure because of contested views on its cause(s). Some argue it began with subprime mortgages in the US, housing bubbles in a number of countries, weak banking regulation, sovereign debt, government manipulation of economic data, and other factors. This volume is not intended to definitively answer those questions, but rather to reveal how news coverage in European nations addressed such competing interpretative frames and the implications for public opinion, and what public responses they suggested to the crisis.

Who are the players and what do they do?

The effects of the developments brought a number of European institutions into play, notably the European Commission and the European Central Bank (ECB), and it induced major eurozone countries to take action to protect the euro and their own economies and to stabilise the countries with sovereign debt issues through loans and compulsory introduction of austerity measures. A wide variety of institutions and individuals came to play roles in the crisis. Most had official positions, but some thrust themselves or were thrust into leadership positions addressing the crisis even when they were not institutionally placed to do so. Understanding their roles is fundamental in comprehending the news coverage of the crisis and its impact.

National governments played an important role in responding to the crisis, but most of the response was initially at the executive level, which then pushed parliaments to accept and implement policy responses. The European Commission, the executive of the EU, struggled to find a way to react because it had never faced such a significant challenge, lacked many powers of executive branches in member states, and its leadership was constrained.

National central banks and the ECB were active in the crisis. Central banks are national institutions that manage a country's currency, money supply based on the nation's monetary policy, and interest rates, and supervise the reserves and support liquidity of retail and commercial banks operating in the country. The powers of central banks of countries with the euro as their currency are limited because they cannot control monetary policy at the domestic level, even though they still have significant regulatory and interest rate influences. The ECB is an institution of the EU that acts as the central bank for the euro and implements monetary policy across states that use the euro as their currency. The bank operates independently of the EU institutions and national governments. The ECB traditionally supported states in the eurozone with collateralised loans to their central banks, but it had to respond to the crisis to shore up the euro and began making purchases of national government bonds to do so.

The International Monetary Fund (IMF) responded to the crisis to help stabilise national economies. The IMF is an intergovernmental organisation that works to create financial stability, improve economic conditions worldwide, and promote trade. It provides funding to finance balance of trade payments and to alleviate national economic crunches. During the euro crisis, it supported national governments by lending to governments with debt problems and other governments whose economies were affected by the crisis.

Private financial institutions holding governmental debt played significant roles relative to the countries with high sovereign debt. These institutions – banks, investment funds, and so on – purchase governmental bonds from national governments at specified rates of return, effectively lending money to governments to carry out projects and operations. They expect to make a profit on the activity and the amount is based on the degree of risk and return expected. Government bonds for European countries have traditionally been relatively safe investments. During the crisis, these financial institutions suffered from the subprime mortgage crisis, the banking crisis, and the recession, which led them to be highly demanding in dealings with governments that owed them money.

During the initial bank-related aspects of the crisis, domestic prime ministers and central bank leaders played significant roles. The response to the sovereign debt aspects of the crisis differed, however. Because of the lack of strong leadership in the European Commission, several European leaders – notably the Chancellor of Germany and the President of France – became de facto European leaders in attempting to resolve the sovereign debt and they aligned with bankers to force change in the nations with debt and budget deficit issues.

A variety of options for addressing the sovereign debt and budget deficits existed. In simplest terms, three approaches could be taken: austerity policies, economic growth policies, or a combination. Austerity involved profoundly cutting government expenditures – including social services – to balance budgets and reforming labour policies and structures. Growth policies would involve expenditures designed to spur economic development. The leaders responding to the crisis and bankers chose the first, which stabilised the euro and their national economies, but sacrificed the national economies of the nations with debt problems and pushed them deeper into recession with high unemployment and few social benefits for citizens.

Major developments in the crisis

The 28 member states of the EU were affected differently and in varying time frames by the crisis. Some were intimately involved; some only peripherally. Some faced domestic economic emergencies; for others it was an external issue. Some were involved in creating solutions; others were not. Two-thirds of the members used the euro; one-third did not. Nevertheless, all countries felt some economic and political effects.

The major developments involving European governance and intervention occurred between 2010 and 2012. Eleven developments or developmental points are particularly noteworthy:

- The EU summit regarding the role of European governments and the IMF in crisis intervention on 11–12 February 2010.
- Eurozone members and IMF agreement for €100bn intervention for Greece on 2 May 2010.
- Changes to the EU Contract made 16 December 2010 that allowed establishment of an emergency fund for the eurozone.
- ECB requires Italy to implement increased austerity measures, 5 August 2011.
- Greek general strike against austerity measures, 5 October 2011.
- EU summit increases the stability fund, extends new aid, and requires banks to raise new capital, 26–27 October 2011.
- Berlusconi resigns as Italian prime minister and Monti appointed, 12–13 November 2011, and French austerity measures begin.
- European Commission issues Green Paper on stability bonds and proposes bringing national budgets under EC control, 23 November 2011.
- EU summit to boost economic growth and balance austerity measures, 23 May 2012, attention begins focusing on Spain's economic conditions, and the UK holds governmental meetings to protect its financial system.
- Spain formally requests assistance (25 June 2012); German Chancellor Merkel calls the eurobonds 'economically wrong and counterproductive' (27 June 2013), EU summit on sovereign debts (28–29 June 2012).
- Merkel affirms need for member states to adhere to budget targets and for European monitoring of compliance, 15 July 2012.

These developments are the focus of this book, but they occur within the wider context of developments between 2007 and 2013, such as the banking crises, implementation of austerity programmes in many countries, the fall of governments in some countries, and requests of governments for aid. The decision to look at the coverage surrounding these particular events was made in order to focus our inquiry into the issues of European identity and cohesiveness, and the roles of European institutions in the crisis.

Economic evidence of the crisis

Regardless of what causes or beginning date of the crisis one accepts, developments in the crisis had clear effects on indicators of the economic and financial conditions of Europe and the euro. Although this book is not about economics and financial performance per se, it is important to recognise the effects as shown in important economic indicators: the value of the euro, gross domestic product, sovereign debt, labour costs, unemployment, and trade balances. These are the indicators that policy makers, economists, bankers, and the public used to assess the crisis.

The performance of the euro as a currency provides a palpable view of the perception of its strength and stability held by active traders, financial institutions, and investors, but it also vividly illustrates the volatility that created the currency aspects of the crisis. Two indicators provide this perspective: the exchange value against another currency and the price of a valuable commodity. The euro value against the US dollar has varied considerably since 2008, with particular volatility in 2009 and 2010. If the euro is strong, it will require fewer euros to purchase dollars; when it is weak, it will take more. Thus, upward peaks in the exchange rates indicate lowered confidence in the euro. Figure 1.1 reveals evidence of the crisis is seen in the volatility of the exchange rates and the peaks in rates in late 2008/early 2009, mid-2010, and mid-2012.

Gross domestic product (GDP), the primary measure of economic growth or decline, fell from 3% to below −4% in the 28 EU countries between 2007 and 2009, rising in 2010 but declining again in 2011 and 2012 (Figure 1.2).

Economic performance varied across Europe, as shown by the variations of the countries reviewed in this book (Figure 1.3). The differences were caused by the extent to which national banking

Figure 1.1   Monthly average exchange rates of the euro to the US dollar

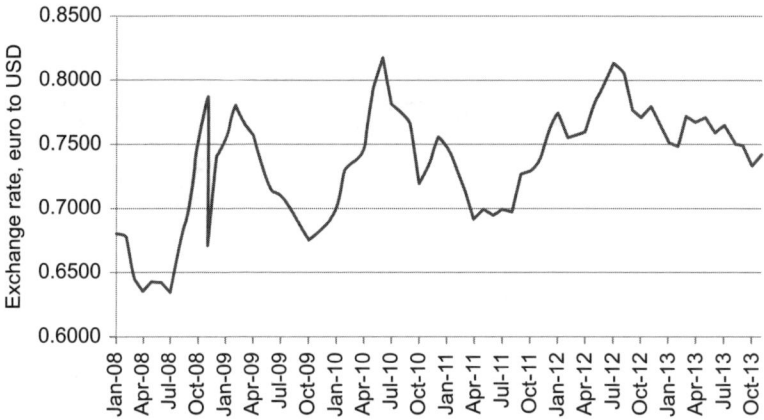

Source: http://www.x-rates.com.

Figure 1.2   Gross domestic product in the European Union (EU 28)

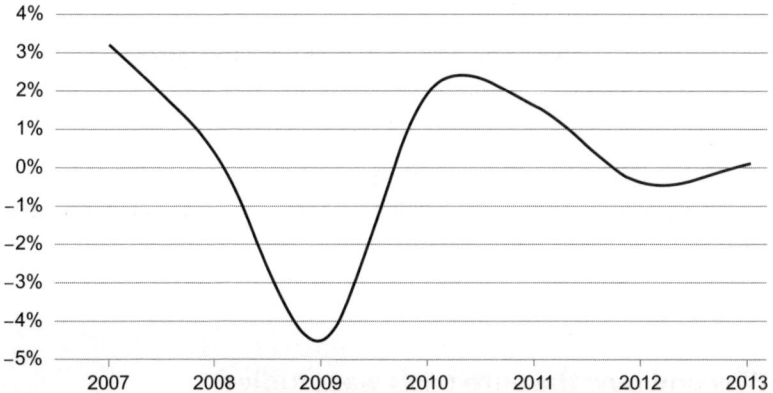

Source: Eurostat.

institutions were affected by the banking and subprime mortgage crises and then by austerity measures instituted in response to sovereign debt problems. Such national differences would be expected to influence how the crises were viewed domestically.

The levels of national debt varied by time period and country, as well. Figure 1.4 shows that the effect of debt acquisition overall raised indebtedness as a percentage of GDP to high peaks in Greece and Italy, well above those for other countries.

Figure 1.3 Development of gross domestic product by country

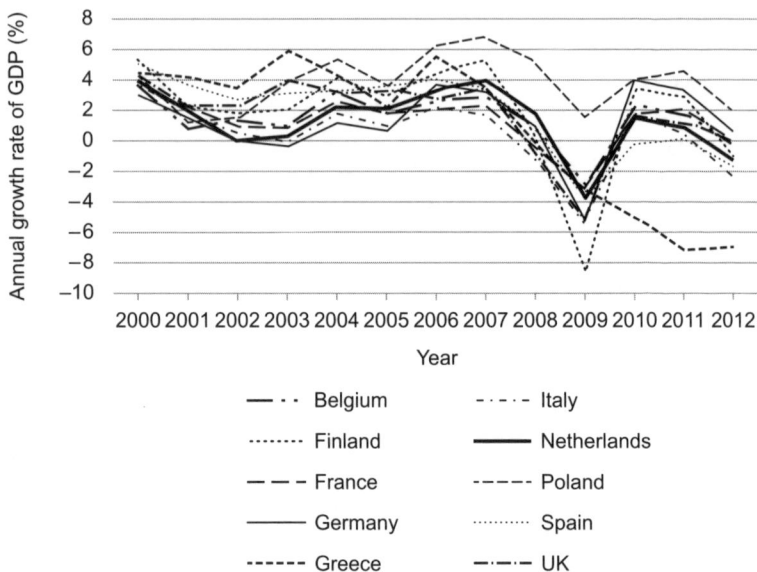

Source: OECD, retrieved from http://stats.oecd.org/index.aspx?queryid=26646# (17 September 2014).

The combination of poor exchange rates, declining GDP, and rising debt generally increased unemployment across the nations during the crisis, but Spain and Greece were affected by rapidly rising unemployment in those two countries as a result of the crisis and its remedies (Figure 1.5).

Why and how the euro crisis was studied

It is widely recognised that functioning polities need information flow to engage citizens and that information is now created, largely, by the mass media and then redistributed and commented upon in social media. In democratic societies, these media can be abrasive, revelatory, and demanding: but they convey a sense of the main events, of the main characters, and of the themes and issues with which the society must grapple. The media thus serve important functions in terms of directing citizens' attention to issues and creating pressures of policy responses (Castells, 2009; McCombs, 1994, 2004; Princen, 2009).

Figure 1.4 Development of sovereign debt by country

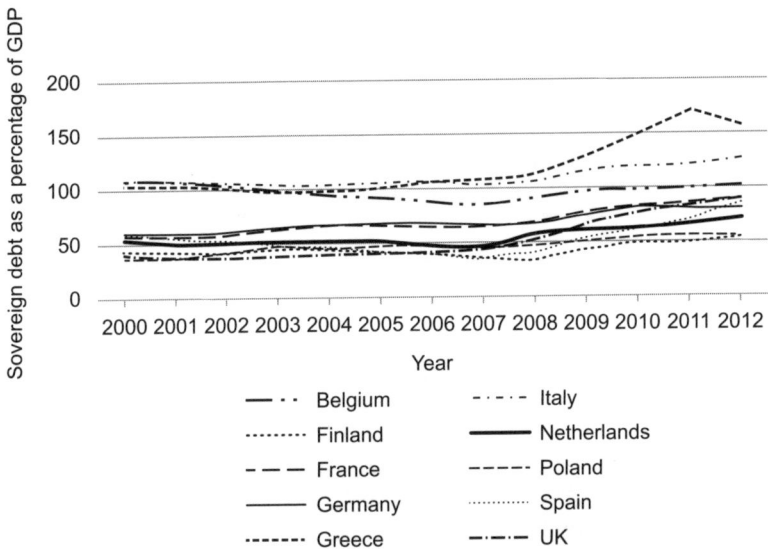

Source: Eurostat, retrieved from http://appsso.eurostat.ec.europa.eu/nui/submitViewTableAction.do (17 September 2014).

Considering the press coverage of the euro crisis is important because there is a link between how news reports, editorials, and columnists frame issues, emphasise certain sources, and portray institutions and how audiences perceive events and form their opinions. These relationships have been well formulated in agenda-setting, framing, and priming theories and approaches in media effects theory (Dearing and Rogers, 1996; McCombs, 2004; McCombs and Shaw, 1993; McCombs et al., 1997; Scheufele and Tewksbury, 2007; Shoemaker and Vos, 2009; Weaver, 2007).

Newspaper coverage is especially important because it is used in deciding what stories should be covered by television news, but newspapers are not alike; large-scale differences exist between general circulation newspapers, tabloids, and financial/business papers, for example, and there are differences among countries in the ways journalism is practised and how newspapers behave. Thus, one would expect differences in the ways they cover the euro crisis and portray the actors and institutions, and comparative analysis is necessary to establish similarities and dissimilarities.

Figure 1.5 Development of harmonised unemployment rate by country

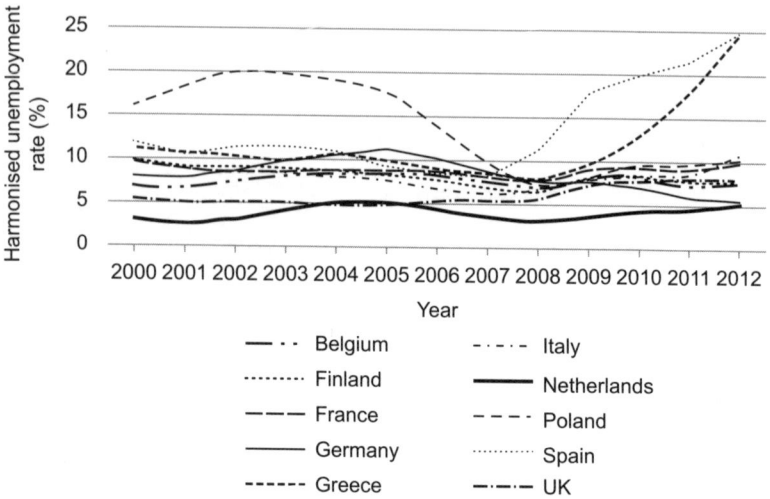

Source: OECD, retrieved from
http://stats.oecd.org/Index.aspx?DatasetCode=STLABOUR# (17 September 2014).

In addition to these fundamental differences in media systems, journalistic culture, and audience expectations, one would expect differences in newspaper coverage of the euro crisis related to the extent to which a country was involved in the crisis. Differences would be expected in coverage of northern, southern and central European newspapers; domestic factors would be expected to influence presentation of news in different countries; variations would be expected in coverage of papers in countries that are part of the eurozone and those that are not; countries with sovereign debt issues would be expected to cover stories differently than those without debt issues.

Media coverage of the crisis has been criticised as shallow and not reflecting its complexities, reflecting narrow national interests and perspectives, and allowing media outside of the eurozone to exert powerful influences on decision-makers (Authers, 2012; Corcoran and Fahy, 2009; Guerrara, 2009). This book illuminates those allegations. It also addresses the extent to which coverage reflected domestic and European perspectives, whether a European or domestic identity was conveyed, how European and national political and financial institutions were portrayed, and the range and quality of the debate.

This book is based on data from a large-scale internationally comparative research project that examined how Europeans understand the challenges facing the euro and workings of the EU and ECB through the news media of their countries. It was directed by Reuters Institute for the Study of Journalism at University of Oxford, which oversaw the work of partners studying coverage in Belgium, Finland, France, Germany, Greece, Italy, the Netherlands, Poland, and Spain, and the UK. Partners include the Institute for Media Studies at KU Leuven, Belgium; the Centre de Sociologie et de Science politique de la Sorbonne Université Paris 1-Panthéon Sorbonne, France; the Institut für Publizistik at Johannes Gutenberg University of Mainz, Germany; Department of Journalism and Mass Communication Studies, Aristotle University, Thessaloniki, Greece; Dipartimento di Scienze Politiche at the University of Perugia, Italy; Communication Research Centre, University of Helsinki, Finland; Institute for Journalism and Social Communication, University of Wroclaw, Poland; School of Communication, University of Navarra, Spain.

In carrying out the research, more than 10,000 articles from 40 newspapers in ten countries were analysed. These included the leading business/financial paper, the leading conservative and liberal papers, and the leading tabloid in each country. The full list of papers is included in Appendix 1. A content analysis was undertaken to identify main themes in coverage, choices of sources, the extent and nature of the coverage, and the scope and balance of the opinions expressed. The research focused on the 11 critical points of time discussed above between February 2010 to July 2012. Full details on the methods, sampling, the coding instrument, and other scientific information about the study are included in the appendices to this book. Core funding for the research was provided by the John Fell OUP Fund at the University of Oxford.

This book is not meant to report full data from the project and does not contain individual reports about domestic coverage in the countries studied. Those can be found elsewhere (see appendices). The focus of this book is on how the fundamental issues of the crisis and its participants were portrayed across Europe and the implications of that coverage for public understanding of the developments and events. It thus focuses on the extent to which newspapers addressed their readers as Europeans and on how they viewed the roles, functions, and effectiveness of European institutions. These are critical to the future of the EU and the extent to which it will be given powers to continue integration.

This approach is important because it will reveal whether the social construction of Europe in the coverage is one of elites or citizens, the extent to which common European debates are carried out across Europe, how European issues are addressed in national discourses and how those debates converge and diverge.

The book is divided into four sections. The first addresses national and European discourses found in the news coverage (Chapters 2–4); the second looks at characterisations and interpretations of the crisis conveyed (Chapters 5–7); the third section focuses on factors that influenced coverage (Chapters 8–10); and the final section addresses the question of where coverage is taking Europe (Chapters 11 and 12).

The initial section explores the discussion in articles revealing how the roots of and solutions to the crisis were presented, national differences in what was covered, and expectations and trust in European institutions portrayed. Heinz-Werner Nienstedt, Hans Mathias Kepplinger, and Oliver Quiring show in Chapter 2 that coverage in most countries presents national economic policies as the roots of the crisis but that European institutions are often seen as responsible for addressing it. Hans Matthias Kepplinger, Christina Köhler, and Senja Post then show in Chapter 3 that news coverage in different countries is characterised by different dominant views of the origins and causes of the crisis, and that these dominant views in most cases remain unchanged, even as events pile up and the crisis unfolds over time. In Chapter 4, Giovanni Barbieri and Donatella Campus note that while centre-left and centre-right tabloid and financial newspapers cover the euro crisis differently, there is considerable intra-country homogeneity, with otherwise different newspapers from the same country often sharing an overarching consensus in terms of how they cover the European institutions.

Chapters in the second section investigate the national and European sources relied upon for information in stories, importance given to the range of issues and ideas about developments, and the language used to describe the crisis. Nicolas Hubé, Susana Salgado, and Liina Puustinen focus on the actors and sources featuring in coverage of the euro crisis and show that leaders of national governments and a few prominent heads of European institutions loom large, especially and far more than anyone else the German Chancellor Angela Merkel, who appears in the news across the continent. In Chapter 6, Susana Salgado, Heinz-Werner Nienstedt, and Lennart Schneider use statistical techniques to identify a similar pattern of considerable internal consonance, in terms of how the causes of and possible solutions to the crisis are covered in different countries, but considerable differences in terms of the internal and external plurality of the coverage from country to country. Willem Joris, Liina Puustinen, Katarzyna Sobieraj, and Leen d'Haenens identify five different metaphorical framings in Chapter 7, showing that the crisis was portrayed as (a) a war, (b) a disease, (c) a natural disaster, (d) a problem of construction, (e) a game – with the war frame most frequently used across the ten countries analysed.

The third section examines the extent to which factors such as the type of newspaper, country involvement in the events, and media systems and journalistic culture were meaningful in explaining coverage of the crisis. In Chapter 8, Ángel Arrese and Alfonso Vara analyse similarities and differences between different kinds of newspapers within each country and show not only that popular, up-market, and financial newspapers have covered the crisis differently, but also that financial newspapers have far more similarities in terms of their coverage across countries than other kinds of newspapers. Paolo Mancini and Marco Mazzoni investigate the idea that a common, Europe-wide event – like the euro crisis – could help create a shared European public, but their work in Chapter 9 reveals that the discussion throughout the crisis has remained primarily national and is far more 'domesticated' than 'Europeanised'. In Chapter 10, Robert G. Picard and Susana Salgado compare the results from the extensive cross-country content analysis conducted here with existing frameworks for comparative media research and find that existing typologies of 'media systems' and 'journalism cultures' only to a limited degree help explain the patterns identified in this book, suggesting we need a more dynamic approach, with more attention to strategic actors and to contextual factors including economic differences.

The extent to which a European sphere was evident in the crisis and overall conclusions are reviewed and discussed in the fourth section. In Chapter 11, Juha Herkman and Timo Harjuniemi show that, though no clear European public sphere appears to have formed, there is some degree of 'vertical Europeanisation' of discussions around the euro crisis, where largely domestic political debates are linked to Europe-wide discussions via coverage of leaders of other governments (especially Merkel), of select European institutions, and in the emphasis on Europe being part of the solution to European problems. The final chapter then shows what the research in aggregate tells us about the contemporary nature of news coverage of European issues and European institutions and its implications for a common identity and locales in which to connect and interact as Europeans.

Part I

National and European Discourses

2

What Went Wrong and Why? Roots, Responsibilities, and Solutions of the Euro Crisis in European Newspapers

Heinz-Werner Nienstedt, Hans Mathias Kepplinger, and Oliver Quiring

During the euro crisis, the European Union (EU) faced the most severe challenge to one of its central institutions – the euro. The finance sector was not willing to take further risks in financing the heavy sovereign debt of some of the euro countries at all or at bearable interest rates. That opened up the possibility of states' bankruptcy, the breaking up of the eurozone as a consequence, and of chain reactions which might have led to disastrous economic problems in all European nations.

To preserve the euro system, political institutions on the national as well as the European level established new mechanisms for decision processes, installed new institutions and new policies, and implemented common rescue measures without historic precedent in Europe. People in the most affected nations suffered severe personal economic setbacks in the course of the crisis and as a consequence of the rescue measures, and other European nations were confronted with heavy burdens to bail out the countries with sovereign debt problems. National political institutions such as parliaments actually lost power and sovereignty to what heads of states and ministers had decided in summits of the eurozone members. All that had the potential for clashes of interest and tensions between nations and people in Europe to an extent not seen for a long time.

The question here is whether the press in the various European nations contributed to building, and at the same time reflected, public opinion in a way that supported preserving or further developing the

European identity and fostering European integration or contributed to erode it through positions shaped by national interests.

This chapter provides a comparative overview on the reporting of European newspapers about some fundamental questions raised in the context of the euro crisis. We selected the following issues for the analysis of their portrayal by the press:

- *What was the attitude towards the euro system?* A positive view of the euro system would support and explain efforts to rescue and preserve it. A negative one would question the sense of the rescue burdens.

- *What are the fundamental roots of the crisis?* In order to deal with the ongoing political, economic, and social turbulence affecting the people, the press should have helped the European public to understand the fundamental roots of the crisis, to support communicative rationality in and between the countries involved. Concerning national versus European views of the press, one could expect that, in case of national views, most articles published in countries with sovereign debt problems like Greece, Italy, and Spain would place responsibility on factors other than domestic policies and economics and most articles of leading European economies like France, Germany, or the UK would blame the domestic policies and economics of the countries with sovereign debt problems.

- *Who benefits from and who bears harmful consequences of the euro system and the euro crisis?* While the discussion on the fundamental roots of the euro crisis is about politics and economics and thereby on more abstract and systemic issues, reporting about beneficiaries and victims of the situation also has emotional implications and consequences for public opinion (see Chapter 5). The reporting on victims and beneficiaries also has significant political and economic implications: for those who suffer – and are not able to help themselves – the perception of being a victim or others being beneficiaries is a justification for claiming help and solidarity. If suffering is experienced by other nations it is a justification to provide help. One's own suffering may also serve as an argument to limit one's own contribution to help.

- *Which institutions or countries should take the main responsibility for solving the crisis?* The Maastricht treaty, which defined the fundamental rules of the euro system, was based on the non-bailout principle. Instead, the euro countries as a group took over responsibility for solving the sovereign debt crisis. As a consequence, the tax payers of donor nations risked having to pay for the debt of the recipient nations. The question is how far the press supported this fundamental change in European policy. In the case of views purely driven by national interests, it could be expected that most articles from leading European economies would portray the solution as domestic to countries with the sovereign debt problems rather than other nations or institutions and that most articles from countries with sovereign debt problems would portray the solution to the problem as external rather than domestic.

- *What should be the main political and economic responses?* The euro countries responded to the crisis with massive financial support for the countries that were in trouble. The help was provided together with imposed conditions for the recipients limiting their sovereignty. Conditions mainly demanded immediate austerity policies to prevent a further increase of the fiscal debt burden in the short term and reforms to liberalise the domestic markets as a prerequisite for future growth in the long term. The negative consequences of austerity policies in terms of unemployment and worsening of public welfare caused public uproar where they were blamed on the donor countries, especially Germany, which insisted on austerity policies. We look at the role of the press in this respect, whether it predominantly supported these policies as common European ground or instead portrayed growth policies with increased debt as appropriate – what is proposed fiercely by many voices today – or the reintroduction of local currencies in the countries with sovereign debt problems to lower the debt burden and gain competitiveness through devaluation of the currency. This would have supported a break up, possibly the end of the euro, with unknown but potentially high risks for the EU as a whole.

- *Which outcome of the crisis is expected?* Clearly the forecast of a positive outcome of the rescue measures would support them and make intermediate setbacks easier to bear.

To start with, we first provide an overall picture about the press coverage of the euro crisis. We present what the total magnitude of reporting about the crisis has been in the ten nations and what the dominant issues have been on a European level.

The analysis in this chapter is based on aggregated data for each country and over all 11 time periods which were covered.[1] Data for single nations indicate the total reporting of all four newspapers of that country. This aggregation level is relevant for two reasons: one can assume that the reporting in the most important newspapers of a country influenced the reporting in many other newspapers and news media and initiated a co-orientating process among journalists (Bach et al., 2013; Breed, 1955; Noelle-Neumann and Mathes, 1987; Reinemann, 2003). We can further assume that the number of news items pointing in a specific direction is a relevant factor and indicator for the perception of the public about this issue, furthermore that the proportion of articles portraying specific views in regard to an issue provides an indication of the relative relevance of these directions in the political discourse (for an explanation of so-called 'agenda building', see, for example, Nisbet, 2008). We first present the empirical results and then discuss them.

Differences in amount of coverage

We examined 165 publishing days of four newspapers in ten countries, resulting in 6,600 newspaper editions, and identified a volume of 13,718 relevant articles.[2] They represent an average of more than two articles about the euro crisis in each edition. This is impressively high and shows the importance the press devoted to the crisis. But the amount of reporting varied significantly between the countries under study[3] (Figure 2.1). Since we looked at the same number of newspapers in each country and over the same time period, there was no striking technical reason for this variation. Thus, one might assume that the amount of reporting reflects mainly to what extent the journalism of these nations cared about the euro crisis.[4]

Looking at the northern members of the eurozone, Germany and France had the biggest amount of reporting. It is between 2.6 and 3.4 times the volume of the reporting of Finland, the Netherlands, and Belgium. In the southern euro countries, Italy had the highest amount of reporting. Nevertheless, Spain and especially Greece had a fairly high volume level compared to the small northern euro countries – no wonder, since the southern countries were in the eye of the hurricane.

The high UK interest in the euro crisis compared to that of Poland may have been influenced by its fundamental internal discussion about its EU membership and its role as the premier European financial centre.

Figure 2.1   Euro crisis coverage by country

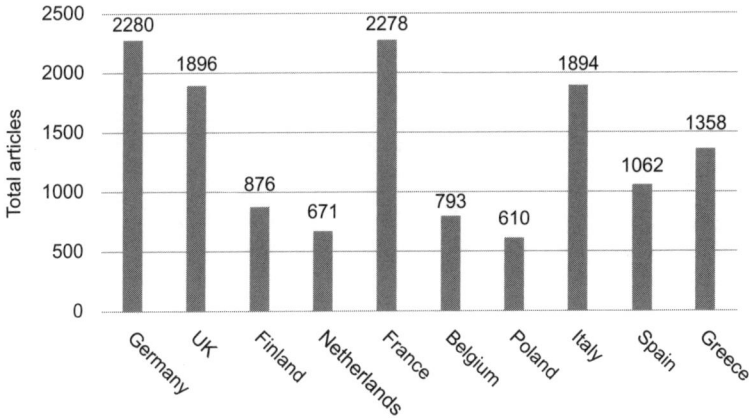

Note: Weighted number of article codes per country. Total number of articles: 13,718 (all countries).

Dominant issues in the media coverage

The press most often dealt with the question: who primarily suffers or will suffer economically or politically from the euro crisis – who are its victims (Figure 2.2)? Compared to the large number of these articles, the small number dealing with the beneficiaries of the crisis seems to be nearly negligible. How to fix the problem, meaning who should take over the responsibility of solving the crisis and what measures should been implemented in terms of short-term specific mechanisms as well as broader long-term responses, was also at the centre of interest, followed by forecasts of the outcome and the portrayal of fundamental roots of the crisis. The discussion about the euro system itself, its harms and benefits, played a role in 17% of the articles.

Reporting about the euro

Since a high proportion of articles dealt with the rescue of the euro, the question is whether the euro is presented as something that is worth rescuing. The count of press assessments in most countries raises doubt about that. In a total of 2,369 articles, twice as many were negative (harms)

Figure 2.2 Dominant issues of the euro crisis coverage – all countries

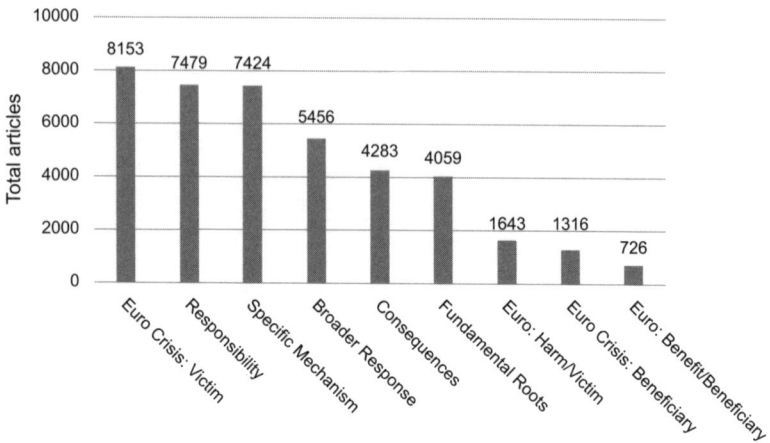

Note: Number of articles coded for each category. Total number of articles: 13,718 (all countries).

than positive (benefits)[5] (Table 2.1). Only in the German and, to a lesser extent, in the Belgian press does one find more positive than negative articles about the euro; the Finnish press is balanced in that respect. The press in Spain, but especially in Italy, have a stronger tendency towards the harms than the average. The critical attitude of the UK towards the euro is reflected in its 3.3 ratio of negative to positive articles.

Reporting about the euro crisis: fundamental roots

Fundamental roots have been portrayed in 30% (*n* = 4.059) of all articles about the crisis. In terms of the number of articles, roots were most broadly discussed in the German press, followed by Greece (Table 2.2). A somehow different picture emerges if one takes into consideration the different number of articles on the euro crisis in the ten countries: the percentage of articles dealing with the roots of the euro crisis is higher than average in Belgium (55%), Greece (47%), the Netherlands and Spain (both 40%), as well as Germany (36%), but lower in Poland (8%), Italy (18%), the UK (19%), and France (20%), and medium in Finland (31%). This sheds light on the relative effort that the journalists of the various countries undertake to try to explain the causes of the crisis

Table 2.1 Harms and benefits of the euro

	Harms	Benefits	Ratio of harms to benefits
Germany	158	218	0.7
UK	119	36	3.3
Finland	20	21	1.0
Netherlands	161	73	2.2
France	88	40	2.2
Belgium	42	47	0.9
Poland	5	5	1.0
Italy	592	108	5.5
Spain	142	46	3.1
Greece	316	132	2.4
Total	1,643	726	2.3

Notes: Columns 2 and 3: Total number of articles coded for each category. Column 4: Total number of harms divided by total number of benefits.

to the public and thus provide analysis beyond reporting on current events.

Concerning specific causes, the appearance of 47 different potential fundamental roots in the articles can be identified based on the codebook developed for this study (see Appendix 3). We mainly look at them in an aggregated form with six major topics as presented in Table 2.2 and then also comment on some peculiarities behind these aggregates where necessary, but especially when single countries deviate significantly from the average of the others.

National economic policies, which include fiscal and social policies like governments' deficit spending as well as industrial developments like those concerning the competitiveness of industries, have been addressed most often as the main cause in all euro countries except France – in total in 1,410 or 35% of the 4,059 articles that deal with roots. In the Finnish, the German, and the Greek press, they were by far the dominant reported cause of the crisis (Table 2.5). Europe-wide, 76% or 1,070 of these articles were about *fiscal and social policies* and 24% or 340 articles about *industrial developments* in the crisis countries. Only in Spain were both of these fields written about equally often.

Table 2.2 Fundamental roots of the euro crisis

	National economic policies	Structure of euro system	Private financial actors' misconduct	Political deficiencies	General economic conditions	Central banks' policies	Other	Total articles (n)
Germany	46	13	23	9	5	2	2	816
UK	9	40	26	13	3	3	6	369
Finland	47	16	14	5	4	1	12	268
Netherlands	28	23	15	21	2	1	10	271
France	33	34	17	12	3	1	1	452
Belgium	38	13	23	18	3	2	3	433
Poland	19	49	6	17	4	2	2	47
Italy	29	22	24	13	3	2	7	338
Spain	27	20	20	22	7	0	4	426
Greece	40	13	4	23	18	1	1	639
Total (%)	35	21	18	15	6	2	4	4,059

Notes: Columns 2 to 8: Fundamental roots of the euro crisis as a percentage of all articles concerning roots of the euro crisis.

Looking further into the structure of the reporting on *fiscal and social policies*, it is not surprising that debt making was predominantly addressed as the major cause of the crisis (652 out of the 1,070 articles). Contrary to the other countries, the Greek and especially the French press pointed much more frequently to the overall debt level of all countries, instead of putting attention on the crisis countries. This encourages contemplation of Europe-wide development including the northern countries. In Germany, in contrast, these two aspects have been written about equally often. The generous state apparatus of the countries with sovereign debt was hardly identified as the root of the euro crisis (28 articles in all countries, 12 published in Italy, one in Greece) in the context of the euro crisis.

When it comes to *industrial developments* (340 articles in all countries), the inability to build up competitive industries in the countries with major sovereign debt problems was one of the two major causes in terms of numbers of articles (106) along with addressing general national industrial policies and developments in these countries (117 articles). The Spanish construction industry bubble was explicitly mentioned in only 65 articles in this context.

More specific issues within the topic of national economic policies that contributed to the deterioration of the southern countries' competitiveness and that directly affected the social situation of people found less attention in the press. High wage increases compared to productivity gains received almost no mention: in total 32 articles, 13 from Greece, one from Italy, none from Spain. Economists deem high wages to be one of the driving forces behind the increasing lack of competitiveness of the southern countries before the crisis. (For detailed information on the development of real-world economic indicators and the crisis, see Chapter 1.) Only 26 articles portrayed the lack of reforms of labour markets in countries with major sovereign debt problems as a topic concerning the roots; three of them appeared in the southern countries. Only 39 articles were found in the ten European countries dealing with social grants in the southern countries that they could not afford; 13 of them appeared in these countries.

The *structure of the euro system* was portrayed as a fundamental root of the crisis in 837 or 21% of the articles that dealt with the roots of the crisis. It was seen as the clear number one cause by the two countries which are outside the euro system – the UK and Poland – but also by France. The German, Belgium, Greek, and Finnish press in contrast were the least critical about the euro system in this respect. The structural problems included the wrong starting conditions of the euro system (347 articles), the crisis countries not having been ready to enter the system (177 articles), and the incompatibility of one currency on the one hand and fiscal and economic national sovereignty of nations on the other hand (148 articles). The Maastricht treaty itself, which defined the rules and regulations of the euro system and, for example, restricted the deficit and debt ratios, was rarely mentioned as a primary cause of the crisis – it had been weakened and broken without sanction during the history of the euro and especially during the euro crisis.

Private financial actors' misconduct was indicated as a cause of the crisis in 734 or 18% of the articles about fundamental roots, overall ranked as the number three cause. In this respect the blame was especially put on banks for having financed too much fiscal or private debt. Out of the 431 articles that reported this as a major cause, 138 appeared in Germany and 76 in Spain, the two countries that reported most critically about the banks. This is surprising in the case of Germany, but not in the case of Spain, where banks financed and pushed the construction bubble. Speculation against the euro and against countries with sovereign debt problems (303 articles in total) on the other hand was the dominant issue in the UK (68 articles).

Political deficiencies, overall ranked number four with 607 articles or 15% of the articles about roots, was the number two most important cause of the crisis in the Greece and Spanish press. Within this class of causes, the failure of the political class in the problem countries was most often addressed as a specific cause (225 articles Europe-wide). In the southern countries this aspect was relatively often addressed in Greece (79 articles), less often in Italy (24 articles), but not at all explicitly in Spain (2 articles).

General economic conditions, including the recession after the world financial crisis of 2008 and the influence of globalisation (249 articles or 6%), did not play an important role in the European press except in Greece, where 112 articles or 18% of those on roots focused on this aspect. In that respect the Greek press pointed more strongly than the press in the other countries to a cause that could not be influenced by their own country.

Central banks' policies, namely the loose *monetary policies of the ECB* and the lack of the national authorities' supervision of the banks, were rarely reported during the phase of the euro crisis covered by this research (41 articles or 2%).

Beneficiaries and victims of the euro and the euro crisis

When it comes to the names of countries or regions that are portrayed as the main beneficiaries of the *euro crisis,* 611 articles dealt with this issue. Germany was mentioned most times as winner in this context (Table 2.3). It is worth recognising that 127 or 44% of 287 articles on Germany being the beneficiary of the crisis were published by German newspapers. There were more than ten times more articles portraying countries suffering from the euro crisis than articles pointing out countries that benefited: 6,720 compared to 611. More than every other article (3,897) pointed to the southern countries, especially to Greece, which was addressed in 1,687 cases as the main sufferer of the crisis. One-fifth (1,380) addressed the EU countries in general as sufferers.

There was a clear national perspective in the reporting of sufferers. More than 70% of those articles which denoted Germany, Finland, the Netherlands, and Belgium as victims were published by the press of these countries. Although not to the same extent, one can also observe this national perspective in the press of the southern countries: Italy (57%), Spain (30%), and Greece (32%), but also France (36%), mentioned their own countries as victims of the crisis. Concerning the institutions and parties who were beneficiaries of the euro crisis, more than half of the 1,316 articles that addressed this issue saw private economic actors as having profited from the crisis, nearly all of them speculators, hedge funds, large investors, and private banks. In contrast, the majority of the 8,153 articles about institutions or parties who suffered point to specific countries and their population (6,237 articles), private economic actors (1,068 articles), especially banks and political and financial authorities (372 articles). Concerning the latter, especially the German and Italian press portrayed the national governments as having lost influence.

When one looks at the beneficiaries of the *euro system* itself, 59% of all articles that mention a specific country or region receiving harm from the euro point to the southern countries (Table 2.4). Germany, on the other hand, is deemed to be the main beneficiary of the euro (32%).

Possible causes for the coverage of victims of the crisis

Theoretically, the coverage of the euro and the euro crisis can be explained by factors located within the media or in the world outside of the media

Table 2.3 Origin of the beneficiaries and victims of the euro crisis

	EU countries in general	Northern countries	Germany	United Kingdom	Finland	Netherlands	France	Belgium	Poland	Southern countries	Italy	Spain	Greece	Other	Total
Beneficiary	51	34	287	8	6	5	6	2	8	7	29	12	18	138	611
Victim	1,380	39	425	144	49	19	157	44	15	1,126	617	467	1,687	551	6,720
Ratio	65.7	1.2	1.5	18.0	8.2	3.8	26.2	22.0	1.9	160.9	51.4	38.9	140.6	4.0	11.0

Notes: Rows 2 and 3: Total number of articles that mention a specific country/region as a victim or beneficiary of the euro crisis. Row 4: Victims divided by beneficiaries.

Table 2.4 Origin of the beneficiaries and victims of the euro

	EU countries in general	Northern countries	Germany	United Kingdom	Finland	Netherlands	France	Belgium	Poland	Southern countries	Italy	Spain	Greece	Other	Total
Beneficiary	134	18	151	4	6	8	4	0	2	19	17	15	47	45	470
Victim	173	9	65	23	5	10	35	0	2	147	141	98	221	100	1,029
Ratio	1.3	0.5	0.4	5.8	0.8	1.3	8.8	–	1.0	7.8	8.3	6.5	4.7	2.2	2.2

Notes: Rows 2 and 3: Total number of articles that mention a specific country/region as a victim or beneficiary of the euro. Row 4: Victims divided by beneficiaries.

Table 2.5 Country interest rates and articles with one's own country as a victim

Country	Interest rates of ten-year government bonds in July 2012 (%)	Articles: Own country suffers from euro (%)	Articles: Own country suffers from euro crisis (%)
Germany	1.24	1.05	14.12
Finland	1.55	0.34	4.34
Netherlands	1.75	1.49	2.24
France	2.28	0.53	2.46
Belgium	2.69	0.00	3.91
Italy	6.00	4.96	18.48
Spain	6.79	2.17	13.37
Greece	25.82	8.32	39.54
Spearman's Rho*		0.619	0.452
Significance		0.260	0.233

Notes: *Spearman's Rho correlations with interest rate. Columns 3 and 4: Percentage of articles describing one's own country as sufferer of euro or euro crisis of all articles for each country.

(Kepplinger, 1992, 2011; Kepplinger and Roth, 1979). Of course, we will not be able to present a comprehensive or exhaustive analysis of these causes. Nevertheless, we will outline and illustrate some possibilities. With respect to the world outside of the media, two aspects have to be distinguished: hard economic facts like the cost of living, inflation, or interest rates; and statements by politicians, speakers of interest groups and so on to justify their claims, complaints, and demands. The following examples might illustrate this.

If hard economic facts explained the number of articles dealing with harms of the euro, one would expect a positive correlation between the interest rates for government bonds, as an indicator of the exposure to the sovereign debt crisis, and the percentage of articles presenting the country as victim of the euro, respectively the euro crisis. Included in the analysis are the eight members of the eurozone. To exclude an influence of the different intensity of coverage in the eight countries, the calculations are based on percentages (Table 2.5). As expected, we find positive, although due to the small number of cases not significant, correlations between hard economic facts – interest rates in this case – and the percentage of articles presenting their own country as a victim of the euro (0.619)

Table 2.6   Influence of national sources quoted on presenting own country as victim

	Articles on euro*		Articles on euro crisis**	
	National source	No national source	National source	No national source
Statement presenting own country as victim (%)	55	27	43	18
No statement presenting own country as victim (%)	45	73	56	82
Totals (%)	100	100	100	100

Notes: $^*\chi^2 = 15.670$ $df = 1$, $p = 0.000$; $^{**}\chi^2 = 107.393$ $df = 1$, $p = 0.000$;   Cramer's $V = .271$, $\eta = .271$; Cramer's $V = .271$, $\eta = .271$.

and of the euro crisis (0.452) (Table 2.5). Therefore, hard economic facts can be regarded as a relevant cause of the type of coverage in the eight countries. But it has to be noted that these facts explain at best 36% of the coverage mentioned. Therefore, there must have been other relevant factors influencing the amount of coverage on victims.

If statements of politicians, speakers of interest groups and so on explain the large number of negative articles, one should expect the percentage of articles on harms to be especially high if they refer to politicians and representatives of interest groups. As can be seen from Table 2.6, there are significant connections between the presentation of their own country as victim and the type of sources quoted. If national sources are quoted, it is more likely that their own country is presented as a victim of the euro and the euro crisis compared to articles lacking national sources. Therefore, the presentation of their own country as a victim can at least partly be traced back to the activity and presence of national actors.

With respect to factors located within the media, the large number of articles dealing with victims of the euro and of the euro crisis might be explained by the preference of the media for negative news (Eilders, 2006; Shoemaker et al., 1991). The hypothesis is supported by the fact that in all countries except two (Germany and Belgium), the newspapers under investigation published more articles on the harms than on benefits of the euro (Table 2.1). Not surprisingly, the negative tendency was even stronger in the coverage of the euro crisis and – maybe a little surprisingly – it was present in the press coverage in all countries under investigation (Table 2.3). The preference of the media for negative news might be related to the dominance of national sources presenting their own country as victim, mentioned above: because the media prefer negative news, national politicians and representatives of interest groups who complain about the euro and the euro crisis might have better chances of being cited than actors who refer to positive consequences.

Responsibility for solving the euro crisis

Although the fundamental roots of the euro crisis have been overwhelmingly assigned to the problem countries themselves, the responsibility for solving the problems is in most articles in the press of all countries attributed to the eurozone members as a group or to the institutions of the EU (Table 2.7). Of the 7,449 articles dealing with this issue, 54% name one of these two possible actors as the necessary problem solvers, which will not only imply political but also monetary burdens for them. More than two-thirds of these articles name the eurozone members as a group, less than one-third an institution of the EU like the European Commission, as the problem solver of choice. This could indicate that the established EU institutions were not seen to be appropriate for this specific task (compare Chapter 4), or that the members of the eurozone were regarded as a community acting in solidarity.

The responsibility of the struggling countries to solve the problems on their own is only portrayed as a possible solution in one-fifth of the articles concerning this issue, but relatively more often in Greece and Spain. Less than one-tenth indicated that the countries without sovereign debt problems should take the responsibility exclusively. Although the ECB played an increasingly strong role as trouble-shooter in the rescue process, only one-tenth of the articles portrayed it as responsible for solving the crisis in the whole period under study. The private holders of debt, who were portrayed to be one of the roots of the crisis, were extremely seldom portrayed as responsible for solving the crisis. Nevertheless, they had to accept relief of Greece debt, called a 'haircut' (financial jargon for a reduction in the stated value of the debt), worth €106.5 bn in the beginning of 2012.

Short-term responses to solve the euro crisis

When it comes to policies to solve the crisis, we found that nearly every second article suggested loans from the EU countries or the ECB in this

Table 2.7 Responsibilities to solve the euro crisis

	EU/euro members as a group	Struggling countries themselves	Central banks	Countries without debt problems	Private debt holders	Other	Total articles (n)
Germany	44	20	10	12	7	7	1,198
UK	55	9	17	2	1	16	326
Finland	63	20	8	0	2	7	579
Netherlands	62	15	15	3	1	4	538
France	66	12	11	6	4	1	772
Belgium	61	19	12	1	3	2	565
Poland	69	10	6	12	2	1	226
Italy	52	20	14	5	3	6	1,422
Spain	48	28	9	13	1	1	663
Greece	49	37	7	5	2	1	1,190
Total (%)	54	21	11	6	3	4	7,479

Notes: Columns 2 to 7: Responsibilities to solve the euro crisis as a percentage of articles concerning responsibilities to solve the euro crisis.

Table 2.8   Short-term responses to solve the euro crisis

	Loans from euro countries and ECB	Austerity measures	Growth stimulus policies	Hair cut	Other	Total articles (n)
Germany	56	16	8	7	12	1,426
UK	35	20	18	5	23	626
Finland	65	12	6	5	13	503
Netherlands	50	18	5	8	20	446
France	58	24	9	4	4	720
Belgium	46	32	6	6	11	529
Poland	50	31	5	7	8	196
Italy	54	17	13	5	12	1,284
Spain	41	23	14	9	13	571
Greece	33	28	18	14	6	1,123
Total (%)	49	21	11	7	12	7,424

Notes: Columns 2 to 6: Short-term responses to solve the crisis as a percentage of articles concerning short-term responses to solve the crisis.

respect (Table 2.8). From these articles, 31% portrayed loans provided by the ECB and 69% loans from other countries. If loans were suggested, most articles (58%) asked for loans from other countries with supervision (e.g. by the so-called troika, meaning the group of representatives of institutions involved in the financing of the bailout programmes: the European Commission, the International Monetary Fund and the European Central Bank) as the main short-term response. The highest ratio of articles that recommended loans from other countries with supervision came from the UK (96%), Germany (89%), and Greece (84%). Obviously, the Greek press in principle supported the idea of the troika.

Austerity measures to cut budget deficits were ranked second of the recommended policies. Some way behind at number three were articles asking for growth policies and fiscal stimulus. The percentage of articles recommending that was highest in the UK (18%), Greece (18%), Spain (14%), and Italy (13%). The ratio of articles pleading for austerity measures to those for growth policies was 1.9 for all the countries. In Germany, it was only slightly higher (2.1). Since critics of the austerity policies mainly blamed Germany for the enforcement of such measures, at least the reporting in the German press does not justify that interpretation.

Long-term responses to solve the euro crisis

National structural reforms have been by far the most frequent long-term response recommended by the European newspapers. From 5,456 articles which mentioned broader responses to the crisis, nearly every second one pleads for structural reforms in problem countries. This kind of response was reported about more than average especially in Germany, the UK, and the Netherlands but also in Spain. The Greek press was average in this respect but Italy was below average (Table 2.9). More power to be transferred to the EU institutions ranked second in the ten countries. Especially the press in France, but also in Poland and Belgium, where this was the number one long-term response, covered this aspect and gave space to more EU-centric voices.

Table 2.9 Long-term responses to solve the euro crisis

	National structural reforms	More EU power	Breaking up the eurozone	Other	Total articles (n)
Germany	56	18	8	18	1,086
UK	54	15	12	20	470
Finland	32	28	11	28	260
Netherlands	44	40	5	10	367
France	30	56	10	4	648
Belgium	40	42	6	11	376
Poland	37	45	8	9	193
Italy	39	21	20	21	964
Spain	46	28	12	14	437
Greece	43	39	13	5	655
Total (%)	44	31	11	14	5,456

Notes: Columns 2 to 5: Long-term responses to the crisis as a percentage of articles concerning long-term responses to the crisis.

Breaking up the eurozone was far outranked by the other two issues, and numbered third amongst the broader responses. The bulk of these articles, about 80%, suggested the problem countries leaving the eurozone; only about 20% suggested the countries with strong economies leaving the eurozone. The Italian press gave voice to breaking up the eurozone to a much higher degree than the average – 20% instead of 11%.

Forecast of the consequences of the crisis

A significant part of all articles, 31% (n = 4,283), dealt with the consequences of the crisis. Nearly one-third of these articles predicted the preservation of the eurozone (25%) or even a stronger euro (6%). Only 15% forecast that the problem countries would leave the euro, even less (6%) a final breakup of the eurozone (Table 2.10). The most optimistic countries in this respect, measured by the ratio of positive to negative forecasts, have been Germany and Greece, the most pessimistic Poland and Italy. In some countries, the newspapers under investigation present specific views. For example, in Belgium, Finland, the UK, and Italy, the newspapers forecast an increase of power to the EU institutions. It is remarkable that nearly every sixth article that appeared in the Greek press about the long-term consequences of the euro crisis predicted an enduring transfer system as a consequence.

Discussion

Summing up the results, our data provide evidence for well-known patterns of economic crisis coverage (see also Quiring et al., 2013), for national views and European cleavages but also for significant fields of common European ground in the reporting of the press across Europe.

The euro crisis and ten related political events under analysis triggered extensive media coverage. Nevertheless, there were large differences in the emphasis and thereby the sense of urgency given to the euro crisis in the newspapers of different countries. Measured in terms of the number of articles, the biggest euro countries (Germany, France, Italy) gave by far more attention to the crisis than smaller countries of the eurozone (Belgium, the Netherlands, Finland). The most affected countries (Greece, Spain) were to be found in the middle between these extremes. The

Table 2.10 Consequences of the euro crisis

	Eurozone preserved	More power for Europe	Problem countries will drop the euro	Enduring transfer system	Final breakup	Stronger and more stable euro	Europe-wide inflation	Other	Total articles (n)
Germany	33	15	11	6	3	9	4	19	914
UK	16	34	26	3	4	3	3	11	158
Finland	8	37	6	11	9	8	4	16	237
Netherlands	31	29	17	9	4	2	2	6	245
France	27	20	17	5	14	10	3	4	408
Belgium	21	50	6	3	4	3	4	9	233
Poland	11	11	38	5	20	5	6	5	88
Italy	11	33	20	4	16	4	2	11	758
Spain	25	23	15	9	9	4	1	14	379
Greece	36	12	15	17	5	7	2	7	863
Total (%)	25	23	15	8	8	6	3	11	4,283

Notes: Columns 2 to 9: Consequences of the euro crisis as a percentage of the total number of all articles.

attention and intensity of the media's public opinion-building towards the crisis seem to correlate with effective or aspired political power amongst the euro member nations. The UK, though not being a member, had a high amount of reporting comparable to the bigger euro members, which can be explained by its role as a key finance centre and its ongoing internal discussion about the sense of its membership in the EU.

Cleavages can also be found in the discussion about winners and losers, beneficiaries and victims of the euro and the euro crisis. Here we find a tendency for each country to deem itself to be a victim to a higher extent than others. The different intensities of the coverage of victims of the euro and the euro crisis in the various countries can be explained by their exposure to the sovereign debt crisis, the frequency of claims of politicians and speakers of interest groups in the media, and a more or less distinctive preference of the press for negative news. On the other hand, there is common ground and a consensus in the reporting that Germany is on the side of the beneficiaries and the southern countries are on the side of the victims. Benefits that the southern countries had from the euro, for example in the low interest rates until the crisis became manifest, are hardly portrayed by the press.

We find strong indications towards more European integration when it comes to reporting about the responsibility to solve the crisis but also the responses to the crisis. The responsibility to solve is portrayed to be with the EU or the euro members as a group by the majority of all articles in all countries. Nonetheless, compared to all other countries, the relation of articles that point to one's own responsibility to fix the problems to those that demand European help for the countries affected most by the crisis, was highest in Greece and Spain. Loans from the euro countries and the ECB to the crisis countries are by far the most recommended short-term response.

The latter two aspects are in sharp contradiction to the spirit of the Maastricht treaty, which did set rules but was based on national sovereignty on the one hand and the non-bailout principle on the other. Our data show that deviating from that principle seemed to be considered common sense all over Europe.

The consonant demand for more European integration can also be found in the demand for more power for Europe, which is the second most mentioned desirable long-term response as well as a frequently forecasted consequence of the euro crisis. The press in nearly all countries portrayed and forecasted a significant shift of political responsibilities to forces outside their own nation, resulting in deeper integration and the transfer of national sovereignty to European institutions. In the national context the population usually asks national political actors to solve problems. As a consequence of the euro crisis responsibilities of national political actors have become increasingly transferred to European political actors and institutions as well as to other nations, with still unclear consequences for the institutional and political stability of the EU.

At the same time, a reported dominant view in the press of all euro countries was that the national policies of the problem countries had been the main cause of the crisis. Looking from the outside, UK and Poland in contrast most often reported the structure of the euro system to be the dominant cause of the crisis. This supported a view for their countries that it was wise not to have joined the club.

National structural reforms (labour markets, education, tax structures) in nations with problems are most often written about as the adequate long-term response in all euro countries except in France. But industrial policies, lack of competitiveness, and social policies including wage policies were hardly discussed as causes of the crisis, leaving the necessity for such reforms in the dark for the audience. Instead, the portrayal of the economic causes of the crisis was concentrated on the lax fiscal debt policies.

Nearly twice as many articles indicated that austerity measures should be the main short-term response instead of growth measures. There seemed to be an astonishing consensual support for austerity policies across Europe, which are normally attributed to Germany only.[6]

Breaking up the eurozone played a minor role as a long-term response to the crisis but more so in Italy. Except in Italy and – outside the euro system – in the UK and Poland, the press in all other countries more often portrayed forecasts whereby the eurozone would be preserved and even become stronger than forecasts where it would break up. On the other hand, the press in most countries provided a negative picture of the euro itself. The euro was portrayed as causing more harms than benefits all over Europe except in Germany, Belgium, and Finland. This conveyed a message to the public of most euro countries that they were caught in a system that was detrimental to their interests and may have caused feelings of distance and aggression.

This overall picture of roots, effects, responsible actors, and measures presented by the total number of articles did not necessarily meet the conditions of a consistent picture of cause and effect or storylines of the press. Examples of inconsistencies are the responsibility for solving the crisis (and paying) being attributed to all euro countries for problems that were reportedly caused by the crisis nations, the euro as a detrimental system to their own interests but forecasted to survive the crisis, the blame on the private financial actors' misconduct but the absence of their bearing responsibility to solve the crisis, the aim of more European power but the complaints of a loss of sovereignty.

These contradictions can be partly traced back to the fact that all these aspects were not raised together in single articles. Instead, they were raised in different articles that were triggered by different cues. These articles may all have been self-consistent. Nevertheless, the collection of contradicting standpoints reached the audience and became part of public opinion contributing to uncertainty and disappointment about economic, political, and social circumstances. This is common in a plural public discourse but stimulates tensions in and between societies when massive material interests are involved.

Real-life consequences of the portrayed building and reflection of public opinion by the media can be observed. In the crisis countries the low amount of discussion on the structural economic causes of the crisis beyond lax debt policies may have made the severe social consequences of austerity measures even less understandable and bearable, encouraging outbreaks of protests and political instability.

The call for solutions to be provided by others opened the option to blame them for the negative consequences of policies undertaken to solve the crisis, especially those from austerity policies, with Germany being at the centre of the blame.

The attribution of the main cause of the crisis to the national economic policies of the crisis countries but the financial burden to others strengthened populist parties in northern countries.

In the Italian press, the voice for struggling countries to have their own responsibilities for solving the crisis as well as for austerity measures and structural reforms was weaker, but the voice for loans from others was stronger than the voice in the Greek or Spanish press. Italy exhibited the strongest Euro-scepticism amongst the euro countries. It had the highest portion of articles that portrayed the breakup of the eurozone as the long-term solution and was the only euro country that cited more forecasts of a breakup of the eurozone compared to forecasts of the preservation of the euro. The opposition of Berlusconi to the rescue measures except to receiving loans and the difficulty his successors faced in cutting deficits and initiating structural reforms can be interpreted in the light of the picture that the press provided.

In France, major economic problems became obvious in recent years. The huge opposition to budget cuts and structural reforms can be seen against the background of the reporting in the French press. It placed the responsibility to solve the crisis with countries without sovereign debt problems to a higher extent, and the responsibility with struggling countries themselves to a lesser extent than the press of any other euro country. National structural reforms as responses to the crisis also played a significantly lesser role than in the press of any other of the countries covered by this study.

To sum up, we found aspects of common ground in the reporting of the European press especially in the plea for more European integration and more power to the EU. The above-mentioned inconsistencies and real-life consequences, on the other hand, mirror the huge tensions within the societies and between nations that were caused by the euro and the euro crisis.

Regrouping of original categories in the codebook used in this chapter

In order to avoid going too much into detail, for the purposes of this chapter we have aggregated the codes provided by the codebook (see Appendix 3) in a meaningful way according to the issues to be discussed.

The numbers in this section refer to the numbers of the codes in Appendix 3: Codebook. These codes define the categories that are used in this chapter.

14. **What does the article indicate is the main fundamental root or cause of the crisis?**

10+60+61	Structure of euro system
20,30	National economic policies
40–42+45–46	Private financial actors' misconduct
50+62	Political deficiencies
43–44+70	Central banks' policies
80	General economic roots
98	Other

15. Which does the article indicate should bear the main responsibility to solve the problem?

01	Struggling countries themselves
02	Countries without sovereign debt problems
03+04	EU/euro countries and institutions
05+06	Central banks
07	Private debt holders
98	Other

16. What does the article indicate should be the main (short-term) response to the crisis?

01+02+03	Loans from other countries and ECB
04	Haircut
05	Austerity measures
06+07	Growth stimulus policies
98	Other

17a. What does the article indicate should be the primary broader (longer-term) response to the crisis?

01	More EU power
02+03+05	Breaking up the eurozone
04	National structural reforms
98	Other

18a. What does the article indicate as the main benefit from the existence of euro currency?

10+20+50+60	Economic advantages
30+40	Political advantages
98	Other

19a. What does the article explicitly indicate as the main harmful consequence from the existence of the euro currency?

10+20+50+60	Harmful economic consequence
30+40	Harmful political consequences
98	Other

20a. Who does the article indicate primarily benefits or will benefit (economically or politically) from the euro crisis?

10+40	Countries and their population
20	Political and financial authorities

30	Private economic actors
98	Other

21a. Who does the article indicate primarily suffers or will suffer costs (economically or politically) from the euro crisis?

10+40	Countries in general and their population
20	Political and financial authorities
30	Private economic actors
98	Other

3

Do Political Events Change National Views?

Hans Mathias Kepplinger, Christina Köhler, and Senja Post

Our capacity to receive and process information compared to the complexity of information given is far too limited. Therefore, we have to 'pick out what our culture has already defined for us, and we tend to perceive that which we have picked out in the form stereotyped for us by our culture'.[7] Lippmann's analysis does not only apply to the 'man on the street' but also to the 'well informed citizen' (Schütz, 1964), among them journalists covering the euro crisis. The worldview of journalists, their attitudes and opinions, guides their perception of reality and their coverage, especially about crises and conflicts. Since 1950 this has been documented in numerous field studies (Flegel and Chaffee, 1971; Kepplinger and Lemke, 2013; Larcinese et al., 2011; Molotch and Lester, 1974; White, 1950). These findings can be explained by the theory of instrumental actualisation (Hartung, 2008; Kepplinger et al., 1991) which can briefly be summarised in three claims. First, in every major conflict and crisis a large number of events happen, a large amount of information exists, and a large number of sources are available that support the position of either one or the other opponent. Second, journalists ascribe higher news values to events, information, and sources that support their worldview and conflict position, respectively the editorial line of the news organisation they work for. Third, for the reasons mentioned, the news on topical events, information, and sources seem to support the views of media with different and even opposing positions in conflicts and crises.

Journalists cover topical events, but the 'event as event' has to be distinguished from the 'event as news' (Noelle-Neumann and Mathes, 1987). Journalists tend to perceive and cover spectacular and seemingly unique events in the light of past events. For example, the public reaction in Chicago to General Douglas MacArthur on his return from Asia was restrained, but the coverage was highly coloured by his enthusiastic reception on the West Coast (Lang and Lang, 1953). After the British media, impressed by the violent demonstrations against the Vietnam War in 1968 in Paris and Berlin, had in many articles raised the expectation of similar excesses at the upcoming demonstration in London, they heavily concentrated their coverage on violent acts of about 2,500 radicals who had left the official route of nearly 60,000 peaceful demonstrators, creating the impression of a predominantly violent demonstration (Halloran et al., 1970). One would misunderstand the coverage of the two public events if one interpreted it as manipulation. More likely, the journalists had become victims of the intensive framing of the previous events and the proneness to make sense of future events by interpreting them in the light of past experiences and general convictions (Entman, 1991). Similar factors might have influenced the coverage on major political and economic events during the euro crisis.

In the past 15 years, the national news media have increasingly paid attention to issues, protagonists, and processes at the EU level (Boomgaarden et al., 2010; Brüggemann et al., 2009). Until 2008, they had hardly covered political issues and processes in fellow member states (Kleinen-von Königslöw, 2012). However, the European sovereign debt crisis has intensified national news coverage of issues and processes both at the EU level and in fellow member states (Post and Vollbracht, 2013). Comparative long-term studies on the national news coverage of EU topics indicate that the news media provide similar problem definitions of the issues at stake (Pfetsch et al., 2008). According to analyses of national media coverage of the European Parliament, it largely follows the routine events of the plenary calendar and is therefore largely synchronised across countries (Gatterman, 2013: 447). Nevertheless, at times of crisis, conflict, or unique events, national news coverage often differs across countries because it is embedded in specific national and cultural contexts. For instance, although the national news in Denmark, the Netherlands, Germany, and the UK mutually interpreted the introduction of the euro as an economic (rather than political) issue, the national media of these countries emphasised rather different aspects of it. The German news referred to economic benefits for consumers and the economy as a whole, whereas news in Denmark and the UK referred to the economic disadvantages of not belonging to the financial union (Vreese, 2001; Vreese et al., 2001). Media coverage in Germany and France about EU enlargement and a common EU constitution focused on different issues and actors and attributed responsibility to different actors (Adam, 2007).

News media in various countries discussed Turkey's bid to become a member of the EU from different perspectives. For instance, the press in France related it largely to domestic issues, whereas the British press put much more emphasis on dissent within the EU (Negrine et al., 2008: 55). Examples such as these suggest that, although the transnational news coverage of the EU increasingly assimilated during routine periods, coverage of critical or spectacular events is still largely influenced by specific national perspectives and experiences (for a detailed review of literature, see Chapter 11). In the following, we seek to answer to what degree national views of the euro crisis predetermined national news coverage of major political and economic events during the crisis and how much coverage in several countries differed or converged.

Assumptions

Most likely, in all European countries there exist dominant views of the causes of the crisis, the responsibilities for solving it, and the specific mechanisms needed to solve it. They guide the media's explanation of the causes of the euro crisis, the attribution of responsibility to different institutions, and the demand for specific mechanisms to solve the crisis. For example, statements explaining the causes of the euro crisis by national industrial, social, or fiscal policies in countries with major sovereign debt problems represent a specific view. It directs the attention to specific nations and probably suggests conclusions about mechanisms necessary for the solution of the crisis. Statements attributing the causes of the euro crisis to insufficient economic fundamentals or to the incompatibility of one currency with national economic sovereignty or to the structure of the euro system constitute an alternative view. It directs the attention to political decisions made at the introduction of the euro and so on. From these general notions, four assumptions can be derived:

1. In all European countries there exist dominant views on the euro crisis, colouring the coverage of the euro crisis.
2. Dominant views and the relevant media coverage will differ across countries.
3. Dominant views will minimise the effect of major political and economic events on the presentation of important aspects of the euro crisis.
4. Dominant views are caused by the preference for domestic sources.

To test our assumptions about the relative influence of major political events and of dominant views on media coverage, we will compare the presentation of the causes of the crisis (roots), of the responsibilities to solve it, and of the mechanisms needed for a solution around 11 major political and economic events between 2010 and 2012 (for a detailed description, see Appendix 1). We will proceed in three major steps. First, countries to be included in the analysis will be identified; second, dominant views will be identified; third, coverage on the 11 events under investigation will be compared across countries. The comparison will be threefold:

- *Quasi-experiments:* The 11 political events covered and coded are regarded as stimuli. Differences between coverage before and after the events are interpreted as effects of the events.
- *Trend analysis:* The period under investigation will be divided in three sub-periods with similar amounts of coverage. Changes will be interpreted as trends.
- *Context analysis:* This will be provided to see if the reference to different types of sources coincides with specific dominant views.

Methods

Selection of nations for detailed analysis

We agreed upon the following criteria for the selection of nations for this analysis. They should include (a) members and nonmembers of the eurozone; (b) members of the eurozone with and without debt problems; (c) countries with different views on the crisis (roots, responsibility, mechanisms); (d) countries with a sufficient number of articles. Based on these criteria, the following eight countries were included in the analysis: Belgium, Finland, France, Germany, Italy, the Netherlands, Spain, and the UK.

As a first step, we identified the dominant views on roots, responsibilities, and measures with regard to the euro crisis in each country. They are indicated by the highest percentage of media coverage on one of three types of roots of the crisis, one of the three types of responsibilities for its solution, and one of the four types of measures needed.[8] The newspapers seldom provided information on the roots of the euro crisis.[9] The number of relevant articles ranged from 109 (Finland) to 340 (Germany), with an average number of 194 articles per country. According to the press coverage in France (65%), the UK (73%), Italy (41%), and the Netherlands (43%) the roots of the euro crisis were the *conditions and structure of the euro system*. According to the press in Germany (50%), Belgium (42%), and Finland (51%) the roots of the crisis were *national industrial, fiscal, and social policies in countries with major debt problems*. According to the press in Spain (47%) there were *political roots, including the failure of political elites*. Looking at these percentages, two conclusions have to be drawn. First, the dominant views in the various countries did not exclude other perspectives. They were typical but not exclusive. Second, in some countries, the dominant views were rather distinct – for example, in France and the UK. In other countries, they were less distinct but still existing – for example, in Italy, Belgium, and the Netherlands (see also Chapter 6).

Information on the responsibility for the solution of the crisis was a major topic of the newspaper coverage. The relevant number of articles ranged from 264 (UK) to 1,230 (Italy) with an average of 648 articles per country. According to the press in Germany (47%), France (66%), the UK (55%), Belgium (46%), Finland (57%), and the Netherlands (62%), the *eurozone members as a group* were primarily responsible for the solution of the euro crisis. According to the press in Italy (39%) and Spain (41%), *supranational organisations, like the European Central Bank and the International Monetary Fund*, were primarily responsible. In none of the countries was the responsibility to solve the crisis dominantly attributed to the *countries with sovereign debt problems*. The widespread preference for the solution of the euro crisis by the eurozone members as a group and the low relevance of a solution by countries with sovereign debt problems may indicate the devotion to the idea of Europe as a community of solidarity members.

The main mechanisms needed for the solution was not a major topic, but it was an important one. The number of relevant articles ranged from 100 (Italy) to 1,138 (Germany), with an average of 480 per country. According to the dominant views in France (41%), Italy (32%), Finland (42%), and the Netherlands (51%), *loans from other countries without supervision or abatement of existing loans* were the main mechanisms needed. This differed from the dominant view in Germany (47%) where the newspapers primarily asked for *loans from other countries with supervision*. According to the dominant view in the UK (33%), *loans from the European Central Bank* were needed. The dominant view in Spain (32%) and Belgium (38%) asked for the *reduction of budget deficits*. Table 3.1 illustrates the type of dominant views on roots, responsibilities, and mechanisms needed in the various countries (Table 3.1).

Table 3.1 Typology of dominant views on roots, responsibilities, and main mechanisms needed in various countries

	Roots	Responsibilities	Mechanisms
Germany	National policies	Eurozone members	Loans with supervision
France	Starting conditions	Eurozone members	Loans without supervision
UK	Starting conditions	Eurozone members	ECB loans
Italy	Starting conditions	Supranational organisations	Loans without supervision
Spain	Political roots	Supranational organisations	Reduce budget deficits
Belgium	National policies	Eurozone members	Reduce budget deficits
Finland	National policies	Eurozone members	Loans without supervision
Netherlands	Starting conditions	Eurozone members	Loans without supervision

From a theoretical point of view it would be reasonable to use articles that represent combinations of dominant views on roots, responsibilities, and measures in the various countries as units of analysis. This was not possible because the information provided in the individual articles was not as complex as expected: only 4% of all articles provided information on roots and responsibilities and measures; only 23% included information at least on two of the three aspects. Therefore, we used dominant views of roots, responsibilities, and measures independent from each other. In an attempt to base the analysis on clear-cut views we excluded from the analysis all articles in which dominant views on one topic (i.e. roots, responsibility, and mechanisms) were combined with inconsistent views on other topics. For example, articles in German newspapers presenting the dominant view on roots of the crisis (national industrial, fiscal, and social policies) were only included in the analysis when they provided consistent information on responsibilities (eurozone members as a group), the main measures needed (loans from other countries with supervision) – or no information on responsibilities or measures at all. Clear-cut dominant views on responsibilities and mechanisms were identified by the same procedure for each country under investigation. Table 3.2 presents the number of articles

Table 3.2   Number of statements presenting dominant views for each country

	Roots	Responsibility	Mechanism	Total
Germany	72	302	426	800
France	76	302	204	582
UK	93	106	91	290
Italy	30	230	154	414
Spain	27	112	38	177
Belgium	17	80	53	150
Finland	24	196	137	357
Netherlands	36	243	134	413

published in the various countries after the exclusion of a small number of articles presenting inconsistent combinations of dominant views. It should be noted that the figures do not refer to the number of articles but to the number of statements in articles. Theoretically, statements on roots, responsibilities, and mechanisms could be placed in three different articles or together in one article.

The German press dealt more often with the roots of the euro crisis, the responsibility for solving it, and measures needed than the press in all other countries under investigation. This might be traced back to the strong devotion of German politics to the European Community since the Treaty of Rome in 1957. In contrast, the press in the UK, Spain, and Belgium dealt only seldom with the three aspects mentioned. In the case of the UK, this might be explained by the fact that it is not a member of the eurozone. More astonishing is the case of Belgium, because Brussels is the political and administrative centre of the European Community, and because Belgium is economically in a position similar to the Netherlands, where the three aspects raised more than twice as much media attention.

In all countries but one, the newspapers most often dealt with the responsibility for the solution of the euro crisis. The exception was Germany where the newspapers dealt most often with the mechanisms needed to solve the euro crisis. This might be traced back partly to the strong devotion of German politics to Europe and partly to the expectation of some countries to solve the euro crisis with loans from Germany without supervision. In Germany this was regarded as a threat to the stability of the currency. There were remarkable differences in the emphasis given to that aspect. In Germany and France, the newspapers published many more articles dealing with this issue than the press in the UK, Spain, and Belgium. It might be surprising that in all countries under investigation, the newspapers dealt very seldom with the roots of the crisis. But the low number of articles may not necessary lead to the conclusion that the newspapers were not interested in the search for causes of the crisis. Instead, it indicates that the press is not primarily devoted to explaining the past but to describing the present time and to outlining future developments.

Results

Quasi-experiments

For the quasi-experiments, the coverage seven days before the events was compared to the coverage seven days after the events. To make the analysis as easy as possible and in order to obtain a sufficient number of articles for the analysis, the coverage on the 11 events will be summarised. No significant difference between the coverage before and after the events indicates that the events did not cause any remarkable change in the dominant views. A significant difference indicates that the events caused a change in the typical presentations of roots, responsibilities, or mechanisms. In this case, two contradictory possibilities have to be distinguished. The events could intensify dominant views or they could erode them. To facilitate the reading and understanding of the data, in the following text the relevant percentages are mentioned.

Except for Italy, the 11 major political and economic events had no significant influence on the dominant views of the roots of the euro crisis. In the case of the Italian press, the events weakened the dominant view (starting conditions and structure of the euro system are a major cause of the euro crisis) from 3% to 0.6% of all articles. Except for the UK, the 11 major political and economic events had no significant influence on the dominant views of the responsibility for solving the euro crisis. In the case of the British press, the events weakened the dominant view (the eurozone members as a group are responsible) from 7.1 to 3.9% of all articles. Except for Germany and Italy, the major political and economic events had no significant influence on the dominant view of the mechanisms necessary for the solution of the euro crisis. In case of the German press, the events weakened the dominant view (loans from other countries with supervision as the necessary mechanism) from 21.8 to 16.0% of all articles. In the case of the Italian press, the events weakened the dominant view (loans from other countries without supervision and abatement of existing loans as the necessary mechanism) from 11.4 to 5.7% of all articles (Table 3.3).

To summarise the results: there could have been 24 significant influences of the political and economic events on the dominant views of the roots, the responsibilities, and the necessary mechanisms in the press of the

Table 3.3 Dominant views on roots, responsibilities, and mechanisms before and after the political and economic events

	Roots		Responsibility		Mechanisms	
	Before	*After*	*Before*	*After*	*Before*	*After*
Germany Before n = 1,066 After n = 1,214	3.8	2.6	14.5	12.2	21.8^3	16.0^3
France Before n = 1,108 After n = 1,170	3.2	3.4	12.3	14.2	9.9	8.0
UK Before n = 1,002 After n = 894	5.5	4.3	7.1^2	3.9^2	4.0	5.7
Italy Before n = 810 After n = 1,084	3.0^1	0.6^1	13.6	11.1	11.4^4	5.7^4
Spain Before n = 596 After n = 466	2.0	3.2	10.6	10.5	2.9	4.5
Belgium Before n = 425 After n = 368	1.6	2.7	11.1	9.0	5.9	7.6
Finland Before n = 429 After n = 447	2.8	2.7	23.5	21.3	14.9	16.3
Netherlands Before n = 361 After n = 310	5.0	5.8	39.1	32.9	21.9	17.7

Notes: Values are percentages. Calculations based on the number of dominant views that may differ from country to country; superscripted figures indicate significant change: [1] χ^2 = 17,265, df = 1, p = 0.000; [2] χ^2 = 9,000, df = 1, p = 0.003; [3] χ^2 = 12,495, df = 1, p = 0.000; [4] χ^2 = 19,731, df = 1, p = 0.000.

countries analysed. Of these, only four actually occurred, which equals 17%. Two of the four significant changes happened in Italy. All of the significant changes reduced the dominance of the typical views and thus might have contributed to the convergence of views in Italy, Germany, and the UK.

Trend analysis

Major political and economic events may not change dominant views immediately but they might have a significant influence in the long run. Therefore, we divided the 11 events into three periods. Figure 3.1 illustrates the three periods and gives some basic information on the events included and the number of articles dealing with them.

The press coverage in four countries – Germany, the UK, Belgium, and Finland – displayed significant changes in the dominant views on the roots of the euro crisis. In each country, the dominant view became less prominent. For example, in the German press, the dominant view (national industrial, fiscal, and social policies in countries with major sovereign debt problems caused the crisis) was reduced from period 1 to period 3. As a consequence, the public conflict between these countries and the other countries under investigation decreased.

Figure 3.1 Total articles with substantial statements on roots/responsibilities/mechanisms, during three sub-periods

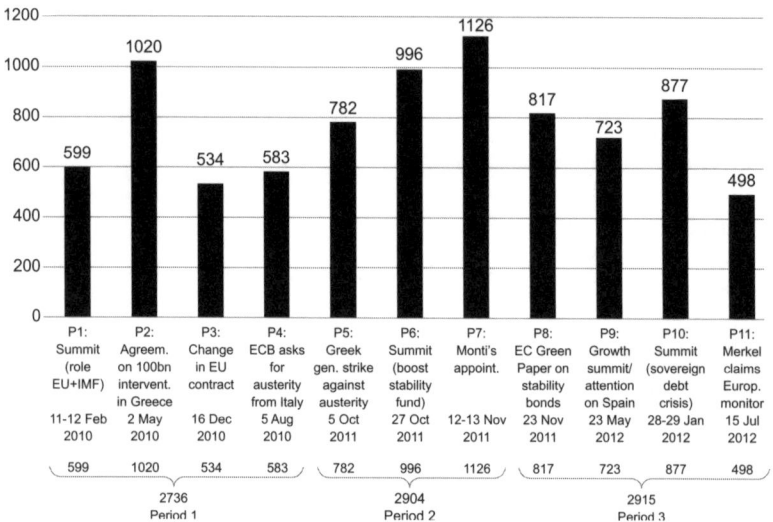

There were also significant changes in the dominant views of the responsibility for the solution of the euro crisis in the press coverage of four countries – Germany, France, Belgium, and the Netherlands. But mostly they ran in a direction opposite to the cases mentioned before. Only in France was the dominant view (eurozone members as a group have to solve the problem) reduced. In Belgium and the Netherlands, the same dominant view became even more prominent. In Germany, the same dominant view reached its peak at the height of the crisis in the second period. From these data, one can conclude that the public controversy between Germany, Belgium, and the Netherlands on the one hand and Italy and Spain on the other hand increased because their dominant views more or less continued to demand opposites.

In five countries – Germany, France, Italy, Finland, and the Netherlands – the press coverage displayed significant changes in the dominant views on the mechanisms needed to solve the euro crisis. In four of the five countries, the dominant views on the mechanisms needed became less prominent. For example, in the German press, the dominant view (loans from other countries with supervision) was reduced from period 1 to period 3. In France, the dominant view (loans without supervision) reached its peak at the height of the controversy in period 2 but fell back to its original level in the third period. Because the dominant view in Germany demanded the opposite of the dominant views in Italy, Finland, and the Netherlands, the reduction in dominant views meant the public controversy between these countries significantly decreased. Contrary to these developments, the public controversy between Germany and France reached its peak in the second period and was calmed down in the third period to its level during the first period (Table 3.4).

To summarise these results: there could have been 24 significant changes of dominant views from period 1 to period 3. Of these, no less than 13 actually occurred, which equals 54%. This was more than double the changes that could be identified within the weeks before and after the events (i.e. the quasi-experimental analysis). The newspapers in Germany (3), France (2), Belgium (2), Finland (2), and the Netherlands (2) significantly changed their dominant views most often. When dominant views explaining the roots of the euro crisis and demanding specific mechanisms were significantly changed, the public controversies between countries were reduced. But when dominant views attributing the responsibility to solve the euro crisis significantly changed, the degree of public controversies increased.

Relevance of sources

The presence and resistance of dominant views might be a consequence of the dominance of national sources in the relevant newspapers. The assumption might be specified in the following way. First, national sources are more often quoted than foreign and international sources (see also Chapter 4) and this might reinforce the presence of dominant views. Second,

Table 3.4 Dominant views on roots, responsibilities, and mechanisms during the first, second, and third periods

	Roots			Responsibility			Mechanisms		
	P1	P2	P3	P1	P2	P3	P1	P2	P3
Germany									
P1 $n = 752$									
P2 $n = 712$	4.0[1]	3.7[1]	2.0[1]	10.9[5]	19.1[5]	10.3[5]	16.8[9]	27.2[9]	13.0[9]
P3 $n = 818$									
France									
P1 $n = 820$									
P2 $n = 694$	3.9	3.2	2.9	16.3[6]	9.2[6]	13.6[6]	7.8[10]	11.8[10]	7.6[10]
P3 $n = 764$									
UK									
P1 $n = 536$									
P2 $n = 682$	8.4[2]	4.6[2]	2.5[2]	7.5	4.8	4.9	6.5	4.0	4.3
P3 $n = 678$									
Italy									
P1 $n = 576$									
P2 $n = 502$	2.1	0.8	1.7	11.1	13.1	12.3	10.8[11]	5.6[11]	7.8[11]
P3 $n = 816$									
Spain									
P1 $n = 321$									
P2 $n = 345$	0.9	3.8	2.8	10.0	11.3	10.4	4.4	2.3	4.0
P3 $n = 396$									
Belgium									
P1 $n = 242$									
P2 $n = 280$	4.6[3]	1.1[3]	1.1[3]	7.9[7]	7.9[7]	14.4[7]	7.9	4.6	7.7
P3 $n = 271$									
Finland									
P1 $n = 260$									
P2 $n = 271$	6.9[4]	1.5[4]	0.6[4]	23.1	22.5	21.7	23.5[12]	16.6[12]	9.0[12]
P3 $n = 345$									

Table 3.4 *(Continued)*

	Roots			Responsibility			Mechanisms		
	P1	P2	P3	P1	P2	P3	P1	P2	P3
Netherlands									
P1 $n = 217$									
P2 $n = 248$	4.6	4.8	6.8	30.0^8	32.7^8	47.1^8	20.3^{13}	24.6^{13}	14.1^{13}
P3 $n = 206$									

Notes: Values are percentages. P1: Outbreak of the crisis in Greece and spread in Europe (February 2010–August 2011). P2: Peak of the crisis (September–November 2011). P3: Establishment of crisis management (November 2011–July 2012). Calculations based on the number of dominant views which may differ from country to country; superscripted figures indicate significant changes: [1] $\chi^2 = 6{,}091$, $df = 2$, $p = 0.048$; [2] $\chi^2 = 22{,}545$, $df = 2$, $p = 0.000$; [3] $\chi^2 = 9{,}577$, $df = 2$, $p = 0.008$; [4] $\chi^2 = 24{,}741$, $df = 2$, $p = 0.000$; [5] $\chi^2 = 31{,}018$, $df = 2$, $p = 0.000$; [6] $\chi^2 = 16{,}694$, $df = 2$, $p = 0.000$; [7] $\chi^2 = 8{,}403$, $df = 2$, $p = 0.015$; [8] $\chi^2 = 15{,}580$, $df = 2$, $p = 0.000$; [9] $\chi^2 = 53{,}617$, $df = 2$, $p = 0.000$; [10] $\chi^2 = 10{,}037$, $df = 2$, $p = 0.007$; [11] $\chi^2 = 9{,}817$, $df = 2$, $p = 0.007$; [12] $\chi^2 = 23{,}827$, $df = 2$, $p = 0.000$; [13] $\chi^2 = 7{,}810$, $df = 2$, $p = 0.020$.

national sources are primarily quoted or referred to with statements fitting the dominant views; foreign and international sources are mostly quoted or referred to with statements differing from the dominant views. Therefore, the dominant views are a consequence of the one-sidedness of national sources. Sources can be politicians, bankers, financiers, economists, and society representatives – major players like Jean Claude Juncker and anonymous representatives of organisations (see also Chapter 5). To keep the analysis as simple as possible, these differences will be neglected and all sources are classified as national, foreign, or international.[10]

The press coverage of most countries under investigation does not support the assumptions. First, only the German and Finnish newspapers primarily published statements from domestic sources. The newspapers in all other countries presented mainly sources from foreign countries. Therefore, in most countries the sheer number of national sources cannot be regarded as a major cause of dominant views. Second, in only four cases are there significant differences between the percentages of statements from the three types of sources. They existed in the coverage of the German, French, Italian, and Finnish newspapers and dealt with the responsibility for the solution of the euro crisis. But, contrary to expectations, in all four cases the highest percentage of statements fitting the dominant views did not characterise the presentation of national but of international sources. Therefore, the one-sidedness of national sources cannot be regarded as a major cause of dominant views. The number of national sources as well as the one-sidedness of national sources might have had an influence on the establishment of the various dominant views, but they were not the most important causes.

To summarise the results: there could have been eight countries in which national sources might have coloured the dominant views, but only in two countries did the necessary condition exist – national sources outnumbered other sources. There could have been 24 differences between the percentages of statements from different sources. Of these, only four differed significantly. All four cases contradicted the assumption: the percentage of information typical for the various countries was highest in quotes from international sources. This might partly be explained by the character of the nationally distributed quality papers and of the economic papers under investigation (see also Chapter 8). They have access to international and foreign sources and inform readers who expect information from a broad range of politicians and experts from all relevant countries. This might be another explanation for the limited impact of major political and economic events on the coverage of the euro crisis (see Table 3.5).

Conclusions

The existence of different dominant views on the roots of the euro crisis, the responsibility for solving it, and the mechanism needed for the solution of the crisis, do not support some of the optimistic findings referred to at the beginning. The differences might be explained by the design and methods of the various studies. We did not concentrate on the emphasis that the media has given to EU-related topics and issues, indicated by their sheer quantity of coverage (see Peter et al., 2003). Instead we focused on the specific content of coverage; we dealt with problem definitions. In addition our study investigated media coverage in times of a severe crisis and not in routine periods like previous studies (see Pfetsch et al., 2008). For these reasons, the divergent results of the studies do not contradict each other. They cannot be adequately compared because they deal with different topics, different circumstances, and used different methods.

We neither analysed a representative sample of the newspapers in the various countries, nor did we distinguish the different types of newspapers included in our sample (see also Chapter 8). Representative samples of newspapers would have been – if possible at all – misleading. There is,

Table 3.5 Dominant views on roots, responsibilities, and measures from domestic, foreign, and international sources

	Roots			Responsibility			Mechanisms		
	Domestic	Foreign	Internat.	Domestic	Foreign	Internat.	Domestic	Foreign	Internat.
Germany Domestic $n = 296$, Foreign $n = 200$, Internat. $n = 60$	3.4	6.0	6.7	14.2[1]	8.0[1]	20.0[1]	18.2	16.0	23.3
France Domestic $n = 178$, Foreign $n = 290$, Internat. $n = 100$	4.5	5.5	2.0	4.5[2]	13.8[2]	18.0[2]	2.2	6.9	6.0
UK Domestic $n = 118$, Foreign $n = 163$, Internat. $n = 53$	4.2	8.0	5.7	9.3	4.3	9.4	4.2	3.1	5.7
Italy Domestic $n = 58$, Foreign $n = 80$, Internat. $n = 30$	6.9	5.0	0.0	13.8[3]	5.0[3]	20.0[3]	10.3	7.5	13.3
Spain Domestic $n = 60$, Foreign $n = 118$, Internat. $n = 45$	0.0	2.5	0.0	5.0	11.9	8.9	6.7	1.7	2.2

(Continued)

Table 3.5 *(Continued)*

	Roots			Responsibility			Mechanisms		
	Domestic	Foreign	Internat.	Domestic	Foreign	Internat.	Domestic	Foreign	Internat.
Belgium Domestic $n=62$ Foreign $n=92$ Internat. $n=48$	4.8	2.2	2.1	8.1	15.2	18.8	6.5	4.3	10.4
Finland Domestic $n=139$ Foreign $n=93$ Internat. $n=53$	2.9	4.3	0.0	20.1[4]	16.1[4]	34.0[4]	18.0	9.7	18.9
Netherlands Domestic $n=50$ Foreign $n=71$ Internat. $n=28$	3.8	1.4	0.0	32.7	30.6	39.3	19.2	13.9	21.4

Notes: Values are percentages. Calculations based on the number of dominant views that may differ from country to country; analysis includes only articles with a single source cited. Superscripted figures indicate significant changes: [1] $\chi^2 = 7,510$, $df = 2$, $p = 0.023$; [2] $\chi^2 = 14,098$, $df = 2$, $p = 0.001$; [3] $\chi^2 = 6,009$, $df = 2$, $p = 0.050$; [4] $\chi^2 = 6,638$, $df = 2$, $p = 0.036$.

for example, no equivalent to the large number of regional newspapers in Germany, the UK, France, and Italy. Differences between the three types of newspapers – national quality papers, economic papers, and tabloids – exist (see Chapters 9 and 10) but they had to be neglected. Otherwise, the complexity of data would have confused the main results of our study on the possible effects of major political and economic events on crisis coverage. Nevertheless, the mentioned differences should be taken into consideration.

Dominant views shaped the coverage of the roots of the euro crisis, the responsibility for solving it and the specific mechanisms needed more than major political and economic events. In only about one-fifth of all cases did the specific character of the events significantly change the dominant views presented in the coverage of the week following these events. If that happened, it contributed to the reduction of different views in the countries under investigation. From these findings one can conclude that the type of coverage about the roots of the euro crisis, the responsibilities to solve it, and the mechanisms needed for a solution in the context of major political and economic events was not predominantly driven by these events. Instead, it was mainly driven by dominant views existing already before the events happened.

The very small influence exerted by the major political and economic events on the press coverage in the week following these events might be explained by the short period of time: maybe the influence of the events on the coverage does not really manifest within one week but needs several months or even years to become visible? This idea is supported by the coverage about the causes (roots) of the euro crisis and the mechanisms needed to solve it from period 1 to period 3. From the beginning of period 1 in Spring 2010 to the end of period 3 in Summer 2012, the public controversies between some of the countries under investigation represented by their leading newspapers diminished. This might be traced back to the influence of the major political and economic events that slowly manifested itself in the framing of causes of the euro crisis and the mechanisms needed. The contrary happened with the coverage on the responsibility for solving the euro crisis. In the long run, the dominant views already existing in various countries became even more prominent, thus increasing the public conflicts between the countries under investigation represented by their leading newspapers. Therefore, with respect to the long-term trend of the press coverage, the results are mixed. When it comes to causes and short-term practical consequences, political and economic events and their consequences might at least partly shape the press coverage. But when the general long-term responsibilities for the solution of the EU crisis are covered, dominant views instead of political and economic events shape the media coverage in the countries. This might be traced back to the fact that the question of the long-term responsibility closely relates to the economic interests of the relevant countries.

The relevance of dominant views is stressed by the analysis of the role of national, foreign, and international sources in the articulation of the views dominant in the countries in which they are quoted. Contrary to the assumption, dominant views were not primarily reinforced by national sources expressing ideas that fit the dominant views but by international sources. The surprising findings might be explained by the theory of instrumental actualisation: the high percentage of international sources supporting the specific dominant views in the various countries could be interpreted as a consequence of the newspapers' preference for such sources as a means of strengthening their own position by prestigious international experts. The general preference for international sources was increased because they had high prestige and were regarded as independent experts – representatives of international organisations. Therefore, the national quality papers and economic papers justified their dominant views especially by quoting or referring to international sources. To put it differently: they were predominantly cited or referred to when their statements fitted the dominant views of the various countries.

From the general practice outlined, which does not exclude the publication of some contradictory voices, two conclusions can be derived. First, the instrumental actualisation of international sources reinforced the dominant views and might have limited the possible effects of major political and economic events on the coverage of roots of the euro crisis and of responsibilities and measures needed to solve it. Second, in every country the readers got the impression that not only national but also international actors supported their domestic point of view. This might have contributed to the growing feeling in many European countries of being the victim of unnecessary, unfair, and dangerous political and economic decisions.

4

Who Will Fix the Economy? Expectations and Trust in the European Institutions

Giovanni Barbieri and Donatella Campus[11]

The euro crisis, because of its cross-national pervasiveness and intensity, has increased the requirements for problem-solving capacity at both national and supranational levels. At the same time, it has raised issues about the attribution of responsibility for facing the crisis. This also involves a reflection on the role of media in the activation and functioning of the accountability mechanisms, so the media not only evaluate their national government performance in handling the crisis but also tend to hold the EU responsible for alleviating the damage in those countries belonging to the eurozone.

This chapter discusses if there exists a common European media approach to the role and the responsibilities of the EU, at least at the level of the quality and business press. A body of research has suggested that the representations of Europe are based on what Risse (2010) has called 'transnational identities and public spheres'. In particular, the activation of some common mechanisms of framing the EU by the media of different national countries seems to provide the basis for the emergence of a Europeanised public sphere (Vreese, 2003; Diez Medrano, 2003; Diez Medrano and Gray, 2010). Diez Medrano and Gray (2010), who carried out an extended comparative analysis on the portrayal of the EU and the process of European integration in a number of member states, have concluded that similarities prevail over differences (even if some cross-national framing contrasts can be detected). Along this line, therefore, one may expect that a common imaginary concerning the role and functions of the EU in facing this worldwide economic crisis will also emerge in our analysis of the press coverage in ten selected countries.

The chapter intends to test if the especially severe economic crisis that started in 2008 has promoted the activation of what can be considered as an embryonic European public sphere, characterised by a unique political agenda and converging interests (Privitera, 2012). If supported by empirical evidence, the existence of a shared view about the role of the EU in handling the economic crisis could reinforce the hypothesis of the emergence of a media-sustained supranational mechanism of accountability. As Schlesinger (1999: 264) has observed, 'by introducing a new, higher political level above that of the nation-state, the shift to a supranational formation begins to transform the established communicative relations between national publics and state-centred systems of power'. Therefore, we may argue that the fact that media and citizens start to look at the EU as a responsible actor for solving problems within the eurozone may be one of the possible consequences of the establishment of a supranational space of political communication.

It should be noted, however, that other contributions on the representation of Europe in national news media do not really support the existence of such a Europeanised public sphere. Rather, they claim that the European public sphere is still segmented (Kleinen-von Königslöw, 2012) and that the different national cultures, along with real political factors, prevent the development of a common view of Europe (Schlesinger, 2003). Models of thinking and discussing European issues are still rooted in the national dimension (Machill et al., 2006; Schlesinger, 2003). If national public spheres give attention to what happens at the EU level, but do not make the effort to connect with other European countries (Kleinen-von Königslöw, 2012), then one may expect that the representations of the EU and its role in handling the crisis will vary across national lines.

Some cross-national divergences in how the media represent the EU are already notorious and incontrovertible. A difference between the UK and all the other countries has been repeatedly stressed by most research on the topic (Diez Medrano, 2003; Machill et al., 2006). But are contrasts limited only to the UK or do they also involve other countries? Chapters 2, 3, and 9 of this book reveal the UK is not alone and that separate national public spheres exist. Does this allow us to argue that the EU is still a part of the domestic media political framework? Or, on the contrary, do cross-national differences pale in comparison with the emergence of a common representation of Europe? And is the citizens' view of Europe somehow linked or does it contradict national media coverage? This chapter will try to answer such questions by illustrating and discussing: (a) how the

European press has described and interpreted the role of the European institutions, that is the EU and the ECB; (b) how the European press has made predictions on possible consequences of the crisis, in particular about the reinforcement of the EU role; (c) how popular trust in the effectiveness of the EU – measured through the Eurobarometer data – is consistent with the emerging trends in the media coverage.

The role of European institutions in the crisis

The starting point of our analysis is how the press has portrayed the two European institutions, the European Union and the European Central Bank. The first element to be taken into consideration is the quantity of the coverage, which means how much each newspaper has been involved in a description and a discussion of the role of the two European institutions in dealing with the economic crisis. The second element concerns the quality of the coverage, that is if there is a predominantly negative coverage, or rather whether the EU and the ECB have been portrayed as key and influential actors.

As for the first aspect, Table 4.1 shows that both the EU and the ECB are quite recurrent elements in the coded news articles, with 39.5% of them devoted to the EU and 27% of them to the ECB. As expected, the ECB, being involved in specific and more technical economic matters, is less mentioned in the articles than the EU.

As for the second aspect, Table 4.1 confirms as well the hypothesis that the press looks predominantly at the European institutions as key actors in charge of addressing the economic crisis. In both the cases of the EU and the ECB the majority of articles describe the two institutions as influential (51% of articles describing the EU and 60% of articles describing the ECB as central or strong and determined institutions). Remarkable in any case is the 47.2% of the articles that refer to the EU as insignificant or powerless or ineffectual. Even if it is not a large difference, it is worth noting that the more technical and less political of the two institutions is less criticised, with 27.8% of articles describing the ECB in a negative way, as insignificant or powerless or ineffectual.

The overall evaluation of European institutions shows a certain degree of variability. Therefore, the most interesting aspects of our analysis will be to examine the diversity of positions across countries and types of newspapers. Are newspapers of certain countries more inclined to cover the EU institutions? Are they more prone to consider them as central and strong

Table 4.1 Portrayal of the EU and ECB

EU	Freq.	Percentage	ECB	Freq.	Percentage
Insignificant in addressing the crisis	201	3.7	Insignificant in addressing the crisis	97	2.6
Lacking capabilities to address the crisis	562	10.4	Lacking capabilities to address the crisis	369	9.9
Ineffectual or confused in addressing the crisis	1,794	33.1	Ineffectual or confused in addressing the crisis	566	15.3
Central to addressing the crisis	2,115	39.0	Central to addressing the crisis	1,732	46.7
Strong and determined in addressing the crisis	652	12.0	Strong and determined in addressing the crisis	495	13.3
Others	99	1.8	Acting within its legal framework	191	5.1
Total	5,423	100.0	Acting at the border or outside of its legal framework	157	4.2
Percentage of articles = 39.5			Others	102	2.8
			Total	3,709	100.0
			Percentage of articles = 27.0		

actors? Is the typology of newspapers (tabloid, quality, business) in each country a key variable to differentiate the quantity and quality of coverage?

Figure 4.1 shows how all the newspapers taken into consideration are located along two dimensions: the quantity of coverage of the EU (i.e. the percentage of articles containing whatever portrayal of the EU) and the assessment of the centrality and efficiency of the EU (the percentage of articles that portrayed the EU with respect to the crisis as central or as

Figure 4.1   Portrayal of the EU

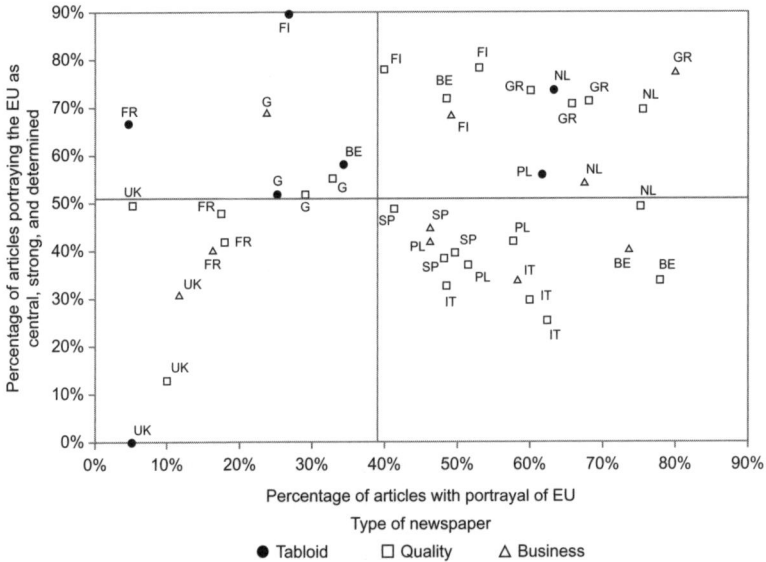

strong and determined[12]). The lines drawn across the chart display the overall data averages, which are 39.5% for the portrayals of the EU and 51% for a portrayal as central or strong and determined.[13] The most salient result shown in Figure 4.1 is the clear intra-country consistency of national newspapers' attitudes toward the EU; that is, in several countries, all national newspapers tend to cover and describe the EU in a similar way. In particular, in the UK, Germany, Greece, Italy, and Spain, newspapers of all types (tabloid, business, and quality newspapers) are grouped together in the same quarter of the figure. For instance, all the four British newspapers are in the first quarter, which means that all four covered the EU less than the average and all four attributed centrality and strength to the EU in a percentage below average. At the opposite quarter of the figure, all Greek newspapers are located together, with a more than the average number of articles and a more than average of articles in the categories of 'central', and 'strong and determined'.

Other countries also show a quite high degree of consistency: for instance, Finland, with three newspapers in the third quarter and just one, the tabloid, in the second quarter. This last one has a number of articles containing a portrayal of the EU below the average, but shares the same views of the other Finnish outlets in terms of centrality and strength of the EU. A high homogeneity also characterises the French and the Polish

Figure 4.2 Portrayal of the ECB

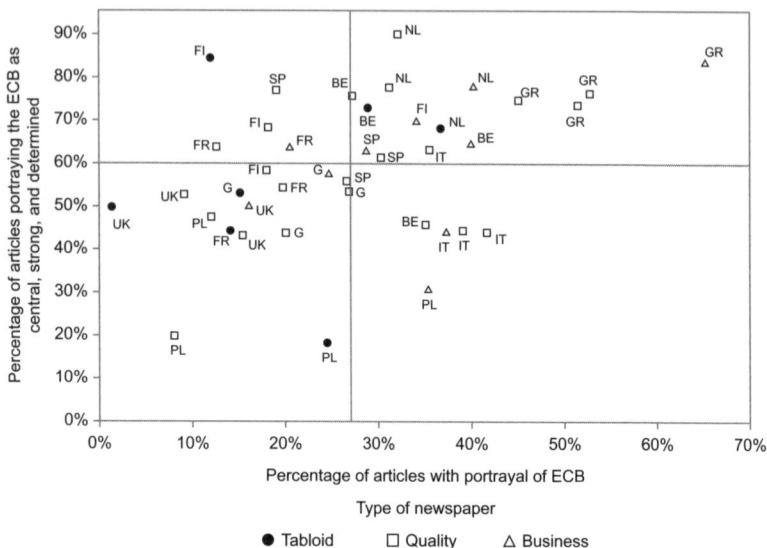

press. In both cases, three of the four newspapers lie in the same quarter while one, the tabloid, is deviant. In the Netherlands, three newspapers are together in the third quarter, while one, the elite *De Volkskrant*, is only slightly divergent, being actually very close to the average line also for the centrality and strength of the EU. Only in Belgium can one observe a true differentiation between the newspapers: the business *De Tijd* and the elite *De Morgen* cover the EU extensively but are mostly critical; another, the elite *De Standaard*, is high on both dimensions; finally the fourth outlet *Het Laatste Nieuws* has a trusting attitude towards the EU action, but covers it less than the others, being in line with most of the other European tabloids, whose majority is below the average of articles with a portrayal of the EU. In this national context, the partisan affiliation may well play a role in making sense of such differences: *De Morgen* is a leftist quality newspaper while *De Standaard* is more centre-rightist, with a lower tendency to question the establishment. Moreover, *De Tijd* and *De Morgen* belong to the same news media company and this helps to explain their closeness in Figure 4.1.

The overall picture of the EU is mirrored by the results on the portrayal of the ECB in Figure 4.2, which is organised similarly to Figure 4.1, with 27% as the average value for the portrayal of the ECB and 60% as the average value for a central or strong and determined portrayal. Here as well, the degree of consistency within individual countries is quite high, even if there is more variability in comparison with the portrayal of the EU. With three or four outlets in the same quarter, there are Belgium, Germany, Greece, Italy, Poland, the Netherlands, and the UK. Only the French press seems to be divided, with two newspapers with a critical attitude and two with a more positive one.

In sum, it should be stressed that, in most of the countries under consideration, the national press shows an entirely or almost entirely consistent attitude toward the EU institutions. This finding is even more striking if one not only considers the diversity in the types of outlets, but also the different partisan views of many of them. In fact, within individual countries, with the already mentioned exception of Belgium, partisanship does not seem to have produced substantially different coverage.[14]

Another observation is that, although the typology of newspapers matters in some degree, this does not emerge as the key factor. The only aspect that can be underlined is a quite functional labour division between the business and quality newspapers, on the one hand, and the tabloids on the other, with the first group mostly placed among those with a number of articles over the average and the second group mostly located on the opposite side. Understandably enough, tabloids focus less on economic matters in comparison with business and elite outlets. However, for a more accurate analysis of the coverage of different types of newspapers, see Chapter 10 of this book.

In light of all this, it is difficult to detect apparent supranational opinion trends. Notwithstanding, one may observe that some countries may be grouped together along some general lines. For instance, it is worth noting that the newspapers of countries not adopting the euro, like the UK and Poland, are among those which express lower expectations about the EU intervention, and, in the case of the UK, even a more limited interest in discussing the role of European institutions. The finding concerning the UK is not surprising since it is well-known from previous research (Diez Medrano and Gray, 2010: 196) that the UK is different from the rest of European countries in its way of representing the EU.

By contrast, the newspapers of countries that are more affected by debt problems and the economic crisis, like Greece, Italy, and Spain, are understandably looking at the EU with more attention than others. Although they have in common a quite large coverage[15] (albeit of different extension), nonetheless they do not appear to share the same view of the European

Figure 4.3 Portrayal of the EU: Greece's peculiarity

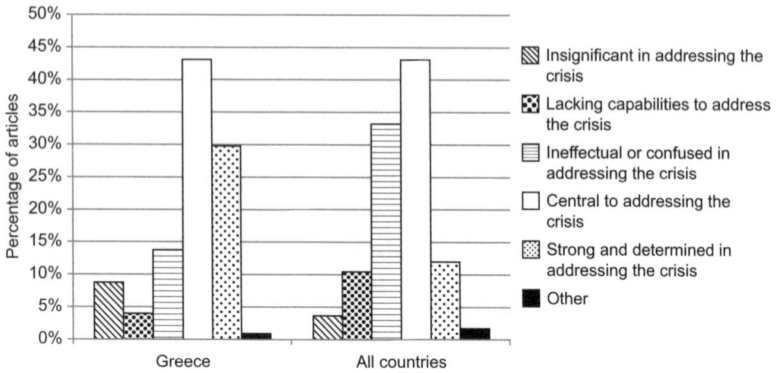

impact on the crisis. While Spain and Italy seem to be more sceptical about the action of the EU and the ECB, the Greek press describes such institutions as much more active. For instance, in Figure 4.3, the assessment of the EU in terms of 'strong and determined' is definitively higher than the average. This may find an explanation in the specific circumstances. In fact, the notable percentage of the category 'strong and determined' can be intended not as a necessarily positive evaluation of the EU but rather as the acknowledgement of the EU intervention in the management of the Greek crisis through the offer of bailout loans conditional on compliance to a number of economic measures by the national government. As a consequence, the Greek press may have developed a stronger belief about the assertiveness of the EU than its counterpart in less troubled countries, like Spain and Italy. In these countries, newspapers may well reveal their worries about the future of their economy and of the eurozone through a high attention to what the European institutions do and what they could do, but they were not facing immediate measures as a consequence of decisions taken at the European level. This line of explanation makes sense of the differences between Greece, on the one hand, and the other countries with serious economic problems, on the other hand.

Trust in a positive solution to the crisis

The analysis of the portrayals given to the EU and the ECB has suggested that the press views seem to be quite differentiated across countries and respond to a number of internal political, social, and economic traits.

Table 4.2 Various forecasts of the consequences of the rescue measures

	Freq.	*Percentage*
Deeper integration/transfer of national sovereignty to European institutions	993	23.2
Stronger and more stable euro	258	6.0
Success/eurozone preserved	1,078	25.2
Final breakup of the eurozone	351	8.2
Failure/countries with sovereign debt problems will drop the euro finally	653	15.2
Establishment of an enduring transfer system to countries with sovereign debt problems	356	8.3
Europe-wide inflation	113	2.6
Other	481	11.2
Total	4,283	100.0
Percentage of articles = 31.2		

We are going to see if such national trends are also reflected in the press analysis of the possible consequences of the crisis.

First of all, in comparison to the portrayals of the EU and the ECB, the percentage of articles coded with reference to the possible consequences of the crisis is slightly inferior to the former and superior to the latter. The overall percentage of 31.2 means that not only has the press given room to the description of the economic crisis, but it has also quite frequently speculated about its possible solutions and outcomes. The most interesting finding is that the predictions about the survival and the recovery of the EU and eurozone exceed more pessimistic forecasts about the consequences of the crisis. In more than half of all articles the press says either that the crisis will lead to a reinforcement of the European powers, with a consequent deeper integration; or that the euro will become stronger and more stable; or that the eurozone will be preserved.

To highlight the general trends of the national press in each country, we have grouped together articles expressing substantial trust in the future of the eurozone and in the reinforcement of European powers (categories 1–3); articles predicting the failure of the eurozone and a weakening of the EU (categories 4, 5); and articles expressing other kinds of worries about the developments of the crisis (categories 6, 7).

Figure 4.4 Forecast of the consequences of the rescue measures by newspaper type

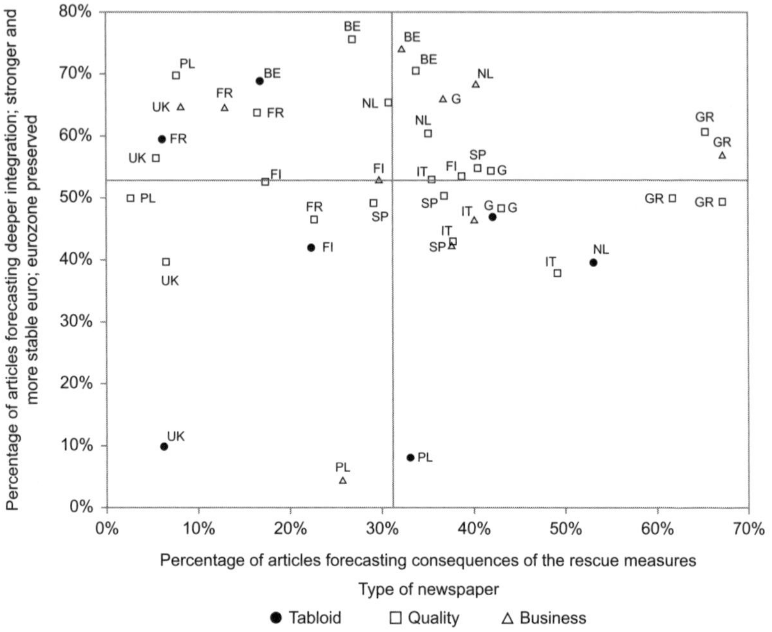

Percentage of articles forecasting deeper integration; stronger and more stable euro; eurozone preserved

Percentage of articles forecasting consequences of the rescue measures

Type of newspaper
● Tabloid   □ Quality   △ Business

Figure 4.4 shows how all the newspapers taken into consideration are located along two dimensions: the percentage of articles dealing with the consequences of the crisis (x-axis) and the percentage of these articles which portrayed the consequences in terms of deeper integration, a stronger and more stable euro, and a preserved eurozone (y-axis). The lines drawn across the chart display the overall data averages, which are 31.2% (x-axis) and 54.4 % (y-axis).

With respect to the previously discussed portrayals of the EU and ECB, the scenario here appears characterised by less intra-country homogeneity. If, in some cases, all newspapers of the same country are still grouped together or are relatively close to each other, in others there are notable differences. A possible explanation can be found in the technical nature of the topic, since assessing possible consequences is a more complex task than simply evaluating the overall performance or expressing trust in an institution. This aspect may produce differences in the coverage of business outlets, for instance, which are mainly placed in the upper quarters; that is, they have a number of articles with an optimistic approach on possible consequences over the average. Moreover, if we compare in each country the business newspaper with the tabloid, in all cases except Poland, the first appears definitively more trusting in a positive ending. This suggests that, albeit in substantial agreement with the other national newspapers on how to evaluate the role of the EU, business newspapers may have offered a more detached assessment based on economic reports and data, while tabloids may have given voice to popular worries about the future in a more emotional way.

Media and citizens: common or divergent views of the EU role?

The analysis of the portrayals given to the EU and ECB has shown that the press narratives in each individual country under consideration are quite homogeneous and seem to be country-specific in the sense that they respond to a number of domestic political, social, and economic traits. Starting from the premise that news exposure and the content of economic news coverage may influence citizens' assessment (Boomgaarden et al., 2011; Hetherington, 1996) and, therefore, that the representation of the EU's effectiveness in handling the crisis by the news media may exert some effects on the public opinion, it may be valuable to compare our results with some measures of European citizens' opinion on the role of the EU in dealing with the crisis. In order to do so, we will analyse some data from five waves of the Eurobarometer (Standard Eurobarometer, 73 (Spring 2010)–Standard Eurobarometer, 77 (Spring 2012)), which more or less coincide with the interval of time taken into consideration by our analysis of the European press.

It should be clear that such an approach does not allow us to test the existence of measurable effects of the media coverage on citizens' views. Simply, we believe that the comparison with the Eurobarometer data might offer an indirect validation (or invalidation) of our argument that in each country a substantially national public sphere has prevailed over a transnational European view. In other words, we are going to explore if there exists a certain degree of correspondence between national media attitudes towards the European institutions and the opinions of the population on the same subject. Will we observe, for instance, that a very critical view or, on the contrary, a substantially trusting attitude of the press is mirrored by the popular opinions? Or will we observe that the press, especially the elite press, is more confident in the EU than its citizens, who, being worried and confused about the dynamics of the crisis, can be more subject to the appeals of anti-euro propaganda?

We have previously observed that the press of individual countries does not share a transnational view and also that notable differences on how the European institutions' role is assessed prevail. If citizens of different countries show the same variability and if, in each single country, there is a certain consistency between media and citizens in their way of looking at the role of the EU, then we may advance the hypothesis that the formation of general views on the EU is a very national matter, that is rooted in the social and political settings of individual national contexts. Of course, this hypothesis cannot be fully tested here with the methodology employed or with the available data; rather our analysis simply intends to provide a background for further discussion and research.

Table 4.3 shows the percentage of respondents who picked the EU as the potentially most effective institution against the effects of the crisis from a study that included also national governments, the International Monetary Fund (IMF), the United States, and G20 among the possible options. In such a way, respondents choosing the EU expressed a higher degree of trust in European institutions in comparison with all the other mentioned political and economic actors. In order to better highlight the results concerning the EU, we have also included in Table 4.3 the percentages of those who picked national governments as the institution that can act more effectively against the effects of the crisis.[16]

At first sight, we may observe that the EU appears to be affected by a general loss of popularity over time, probably due to the worsening of the crisis and its heavier impact on citizens' lives. However, in the majority of our selected countries, the EU is still the institution mostly trusted by citizens to find a solution to the economic crisis. This is true for all countries under consideration except the UK, where the trust in the action of the national government is largely predominant, a finding that is entirely consistent with our results showing the limited trust and interest in the EU institutions of the British press and that confirms previous literature about British exceptionalism (Diez Medrano and Gray, 2010).

It is particularly interesting to pay attention to the countries that have experienced the most evident decline in trust in the EU's effectiveness in handling the crisis, for example Spain and Italy (−10). Here also, we observe a correspondence with our findings. As discussed before, the press of both countries extensively discussed the role of

Table 4.3 Statements of who can act most effectively against the effects of the euro crisis

EU	Sp. 10	Aut. 10	Sp. 11	Aut. 11	Sp. 12	Diff. 10–12
Belgium	36	32	29	32	29	−7
Germany	27	22	20	24	23	−4
Greece	33	37	34	32	28	−5
Spain	33	23	25	25	23	−10
Finland	22	20	23	23	21	−1
France	22	22	18	22	21	−1
Italy	33	29	28	27	23	−10
Netherlands	22	17	16	22	20	−2
Poland	35	35	34	39	30	−5
UK	9	9	10	8	12	3
EU 27	26	23	22	23	21	−5
The (national) government	Sp. 10	Aut. 10	Sp. 11	Aut. 11	Sp. 12	Diff. 10–12
Belgium	10	12	17	13	16	6
Germany	12	17	17	16	18	6
Greece	27	17	13	22	29	2
Spain	16	17	19	21	17	1
Finland	13	12	14	14	13	0
France	19	17	21	22	23	4
Italy	17	16	19	15	14	−3
Netherlands	10	16	16	10	16	6
Poland	13	15	15	13	10	−3
UK	35	40	35	37	34	−1
EU 27	19	20	20	20	21	2

Note: Sp = Spring; Aut = Autumn

the EU, probably because there were expectations about a European intervention to compensate for the perceived national liabilities, but the press assessment of the performance and efficiency of the EU institutions appeared more negative than positive. By contrast, if one looks at the third country with serious economic problems, it appears that the Greek percentages of trust are higher and the decline less (−5) in comparison with those of Spain and Italy. Also, such figures are in line with our results showing that the Greek press was more convinced of the effectiveness of the EU action against the economic crisis.

Further support for our hypothesis of media and citizens' consistent views on the role of the EU comes from Finland and the Netherlands, both countries where the press describes the EU as a central and strong actor and the citizens have stable levels of trust. In contrast, neither French nor Belgian data allows us to speculate about the possible congruence between media and citizens' views. As observed before, the Belgian press gave divergent portrayals of the EU; in France, the press appears more Euro-sceptical than the citizens, who are not affected by a loss of trust, but are also the only group who are equally divided between the EU and national government in their choice of the most effective institution against the crisis (in some ways the second choice is slightly stronger than the first one).

Finally, as for Poland, according to the Eurobarometer data, one may observe a certain decline of trust while the total percentage remains among the highest levels. As previously noted, the Polish press tends to be Euro-sceptical and also not very interested in covering the crisis in terms of its consequences. This can be due to the fact that Poland is an external observer of the difficulties of the eurozone, not having adopted the euro currency; therefore, the issue is not a priority in the media agenda. Notwithstanding, Polish citizens are slowly developing a larger degree of Euro-scepticism after the initial enthusiasm on the EU enlargement.

In summary and with all things considered, including the fact that we are comparing two very heterogeneous sets of data, it would seem that in most countries, citizens' attitudes generally concur with their press narratives. If one could expect a certain divergence between the national newspapers' attitudes (in particular, business and quality press) and the popular view, no particular support is forthcoming from our analysis. Rather, in those countries where citizens seem disillusioned and have lost several percentage points of trust over time, the press also does not seem much more confident in the EU's effectiveness.

A final point that should be stressed is that since the beginning of the economic crisis, there has been a quite generalised decline in trust in the EU, as also highlighted by other data from the Eurobarometer.[17]

In Table 4.3, we observed that citizens of most countries are affected by a loss of trust in the EU; however, even if in most countries there is a parallel increase of trust in government, it is still clear that, on average, European citizens (with the exception of the UK and to a certain extent France) expect to find answers to the crisis by addressing a supranational institution like the EU rather than focusing only on their own internal political resources.

Discussion

What clearly emerges as the main implication of our analysis is that the EU institutions are leading actors in the press narratives of the economic crisis. Even if there are also notable differences in the degree of media attention and of their trust in the EU's effectiveness, the newspapers of the majority of the ten countries under consideration gave coverage to the role of the EU and to the consequences of the crisis for the EU. This confirms our initial hypothesis that the intensity and the pervasiveness of this particular economic crisis have created new expectations on the role of the EU institutions in handling the crisis. However, this does not mean that the presses of all countries form a homogeneous whole in terms of their assessment of the European action. On the contrary, our findings show a certain degree of variability among the ten countries ranging from the Euro-sceptical British press, which gives scarce coverage and expresses mistrust in the EU centrality, to the much more confident Greek and Dutch press.

If the press in different countries has different views on European institutions, the most salient result of our analysis is that there is an evident intra-country homogeneity; that is, all the coded newspapers belonging to the same country share similar attitudes. Our analysis has not met any expectation either of finding large intra-country newspaper differences along partisan views or of registering a notable business–tabloid gap. What emerges as predominant is the feeling that the way of looking at the EU is still forged by domestic predispositions and circumstances and, therefore, all the same-country newspapers tend to align around some general views. In other words, our results do not offer any evidence of the existence of a supranational European public media sphere forged by some types of newspapers or by ideological blocks.

Rather, in each country considered, the press seems to base their narratives of Europe on domestic concerns and national interests. The hypothesis that transnational media networks might form the European public opinion and promote the convergence on some common viewpoints has not received any confirmation in our analysis. As a result we may be more inclined to support the view that the press looks at Europe through a national lens which contributes to different, if not divisive, lines of interpretation within the EU. This suggests that such an unprecedented worldwide economic crisis may have posed notable challenges to the project of a true European integration. So, while the discussion on the crisis may well have an international and, in particular, a European focus, also shown in other chapters in this book, the actual narratives of the press are more country-specific than one might expect. With reference to the literature debate about the existence of a supranational communicative space in Europe, our findings would seem to support a more segmented Europeanisation of national public spheres. The fact that the national press in the individual countries varies in the degree to which it considers the EU as a key actor to solve economic problems reinforces the idea that 'the public spheres remain tied to their national containers' (Kleinen-von Königslöw, 2012: 445).

This is not in full contrast with the idea that the media are promoting a supranational mechanism of accountability. Findings reported in Chapter 2 have already highlighted that the responsibilities of national economic and political actors have become increasingly transferred to European institutions as well as to the eurozone members as a group. In our analysis, the process of shifting or at least integrating the attribution of responsibility for solving the crisis by involving the European level seems to have affected the coverage of the press in several countries under consideration, even if, in others, the specific assessment of the role of the EU has been more dismissive. In summary, we could say that the evidence on this point is mixed.

In this regard, however, further interesting insights have been provided by the comparison of the press attitudes with the citizens' opinions. As already stressed, we were not able to find support for the common hypothesis that citizens, basing their opinions on their subjective worries about the consequences, may develop, especially in times of severe crisis, a more pessimistic view and be less trustful in the action of European institutional actors than the elite press, which is supposed to be more detached and competent in its evaluations. As a matter of fact, in most countries under analysis, it may be observed that the trend of citizens' trust in the EU's effectiveness in handling the crisis is congruent with the way the press has portrayed the role of European institutions.

The important point is that our findings about citizens' views have confirmed that, in most countries, the decline of trust in the EU has not altered the fact that the average European citizen looks more to the EU rather than to their national governments to find effective answers to the crisis. As observed before, our analysis does not allow us to establish any causal relationship between exposure to media and the formation of citizens' attitudes towards the role of Europe during the crisis. However, this is clearly a crucial issue to be explored in further research. The important question could be whether media are able to affect the mechanisms of accountability by leading citizens to consider the EU as an institution increasingly responsible for the state of the economy of countries belonging to the eurozone. As is well-known in the literature on media effects, the media are not only able to set the agenda, but are also capable, under specific conditions, of suggesting the attribution of responsibility (Iyengar, 1991; Iyengar and Kinder, 1987; Iyengar et al., 1982; Krosnick and Kinder, 1990). Such a priming effect has been studied especially in national contexts, but the insights presented in this chapter suggest moving beyond the national framework by extending the analysis to supranational levels of governance. Such an approach will be especially appropriate in situations where the attribution of responsibility for having caused a problem may not coincide with the attribution of responsibility for solving that problem, as may be the case in a worldwide economic crisis.

Part II

Characterisations and Interpretations

5

The Actors of the Crisis: Between Personalisation and Europeanisation

Nicolas Hubé, Susana Salgado, and Liina Puustinen

One of the factors contributing to the complexity of the euro crisis is the number of actors involved. In addition to the European Union institutions and the IMF, there are also the various nations involved, as well as many different actors, from national leaders, to financial actors, or citizens and interest groups, just to provide some examples. All these different types of actors have their own interests and a role to play in this crisis, which is, for obvious reasons, more prominent in some cases than in others. Is the newspapers' coverage giving an accurate reflection of this complexity and including all these actors in the news stories about the crisis, or are some more present in the coverage than others? This chapter discusses these issues and analyses the main actors in the news coverage of the euro crisis. Which actors are in the news and which specific political leaders are more often framed as relevant European leaders? All this relates to the responsibility for solving the problems, but also to the role of the EU institutions in general and to a deficit in the attention given to citizens. Our chapter aims to discuss these perspectives by analysing the news coverage of ten European countries. Do the press reflect these points of view of the predominance of governmental actors as major players in the crisis? At the same time in the fragmented European context we may ask how personalised these actors are. Two interpretative lines will be followed in the chapter: country-specific and changes over time.

Two main ideas that have been discussed in the literature provide context for this analysis of the actors in the euro crisis. The first is related to an alleged relapse in the supranationalisation of the European decision-making processes, and the second to a growing personalisation of politics.

One of the broader hypotheses in European studies since the beginning of the euro crisis has to do with a significant relapse in Europeanisation, that is of the supranationalisation of the decision-making processes. The Lisbon treaty institutionalised a dual constitution, supranational in the single market's policies and intergovernmental in economic and financial policies. However, ever since its entry into force in November 2009, most of the soft phrases of the treaty have had to be addressed. The first was the design of the European economic governance. The implementation of the treaty and the transition from a soft to hard governance actually happened in the shadow of the euro crisis (Dinan, 2011, 2013). Yet, if governments drove this redesigning of financial supervision in the EU, it has paradoxically produced a supranational frame (Hennessy, 2014; Menz and Smith, 2013; Yiangou et al., 2013).

Therefore, despite important decisions in the past towards further integration, the euro crisis seems to have empowered the states (i.e. the governments) over the Commission and some states (e.g. Germany or France) over the others (Crespy, 2013; Ondarza, 2013). This 'intergovernmental turn' taken during the crisis points to a depreciation of the European institutions' role and work. This absence of an integrated voice is prejudicial to the EU's image and to its ability to manage the crisis and gain public support. It also causes structural difficulties in solving the most basic problems of European communitarian action.

However, scholars also insist on a paradoxical effect. The inter-governmental management that seems to weaken the EU institutions also reinforces the supranational nature of European governance; therefore, it is contributing to the legitimisation of new control powers for the European Commission (Copeland and James, 2014; Fabbrini, 2013; Hodson, 2013).

In addition, on the national level, governing leaders have been challenged by both strong personalisation and domestic conflicts. Some have used the crisis to capitalise on their successful role; some have been pointed to as being responsible for it. The 'summitisation' of the euro crisis management has also been criticised (Dinan, 2013: 89) and Heinrich and Kutter (2013) show that this process is reflected in the mediated narratives of the crisis.

In general, the news coverage of European issues fails to provide accurate information on the role of the different EU institutions. In fact, these topics are rarely addressed in the mainstream media. Usually, it is only in times of crisis (such as the resignation of the Santer Commission in 1999 (Georgakakis, 2004) or the euro crisis) that a single issue is actually covered on a European scale. Overall, the treatment of European questions remains largely dependent on national perceptions (for a synthesis, see Vreese and Boomgaarden, 2012).

Media coverage is most intensive during European summits, where heads of state and of government meet, because these events provide an opportunity to speak about the national leaders in the European context (Guillaume and Le Torrec, 2003). The European institutions and actors (the Commission, the President of the Commission and of the European Council, the European Parliament and the MEPs, etc.) are significantly under-represented if not altogether ignored. Baisnée (2013) explains how this gulf between EU journalism and conventional political journalism grows ever wider. Even though the supranational union is clearly political and of great substantial importance, its political processes provide a poor fit for forms of political journalism that are only oriented towards some well-known actors and concerned with some kinds of events. Consequently, media coverage is typically highly personalised and dominated by national government leaders, whereas other actors tend to disappear.

The relative personalisation of the European actors

The news media are often blamed for European citizens' disinterest in European issues in general and in the European institutions' decisions in particular (Badouard, 2010; Harrison and Wessels, 2009; Koopmans and Statham, 2010). European affairs are presented by the media as 'an elite business' and European citizens are not usually called to intervene or to give opinions. European integration is definitely an elite-driven process (Best et al., 2012; Haller, 2008). But these elites are divided between those working at the communitarian level and those working at national levels. Within these European domestic elites, national frames of perceptions (and to a lesser extent ideological ones) are driving elites' actions and positions concerning European integration (Gaxie and Hubé, 2013).

At the same time, Pérez (2013) has drawn attention to other problems. To this author, there is a deficit of politicisation within European politics and the EU is a 'pseudo-confederation full of anti-publicity bias and elite-driven integration'. This disconnection between European institutions and citizens may therefore be explained by more reasons than just simply a 'communications gap', what the latest qualitative surveys identify as a 'euro-indifference' and not as a politicised Euro-scepticism (Duchesne et al., 2013; Gaxie et al., 2011; White, 2010).

Although evidence is still far from being definitive, over the last decades there has been a persistent idea in the literature pointing to increasing levels of personalisation in the media coverage of political news (e.g. Mazzoleni, 2000; McAllister, 2007). 'The general belief is that the focus of news coverage has shifted from parties and organisations to candidates and leaders' (Van Aelst et al., 2012). This trend has been so discussed that Van Aelst and colleagues (2012) have decided to review the concept, its operationalisation in different research, and the key findings of these existing studies, with the objective of proposing an inclusive conceptualisation and operationalisation for furthering comparative research and the cumulativeness of results regarding the personalisation of news.

It is important to acknowledge that, although personalisation of politics is not something entirely new, it was enhanced by a growing mediatisation of politics, with the media as the most important intermediaries between politicians and citizens. Moreover, the increasing economic and political interdependency of nations and the enhancement of the complexity of both political issues and media environments also provide a basis to comprehend the tendency for a growing personalisation of power in liberal democracies. In literature, personalisation is usually related to the mediatisation effects (Esser and Strömbäck, 2014; Strömbäck, 2008). Salgado (2012) draws attention to some of the effects of the mediatisation of politics: an acceleration of political decision times due to media and public opinion pressures; the media agenda-setting function influencing the management and setting of political priorities; a simplification of political discourses and issues to be adjusted to media formats; and an enhancement of the personalisation of politics (2012: 241). According to Swanson and Mancini (1996), an important effect of modernisation is the dilution of 'polyarchies' around single political leaders and therefore the empowerment of individual political figures at the expense of the authority of political parties and institutions.

Given the magnitude and nature of the euro crisis and the general trends of political news coverage previously suggested by different research and authors, we expect to find high degrees of personalisation in the news coverage of the euro crisis. At the same time, regarding the previous remarks on lack of identification with the EU, we could also expect quite the opposite result.

Regarding our research on the euro crisis news coverage, it is important to see if news stories introduce different actors, which actors are actually included, and the weight that each actor has in the coverage. We started by looking at the presence of actors and the type of sources quoted in the news stories about the euro crisis. A preliminary analysis (see Table 5.1) shows that, in a sample of 10,492 news stories, there were 20,459 mentions of actors. The analysis also points to an overall percentage of approximately 80% of news stories with actors. Greece and Italy stand out as the countries with more news stories mentioning and quoting actors, and conversely Dutch journalists have covered the euro crisis with less inclusion of actors in their news stories. In the remaining countries, there is not much variation to be noted; the percentages are similar, with between roughly 72% and 82% of news stories on the euro crisis including the presence of actors.

Nevertheless, it is interesting to note that, although having mentioned actors, about half of news stories did not quote any actor specifically (see Table 5.1). In this case, cross-country variation is more expressive and different groups of countries emerge: Italy, Greece, Spain, and mainly Finland have the highest percentages of news stories with quotes from actors, while the UK, the Netherlands, and Poland have the lowest

Table 5.1 Articles dealing with and naming actors

Dealing with actors		Naming actors	
Italy	93.6	Finland	78.7
Greece	92.9	Spain	68.1
Germany	81.9	Italy	66.9
Finland	81.1	Greece	66.6
France	77.8	Germany	52.4
Spain	76.5	France	45.8
Belgium	76.3	Belgium	43.0
Poland	73.6	Netherlands	28.0
UK	72.4	Poland	24.4
Netherlands	65.1	UK	21.9

Notes: $N = 10,492$. Values are percentages.

percentages of quotations. Germany, France, and Belgium have results in between. Overall, there were 11,172 quotations and references to actors quoted directly. The coverage of the crisis shows a tendency of relative non-personalisation of the actors. If 20,459 actors are quoted, only 11,172 are done by name. This is probably due to the presumed lack of knowledge on European affairs and the national orientation of the readers. Journalists are tackling the issue by naming well-identified institutions (e.g. the ECB) and not the actors (e.g. Jean-Claude Trichet). Also, it is interesting to note that non-EMU members (UK and Poland) are those who pay the least attention to these actors.

The next step of our analysis is to identify the actors that journalists refer to most often and to examine in more detail the implications of these newsmaking choices.

Politicisation and nationalisation of crisis management

Looking at the total of 20,459 actors quoted, it is possible to see that the national political leaders clearly dominate the press coverage (see Table 5.2). They represent more than four out of ten actors (42.2%). At the same time, major actors like EU and IMF officials represent approximately one out of ten actors (11.7%). Economic actors and experts form the second major group of actors presented in the press. They represent around three out of ten actors (29.6%). This validates the hypothesis of a crisis managed at the intergovernmental level, by national political leaders. It also confirms some previous analysis: the management of the crisis can *only* be done by major national politicians under control of the business experts, commenting on the decisions and arguing against the Europeanised (and supranational) solutions but from national economics perspectives (Heinrich and Kutter, 2013). This

Table 5.2 Types of actors in the news stories

National political leaders	Economic actors and experts	EU and IMF officials	Society representatives	Others
42.2	29.6	11.7	9.5	7.1

Notes: N = 20,459. Values are percentages.

framing of the crisis is probably a mixed effect of the traditional patterns of EU coverage (Vreese and Boomgaarden, 2012) and of the specificity of the crisis discourse, 'a surfeit of summits' (Dinan, 2012: 86, 2013). On the same line, it is not surprising that the civil society is not that much represented (9.5%).

Similar results were found by Schiffrin and Fagan (2012) when they studied the US economic press coverage of the stimulus package in 2009 after the bank crisis. They reported that government sources were the most frequently quoted (76.9%), followed by business sources (21.7%), while the public was nearly absent (4.7%). Also, many other studies focusing on the economic press (e.g. Parker, 1997) have found that economic journalism devotes a high volume of coverage to government, whereas ordinary people are nearly excluded from the daily news (see also Chapter 8).

Schiffrin and Fagan (2012) argue that stories about economic indicators, corporate earnings, financial markets, and banking focus on short-term news, not on the larger social implications of the events. The sources that journalists turn to are traders, fund managers, government officials, analysts, businessmen, PR people, and press officers. Parker writes that government data are the main source for economic journalism, which routinely interprets economic information in the light of its impact on political actors and trends. 'As a consequence, readers and viewers find the "frames" through which "economic" news is presented almost ineluctably bound to "politics" and government' (Parker, 1997: 5–6). In the same vein, Kutter (2014) explains that the German business press distinguishes itself from the elite and the tabloid press by insisting on business-oriented solutions. This is confirmed by the cross-tabulation of actors and type of press (see Table 5.3 and also Chapter 8). Economic actors are overrepresented in the business press and elite and tabloid presses are quite similar in their choice of actors, with small differences: the tabloid press has less EU and IMF officials and a few more civil society actors.

Thus, the news coverage is mainly based on an overpoliticisation of the crisis (see Figure 5.1; the horizontal line represents the 11 periods coded) and is also strongly 'event dependent' (Baisnée, 2013).

Figure 5.2 shows the difference in treatment between national political leaders and the economic actors. The differences between politicians and EU and IMF officials are less event-dependent and also positive, with politicians' overrepresentation varying from 19% to 37%.

Table 5.3   Actors in news stories according to type of press

Type of press	National political leaders	Economic actors and experts	EU and IMF officials	Society representatives	Others
Business	32.3	40.6	10.7	9.5	6.9
Elite	46.3	24.4	12.6	9.2	7.4
Tabloid/ Popular	48.4	28.5	7.2	12.3	3.7
Mean	42.2	29.6	11.7	9.5	7.1

Notes: N = 20,459. Values are percentages.

Only in period 1 (4–18 February 2010) are political actors weaker than national economists (34% versus 39.7%). Subsequently, the more the crisis is managed by the European Council until mid-2012 at the 'apex of the intergovernmental moment' (Dinan, 2011; Fabbrini, 2013: 1010) (from period 2 to period 10), the stronger is the weight of national political actors (see Chapter 1). There is not much variation in the coverage of European and IMF officials, but there are two exceptions: periods 1 (4–18 February 2010) and 8 (19–30 November 2011) when the main decisions were taken at the supranational level, so they received more coverage. Business actors are also more consulted by national newspapers when decisions or inputs come from the ECB. When the ECB was asking Italy for more austerity measures (period 4: 25 July–18 August 2011), journalists did not quote more ECB officials but asked more economic actors to react. On the same lines, when Merkel argued for a European monitoring of the crisis outside the intergovernmental frame of the European Council (period 12: 8–22 July 2012) economic experts became central, while EU officials were pushed aside (only 7.8% are quoted).

EU summits are as usual (Guillaume and Le Torrec, 2003) strongly nationalised and centred on the head of government/state. Periods 6 (19 October–2 November 2011), 9 (16 May–5 June 2012) and 10 (18 June–5 July 2012) confirm this. Finally, this overview seems to confirm the general political analysis that the implementation of the Lisbon treaty during the first two years of the crisis reinforced the mediated and mediatised role of national governments, producing a series of hard laws over time with supranational effects (Dinan, 2011, 2012; Fabbrini, 2013;

Figure 5.1 Presence of actors in news stories over time (values are percentages; x-axis represents the 11 coded periods)

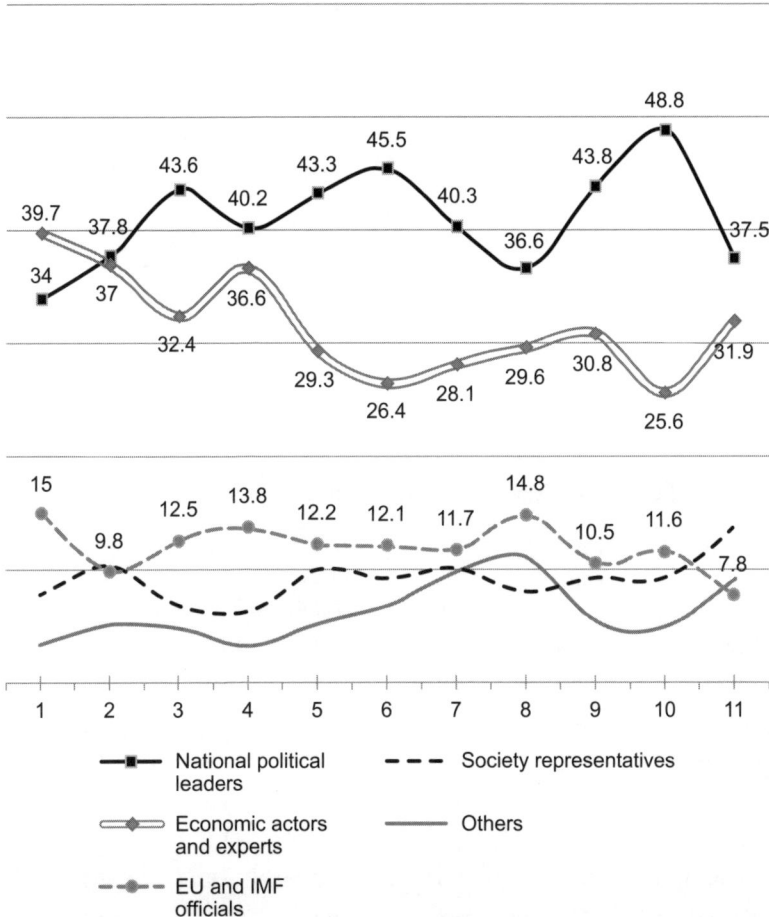

Hennessy, 2014). However, these effects are not reflected in the press (Copeland and James, 2014).

The mediatisation of the managing actors is not only event-dependent; in this case country also matters (see Table 5.4, Figure 5.3, and also Chapter 9). The cross-country variation of the national political actors' presence in the news coverage is significant: from 23% in Poland to more than 50% in Italy. And so is the presence of economic experts, from 17.8% in Greece to 43.7% in the UK. When we look at the difference between the presence of national politicians and economic experts

Figure 5.2 Difference in coverage of national political leaders and economic actors over time (x-axis represents the 11 coded periods)

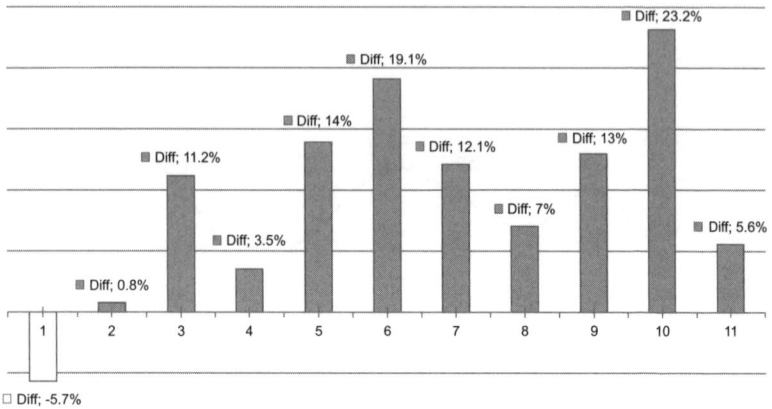

Table 5.4 Types of actors in news stories per country

Country	National leader	Economic actors, experts	EU and IMF officials	Other	Society representatives
Italy	50.9	19.1	10.6	10.1	9.3
Finland	50.0	24.0	10.5	6.9	8.7
France	48.9	32.4	11.3	1.1	6.2
Greece	43.3	17.8	16.8	16.3	5.8
Spain	42.7	31.0	12.2	4.6	9.5
Belgium	42.1	25.6	11.8	13.1	7.4
Germany	39.3	35.5	9.2	6.9	9.2
Netherlands	37.7	28.8	10.1	15.4	8.0
UK	33.5	43.7	10.1	0.9	11.8
Poland	22.9	34.1	20.3	1.1	21.5
Mean	42.2	29.6	11.7	7.1	9.5

Notes: N = 20,459. Values are percentages.

(Figure 5.3), the major pattern of explanation is the EMU membership. Poland and the UK are the only countries where business actors have more discursive power than national politicians, while in the eurozone countries, national political leaders are usually the central actors. There is

Figure 5.3 Difference in coverage of national political leaders and economic actors by country

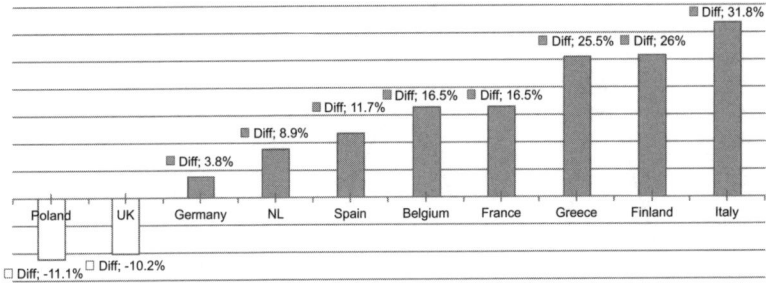

no clear evidence that the more exposed countries have a stronger reliance on national politicians: Finland is a country with a strong nationalised and politicised coverage and Spain is more or less balanced between political and economic actors.

The presence of EU and IMF officials is usually similar in all countries, with only two exceptions. The most exposed country of our sample (Greece) resorts more to these decision-making actors (one-sixth of all actors). The Polish press, belonging to a non-EMU country but being a candidate to join the EMU, pays similar attention to EU/IMF officials (20.3%) and its national politicians (22.9%). Interestingly, in this case, society representatives (organised civil society, think-tanks, etc.) have also the same opportunity to explain and analyse the crisis (21.5%).

In sum, the management of the crisis is dependent on events and countries, thus showing a strong nationalisation and politicisation of the news. An analysis of front pages can provide additional insights into the journalistic patterns of this coverage. Given that front pages are based on a strong journalistic selection of news and actors, they can be an instrument to measure the discursive power attributed to some actors by the press (Hubé, 2008). The front-page coverage gives us an overview of the main national headlines and issues, and television and radio framings are often similar to newspapers' front pages.

Front pages reinforce the nationalisation and politicisation of the news coverage (see Figure 5.4).[18] National political actors are always dominant (54.8% of quoted actors versus 21% of economic actors and 12% of EU and IMF officials), even in non-EMU countries. Two main exceptions should be noted. The first is related to the event-dependency line: in the fourth period, when the ECB asked Italy for more austerity measures,

Figure 5.4   Presence of actors on the front page over time (values are percentages; x-axis represents the 11 coded periods)

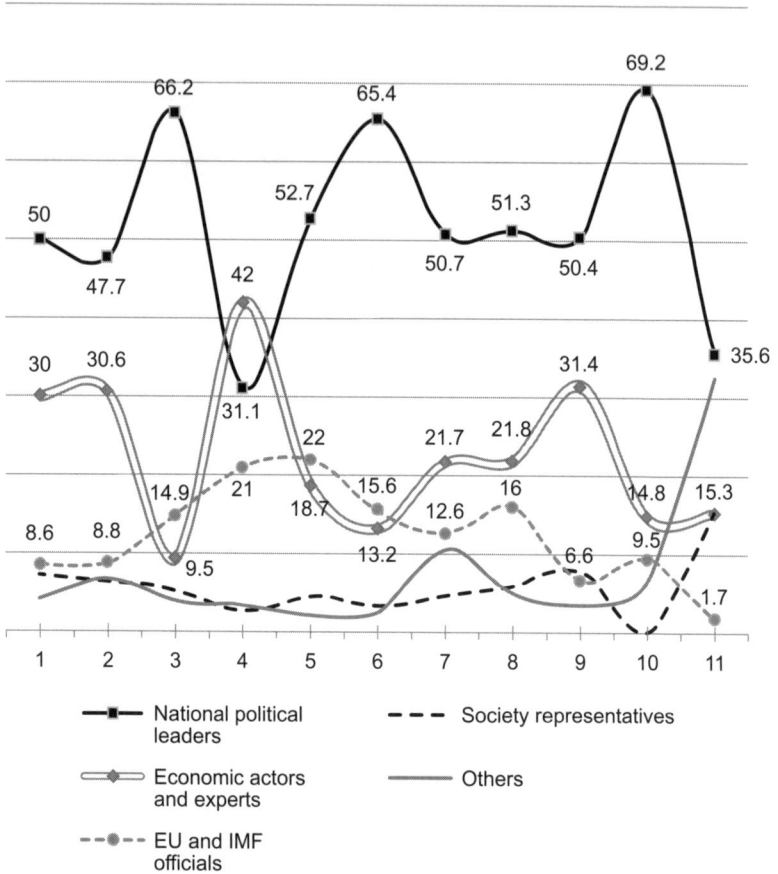

economic actors are central (42%), as well as EU and IMF actors (21%). This is clearly a spill-over effect that exaggerates the tendencies noted before. Something similar happens in period 12, which is characterised by a low presence of politicians (35.6%). The second exception is Belgium's national framing: politicians are less present on front pages than in the rest of the coverage.

This spill-over effect can also be observed by two of the most affected countries, Spain and Greece. In these two cases, front pages give less importance to economic actors and more to EU and IMF officials. The French and German press show a different behaviour: both insist more on the political side of the crisis management and this is probably due to their central position in the crisis management (Crespy, 2013; Dinan, 2013).

Who matters more? Presence or absence of actors

The news coverage of the euro crisis has been highly personalised around political leaders. In this light, the euro crisis was often portrayed merely as political drama, where certain actors play the key roles (Table 5.5). Unsurprisingly, the Chancellor of Germany, Angela Merkel, was the most visible of the national political leaders in the news coverage of all the countries throughout almost all the periods of our study. Only during the period around the EU summit of 23 May 2012 (period 9) does the newly elected French president François Hollande just beat Angela Merkel in number of references. This result was expected, since she has been described as the de facto leader of the EU and the German economy is the strongest of the member countries.

The second most popular source for the press was the two French presidents. Until the end of Nicolas Sarkozy's term (periods 1 to 8), he was said to co-lead a 'Merkozy-management' of the crisis together with Angela Merkel (Dinan, 2013). More specifically, the 'Merkozy management' refers to the role of the two biggest economies of the EMU and the traditional role the Franco-German engine contributes to push the two leaders into the centre of the play. This management is presented as a clash of Titans, between the French White Knight and the German Iron Lady. Their agreement is then regarded as valid for the whole EMU (Crespy, 2013).

From all governing political leaders quoted, the Italian prime ministers, Silvio Berlusconi and then Mario Monti, come next in the list, showing the importance of EMU countries' real economies (far in front of David Cameron, for example). Italy is the third largest economy of the eurozone and under austerity measures due to the crisis. The peak periods of mentions of the Italian leaders was around the time (period 7: 5–19 November 2011) when Silvio Berlusconi resigned after failing to tackle Italy's debt crisis, followed by the appointing of Mario Monti as the new prime minister. Later, during the period (10) from 18 June to 5 July 2012, Mario Monti was often in the headlines due to his efforts to help the Italian economy recover.

Table 5.5 Named actors over time

	P1	P2	P3	P4	P5	P6	P7	P8	P9	P10	P11	Mean
Merkel (G)	11.9	16.0	19.9	8.8	17.0	16.3	15.8	17.1	12.6	18.3	9.9	15.3
French Pres.	8.8	3.9	8.9	9.1	9.6	15.0	6.7	8.6	15.3	12.3	4.0	9.7
EC	6.0	7.8	5.6	15.0	10.6	5.1	8.3	12.0	5.5	4.8	3.7	7.6
Pres. of ECB	10.1	7.8	9.4	13.6	10.9	6.0	4.1	1.9	3.4	3.4	6.1	6.5
Van Rompuy (ECouncil)	7.0	3.5	3.1	3.6	2.2	3.8	2.8	1.6	2.6	5.5	0.8	3.3
IMF	5.5	7.1	7.9	1.8	2.3	1.7	2.0	0.9	2.7	2.7	2.0	3.2
Cameron (UK)	0.7	0.5	0.8	0.5	2.6	4.0	4.3	0.4	3.4	2.0	2.2	2.2
Greek PM	12.1	8.1	1.8	0.9	4.3	5.5	5.0	0.8	1.1	0.2	0.3	3.7
Italian PM	1.3	1.6	2.5	11.7	1.9	5.1	19.0	12.8	7.0	14.4	11.9	8.5
Juncker (Lux)	5.8	1.3	9.8	2.6	2.4	2.3	3.0	2.5	1.7	2.6	2.5	3.0
Spanish PM	6.8	4.2	2.0	6.2	0.7	1.1	2.5	3.7	6.7	7.9	7.6	4.2
Other	24.0	38.1	28.1	26.1	35.4	34.0	26.5	37.7	38.1	25.9	48.9	32.8

Notes: N = 11,172. Values are percentages.

Among the other dominant actors named in the news, yet much less frequently, the president of the European Commission, José Manuel Barroso, appears next. His role was emphasised in late summer 2011 (period 4: 25 July–18 August 2011 and period 5: 28 September–12 October 2011) in discussing the measures for Italy and Greece. The spotlight is momentarily turned onto the Spanish prime ministers, José Luis Rodríguez Zapatero and Mariano Rajoy, dealing with the difficult situation of the Spanish economy, mostly in the summer of 2012. Also, the then President of the European Central Bank (ECB), Jean-Claude Trichet, is mentioned often in late summer 2011 (period 4) when the ECB asks Italy for more austerity measures.

Other less but relatively often mentioned actors were the President of the European Council Herman Van Rompuy, the head of the International Monetary Fund, the Prime Minister of the United Kingdom David Cameron, Greek Prime Ministers Georgios Papandreou and Lucas Papademos, and the Prime Minister of Luxembourg and President of the Eurogroup Jean-Claude Juncker.

When looking at the naming of the actors of the euro crisis by country, in Table 5.6, we can see a general trend of each national press favouring mention of the leaders of its own country. For example, the British prime minister is most mentioned by the British press, and the Italian prime ministers play central roles in the Italian newspapers. Also the national press of each country notices its own citizens in important EU positions. For instance, Belgian Herman Van Rompuy as President of the European Council is most often mentioned by the Belgian press.

Table 5.6 highlights the great differences between the naming of actors by the press in each country. Finnish and German press have the largest variety of miscellaneous actors and least reference to the most often quoted leaders. Yet, in each country, even when the total numbers might be lower, Angela Merkel and the French presidents dominate the narration of the euro crisis. In total numbers, Angela Merkel is mentioned most often by the Belgian, French, and Polish press. However, German newspapers have far fewer mentions of Merkel, but this is due to the fact that the overall level of actors mentioned is lower in the German press selected in our study. Interestingly, the French press has almost the same amount of reference to their own president (20.2%) as to Merkel, and she scores even slightly higher (20.7%). As expected, the German press mentions Merkel (12.2%) but there is a clear drop to mentions of the French partner (4.2%).

Table 5.6 Named actors by country

	Belgium	Finland	France	Germany	Greece	Italy	NL	Poland	Spain	UK
Merkel (G)	21.5	5.6	20.7	12.2	15.1	17.2	18.8	20.2	17.4	15.2
French Pres.	13.4	3.4	20.2	4.2	8.4	11.2	9.1	9.0	11.5	10.2
ECom	11.6	6.5	7.1	3.3	9.4	7.0	13.8	13.3	5.7	12.5
Pres. of ECB	9.1	1.8	11.8	3.7	4.6	9.0	9.7	4.3	6.3	8.3
Van Rompuy (ECouncil)	10.8	1.4	5.8	1.9	2.6	2.6	6.6	8.2	2.8	2.2
IMF	3.6	1.0	6.5	1.0	4.4	2.0	4.4	8.6	3.4	4.8
Cameron (UK)	2.8	0.3	2.8	0.9	1.1	1.0	1.9	2.6	2.1	12.4
Greek PM	3.9	1.6	5.0	2.1	5.3	2.9	3.1	7.3	3.8	6.6
Italian PM	10.1	2.9	8.3	3.0	7.1	19.1	6.9	8.6	6.4	8.7
Juncker (Lux)	5.1	1.1	4.2	3.4	4.1	2.7	3.4	4.3	2.4	2.1
SP PM	4.7	1.7	3.2	1.5	1.8	4.3	6.9	1.3	11.3	3.4
Other	3.4	72.6	4.4	62.8	36.3	21.0	15.4	12.4	26.9	13.7

Notes: $N = 11{,}172$. Values are percentages.

The missing European citizen

The euro crisis was portrayed in the coverage of the European newspapers mostly as a political crisis. The politicisation of the economic crisis in the news can be seen as aiming to steer the power to the people or public squares away from the financial markets, which seem to live a life of their own (see Castells et al., 2012: 11).

Our study shows that approximately 80% of the news stories present some actors involved in the events around the euro crisis, but 50% of the news articles did not mention any actor in particular. This personalisation, on the one hand, and fading out of the actors, on the other hand, contributes to the confusion over the complexity of the field of actors involved in the crisis. Also, it has to do with the differing approaches of journalists and the economists who inform the government and the media.

Journalists tend to personalise events: the actors are seen as essential for the narration of a news story. This journalistic behaviour is well documented in the literature and in news media studies focusing on how journalists report the news. Bennett (2011), for example, explains how journalists tend to focus on the people engaged in issues rather than on the power structures and institutional factors that are often more essential for the understanding of those issues. Furthermore, according to him, personalisation of the news leads journalists to select specific aspects of events that are most easily dramatised, leaving out the others.

Conversely and according to Parker (1997: 15), the economists who explain the crisis to governments value abstract economic rules and forces. They favour moderate observable rules and the absence of individuals in their narratives. The dispelling of human agency is popular in economic theory in general – a good example is the classic expression of the invisible hand of the economy by Adam Smith (Aydinonat, 2008; Kennedy, 2009). Thus, the absence of actors from half of the news stories may imply eliding of responsibility, as the crisis 'just happened' without anyone being responsible (Rantanen, 2012). It was also found by Joris, Puustinen, Sobieraj and d'Haenens (see Chapter 7) that 'natural disaster' and 'disease' were among the most frequently used metaphors of the crisis in the news coverage of the European press. These metaphors imply that the crisis was beyond anyone's responsibility or control, as if it had erupted unexpectedly without any human involvement.

Yet, the crisis touches all European countries totalling millions of citizens, and there is a need to find those responsible to take action. The crisis has not happened in a social vacuum, as Castells et al. (2012) write. They continue: 'Social systems do not collapse as a result of their internal contradictions. The crisis, its conflicts, and its treatment are always social processes. And these social processes, as all others, are enacted and shaped by the interests, values, beliefs, and strategies of social actors' (2012: 7).

Analysing the other half of the data with the personalised actors, we found that the political leaders were the majority of the sources used by journalists when covering the euro crisis, whereas the citizens were nearly always absent. Also, the studies on the citizen perspective on the euro crisis are scarce. One of the few studies on this subject was conducted by Andreas Hepp and his research team (2013); relying on a data of qualitative interviews, half-standardised questionnaires, qualitative network maps, and media diaries, it shows that most often people understand the crisis with patterns of perplexity, anxiety, and speculation. These researchers also discovered that ordinary people have ideas on how to overcome the crisis. From their national political and cultural perspectives, the interviewees display a connection to the European public sphere, in the sense that the overall topics of Europe and the present crisis are noticed or discussed in their everyday life (Hepp et al., 2013: 20).

This public connection is mainly constituted through regional and national media (Couldry et al., 2007). The media coverage thus plays an important part in the processes whereby people construct themselves and are constructed as citizens. But the public sphere is larger than the mainstream media. Citizens may be absent as sources in the established news press, but they are strongly present in what Cardoso and Jacobetty (2012: 200–1) call 'social networking cultures' in the varieties of social appropriation of mediation that occur in our daily lives, ranging from participation in social networking sites, online communities, political or civic activities, user-generated content, file-sharing communities and networks, and so on.

The absence of citizens and the relative disappearance of economic actors confirm our main theses explained in the introduction to this chapter. There were strong national and political patterns in the way the euro crisis problem-solving approach was mediatised. In line with previous researches, the mediatisation of politics is related to strong personalisation. Moreover, this case shows a strong focus on the governmental level of politics. Following the same line, the mediatisation of European affairs is closely linked to events, where the visibility of the actors involved, that is personalisation, is therefore even more accentuated. EU summits and government discussions are decisive moments in which chiefs of government (and only them) play a central role.

If the euro crisis coverage had been more supranational and Europeanised, the analysis would show a stronger presence of non-national political actors and of European institutions leaders, which was clearly not the case. These actors seem to have a deficit of visibility in media coverage and in national public spheres. This leads to an important paradox of the crisis: the euro crisis is a European crisis and therefore – at least at first sight – requires coordinated and European solutions, in which European institutions should be the most central actors; however, the euro crisis is presented as an intergovernmental affair, in which only a very few governmental actors have effective visibility and power. This is another interesting conclusion: not every chief of government is a central actor in the media coverage, only those leading the main European national economies of the eurozone are. This type of framing portrayed without any competitive approaches might be an important explanatory factor for why most European citizens perceive the crisis through national lenses and as a matter of elites only.

6

Consensus or Discussion? An Analysis of Plurality and Consonance in Coverage

Susana Salgado, Heinz-Werner Nienstedt, and Lennart Schneider

'One of the prices we are paying for the spiralling economic problems facing Europe is an erosion of the role of the media', stated former Italian senator, Tana de Zulueta, in a pamphlet publication by the European Initiative for Media Pluralism.[19] Media pluralism is at the base of any healthy democratic environment, especially when citizens, institutions, and countries face additional challenges such as the ones presented by the euro crisis. A crisis situation not only stresses the need for a more inclusive discussion of different perspectives, but also poses additional challenges to media pluralism. Time and again, critical comments on the role of the media in the crisis have been voiced in different countries. Several institutions, among those the media, failed to anticipate the crisis, provided insufficient and inaccurate information on the real crisis situation, and neglected to analyse and contextualise some of the major social problems caused not only by the crisis, but also by the measures implemented to tackle the crisis. Many times, journalists have forgotten to be accountable to their audiences.

Thus, even though the research on the media coverage of the euro crisis has barely started, there are already some signs pointing to deficiencies that highlight the importance of looking closer at these issues. This chapter addresses this concern by examining the levels of plurality in 24 newspapers from six European countries (France, Germany, Greece, Italy, Spain, and the UK) and by hopefully providing new insights into the relationships between plurality, democracy, and crisis. It therefore aims to explore the degrees of plurality (diversity of content) and consonance (the same interpretation conveyed by different media outlets) in the newspapers' coverage of the euro crisis. Are newspapers reporting the diverse reality of their countries or simply giving voice to a few selected views and interpretations of reality? Are there different competing narratives about the crisis or do consonant perspectives dominate the news coverage?

Aiming for comprehensiveness, this analysis takes into account not only the particularities of the economic and political context, but also the nature of the issue covered in the news by investigating diversity and consonance in different types of issues, some closely connected to policy orientations and political decisions and others more related to views and perceptions. Hence, the following topics were analysed: the causes and the solutions of the crisis, and the representations of the victims and the beneficiaries of the crisis. Whenever it makes sense, the relationships between these topics are also identified. For instance, there may be a close link between the causes of and the solutions to the crisis, if low levels of diversity in the causes' news coverage are used as a background justification for advocating predetermined type of solutions.

This chapter examines whether the euro crisis coverage reflects mainly plurality or consonance. Ultimately, these are all pertinent issues in any broader analysis on the quality of European democracy and on the challenges and impact of the euro crisis in the European Union (EU) and its member states.

Why study pluralism and consonance in media coverage?

The higher demand for a greater quantity and diversity of information in times of crisis is well documented in the literature and firmly confirmed in practice (for further discussion on this matter, see, for instance, Fearn-Banks, 2010 or Ulmer et al., 2014). In periods of uncertainty and when feelings of insecurity are growing, citizens and institutions feel the need for more information and tend to actively look for it. McQuail (2000) even argues that, given that media power varies at different times, it may be the case that the media is actually more influential in times of crisis.

It has also been widely demonstrated in studies about news production and theories on news values and 'newsworthiness' that 'conflict' and 'crisis' are among the news organisations' preferences in the news selection processes. Galtung and Ruge's seminal study (1965) proposing a systematisation of the factors (news values) that are more consistently applied in news organisations contributed immensely to a better understanding of the process of news selection and paved the way for significant breakthroughs in this area of research (for developments on this type of approach to journalism studies, see, for example, Staab, 1990 or Harcup and O'Neill, 2001, among others).

Information on the euro crisis seems to have all the characteristics that justify special attention and treatment from European journalists. It is related to a significant crisis that affects not only all European countries – even if some more than others – but also many other parts of the world. The euro crisis has potentially important implications for the future of each of the countries involved, for the future of the European project, and for Europe in general, including the relations among countries. Additionally, information on the euro crisis is usually filled with elements of conflict and suffering that makes it especially interesting for journalists. In fact, journalists usually emphasise these elements and their news reports depict the most difficult moments or the most intense suffering.

All this points to the fact that news outlets should exhibit a tendency to include large amounts of information on the euro crisis in their news reports, which is confirmed by our case studies. However, a substantial amount of information about an issue or an event is not necessarily translated into diversity and pluralism. In view of globalisation, similar journalistic frames of reference, and the frequent tendency of journalists to follow and cite each other's work, which has developed even further with the internet and the new technologies of information and communication, the levels of reinforcement in coverage from different news outlets should not be overlooked.

Timothy Crouse had already noticed this phenomenon in the early 1970s when he was studying the news coverage of the 1972 US presidential campaign (1973), and Ramonet (2002) has more recently referred to this tendency as 'mimetismo mediático' ('resembling media'). With this concept, Ramonet also intended to draw attention to journalistic work constraints, linking the pronounced resemblance often noticeable in the media coverage of different outlets with the competitiveness dimension of the profession and the difficulty of continuously feeding the information chain with news updates, especially considering the rapid pace of change (for further details, see also Salgado, 2010). Ultimately, this can, in his view, contribute to explaining certain homogeneous frames that put forward consonant views of facts and events.

These concepts and observations are closely related to Noelle-Neumann's and Mathes's discussion (1987) on consonance and the effects of consonant media coverage of events. They attribute consonance to the existence of two groups of news media: on the one hand, the opinion-leaders and, on the other, the followers; and it can be established at different levels: agenda-setting (importance attributed to issues); focusing (definition of issues and problems); and evaluating (creation of a climate of opinion) (for further discussion on this, see Salgado, 2014a).

Given that large amounts of attention and journalistic coverage of the euro crisis are not a guarantee of diversity and pluralism, it is thus possible to question whether the information that is made available by the news media is balanced enough for citizens to form their own substantiated opinions about the crisis, its causes, players involved, solutions, and so on. Furthermore, recent studies and opinion polls have also well documented the growing distrust of citizens not only in the mainstream media, but also in European institutions. Due to the crisis, the idea of the EU as something inherently good for all European countries has been more and more questioned, while media outlets have been increasingly said to be mainly reactive (see Chapter 10), acting most of the time as a vehicle of powerful interested parties, instead of being proactive, looking for unbiased information and giving voice to the various interests involved and to all different perspectives. This is all the more important when we acknowledge that the media not only frame the narratives about the crisis, but also shape the citizens' perception of events and issues.

Pluralism, plurality, and diversity

In a democratic system, one of the most important functions of the media is thus to give voice to all different kinds of actors, sensibilities, and interests at stake in any given situation. The media should always reflect a broad range of opinions; that is, it should function as a reflection of inclusive and diverse societies, representing the different social and political groups and providing a space for the public debate of issues. This is a key aspect because these various interests and perspectives should inform and be taken into account in any political decision-making process. The higher the degrees of plurality and public discussion, the more likely decision-makers will try to incorporate a plural approach in their political decisions. Moreover, pluralism is a key ingredient whenever the objective is to strengthen the levels of political awareness and provide citizens with comprehensive information.

'Media pluralism contributes to the richness of European public opinion and identity formation, yet its complexity is liable to ambiguity' (Klimkiewicz, 2009: 45). The existing large body of literature on media pluralism, plurality, and diversity acknowledges the complexities in defining and distinguishing these concepts and often proposes different ways of dealing with the richness of the concepts. Valcke (2011) makes a clear reference to this difficulty: media pluralism, generally referring to the plurality and diversity of media providers and contents, is a complex and multidimensional concept, which has been interpreted in varying ways in different times, geographies, contexts and policy circles. Hence, different authors end up defining and applying these concepts differently and in diverse contexts. While some researchers use pluralism and plurality interchangeably, others do the same with pluralism and diversity, which makes it particularly complicated to define clear borders in each of these concepts.

However, there are also similarities in the work produced so far. Pluralism (and plurality) is typically associated with the presence of free and diverse voices in the media, which safeguards and improves the conditions for democracy. For instance, Terrington and Ashworth (2008) highlight plurality's central role within a media system and point to 'choice, quality and efficiency' as its direct outcomes. Moreover, pluralism is usually considered as more than just the simple existence of several different media outlets; expressly behind the concept is the need to prevent a single voice having too much influence over public opinion and the political agenda. In addition, discussions generally describe a key distinction between external plurality/pluralism, which occurs in the range of suppliers of content, and internal plurality/pluralism, which is related to the expression of multiple points of view in a given media outlet (see, for instance, Klimkiewicz, 2010).

According to McQuail (1992), diversity means 'the variability of mass media (sources, channels, messages, and audiences) in terms of relevant differences in society (political, geographical, social-cultural, etc.)' (1992: 147), which, ultimately, can only exist in a pluralistic media system. Doyle (2002) follows a somewhat similar orientation and posits that media pluralism is generally associated with diversity in the media, highlighting its political dimension: the presence of a number of different and independent voices and of different political opinions and cultural representations within the media (2002: 11). Freedman (2008) tries to further clarify the difference between pluralism and diversity. This author explains that while 'pluralism refers to the wider political context in which media operate, diversity is directly related with the media's ability to acknowledge and express social differences through maximising the choices offered to audiences' (2008: 72).

Karppinen proposes the use of the concepts of diversity and plurality to refer to the empirical fact of plurality, while pluralism should be a value orientation that considers multiplicity and diversity in ideas and institutions a virtue (2013: 3–4). Pluralism is not diversity alone, but somehow an engagement with diversity and plurality.

Hence, diversity is the basis of pluralism; however, as many cases show, diversity in media suppliers does not automatically mean more pluralism in the media system. Elements such as media ownership and media concentration are as important to pluralism as the existence of diverse media outlets. Moreover, there are also significant imbalances in the access of different actors to the mainstream media.

This quick overview of some of the existing literature on these concepts is intended to highlight some of the most important approaches and mainly to provide a theoretical basis to this analysis of the newspapers' coverage of the euro crisis. The objective is not to produce a detailed examination of the ongoing discussion about the concepts, authors' proposals, and its implications, which would certainly need much more space and attention.

Measuring diversity in news content

If there are challenges in the conceptualisation of pluralism, plurality, and diversity in the media, complexity increases even more when the objective is to measure pluralism, plurality, and diversity. Many scholars and policy makers have already largely discussed the issue of how to measure pluralism and different methodologies based on how specific aspects of the concept have been applied in recent years.

The Media Pluralism Monitor[20] uses one of the many existing tools to evaluate the state of media pluralism through empirical data, but there are other methodologies and many possible indicators that can be studied for this purpose (media ownership, levels of media concentration, diversity of media titles and genres, bias and positioning of the existing media outlets, diversity in content, diversity of sources of information depicted in the media, etc.).

The concept of pluralism is extremely rich and complex and includes many possible layers of analysis. Nonetheless, diversity of media content seems to be central to any discussion on media pluralism and its importance is directly linked not only to freedom of expression, but also to the right to information, as well as to citizens' political awareness. It is clearly linked to the construction of perceptions and to the climate of public opinion.

In addition to the discussion on how to measure pluralism, there has also been a debate on whether pluralism can be fully captured through quantitative measures, which according to some criticisms end up reducing dramatically the complexities of the concept and excluding not only important qualitative aspects, but also the relationship between the quantitative and qualitative dimensions of the concept. Nevertheless, a quantitative approach still makes sense in some cases. Given that the objective of this study is to evaluate the levels of similarity and difference in the media coverage of the euro crisis in 24 newspapers from six European countries, the measurement of diversity seems to be well suited for this purpose.

The concept of diversity is central to different fields and it has been used in many contexts and scientific fields, including ecology, geography, economics, psychology, linguistics, sociology, and communication (McDonald and Dimmick, 2003). It has been mainly used in analyses that seek to measure the amount of variation within a *population* with respect to one or more variables and to evaluate the probability of finding agreement and difference (Agresti and Agresti, 1978; Lieberson, 1969). In their comparative study on diversity measures applied to the study of radio and television programmes, McDonald and Dimmick (2003: 74) highlight the two-dimensional nature of the concept: 'One dimension reflects the categories of classification, and the other reflects the distribution of elements within those categories.' A distribution of 80/20 in two categories is not as plural as a distribution of 50/50, as the discussion of several different causes of the crisis is much more plural than focusing the coverage on only two possible explanations, just to provide simple examples.

An instrument that has been commonly used in the measurement of diversity was proposed by Simpson in 1949, but is apparently identical to one first developed by Corrado Gini in 1912 (Agresti and Agresti, 1978; Lieberson, 1969). More recently, McDonald and Dimmick (2003) examined conceptually and empirically different measures of diversity and concluded that Simpson's D is not only one of the oldest and most commonly used, but also one of the best measures of diversity. Basically, Simpson's D reflects the probability that 'randomly paired numbers of a population will be different on a specific characteristic' (Lieberson, 1969: 851).

The present study is concerned with determining if the news coverage of the euro crisis was mainly pluralist or consonant. For this purpose, the levels of diversity present in news stories are measured through Simpson's D, assuming that media diversity manifests itself in the existence of different perspectives in media content. To our knowledge, this is the first study that applies Simpson's D to examine diversity in newspapers' content. The noted communication studies that have applied this measure in the past dealt with diversity of television and radio programming.

At this point, it makes sense to explain in more detail how Simpson's D was applied to study the newspapers' content.

The basic Simpson's D looks at the probabilistic existence of diversity within a *population* (D_w) concerning one specific characteristic.[21] In the present research, it measures, for example, the probability of finding different causes of the euro crisis in two randomly selected news stories that deal with this topic and that were published in a given newspaper and in a given period of time.

Lieberson (1969) developed a multivariate extension of D_w to deal with the cases where a *population* is classified by more than just one characteristic.[22] In our case, the multivariate D_w is, for instance, suited to measure diversity in the news coverage of both the causes and the solutions of the euro crisis within a newspaper.

There is another measure suited for evaluating the levels of diversity between different newspapers. Both Lieberson (1969) and Agresti and Agresti (1978) demonstrated that diversity involving different *populations* can be measured through a simple extension of Simpson's D, named Lieberson's D_b. In our analysis of the euro crisis news coverage, it examines, for example, the probability of finding different causes of the crisis in two randomly selected news stories from two different newspapers in a given period.[23] In addition to being employed to study diversity in different newspapers within a country, it can also be used in cross-national analyses. To put it simply, with this measure, it is possible to analyse diversity on the newspaper level, between newspapers, and between countries. On the newspaper level, we study how diverse newspapers of a country are; on the country level,[24] we analyse how diverse different countries are.

When applying the instruments to measure diversity proposed by these authors to the context of the present research, a set of four different indicators of diversity based on Simpson's D were defined, two at the newspaper level and two at the country level.

Internal plurality refers to diversity within single newspapers concerning one or more characteristics and is measured through the calculation of simple D_w and of multivariate D_w in the case of several characteristics. If the objective is to characterise the level of overall internal plurality of newspapers in a given country (average internal plurality), we calculate the average D_ws of the four newspapers that compose the national sample. Afterwards, the averages of internal plurality in the different countries can be compared.

External plurality refers to diversity within the media system, which means examining how much newspapers differ from each other in a given country, and is measured through the calculation of Simpson's D_bs.[25] If the objective is to evaluate the levels of external plurality in a given country, the average D_b of the four national newspapers is calculated and taken as an indicator. In the next step, it will be possible to compare the level of external plurality of different countries. When analysing the levels of diversity in newspapers within one country, it may also be interesting to look at the differences between external and internal plurality, which can simply be measured by the difference between the average D_b and the average D_w in one country.

Country plurality refers to the diversity within the aggregated news coverage of all four national newspapers and is measured through Simpson's D_w which is now applied to the aggregated data. Country plurality differs from average internal plurality, because in internal plurality each newspaper has the same weight, while in country plurality each article has the same weight. Hence, newspapers with more news stories on the euro crisis influence country plurality more than newspapers with less news stories on this issue. In country plurality, the total news output of a given country is evaluated, so newspapers are not differentiated. Neither country plurality nor average internal plurality look at the differences between country newspapers; this aspect in particular is addressed in external plurality.

Cross-country plurality analyses diversity in the news coverage of different countries and is measured through Simpson's D_b applied to the country's data. Cross-country plurality is examined at several levels: differences between two countries, differences between groups of countries, and the whole European level.[26] We can also examine if plurality increases when more countries are considered by analysing the differences between cross-country and country plurality.

In summary, this study addresses both internal and external plurality, focusing on the levels of diversity in newspapers, but also deals with both country and cross-country comparisons, looking for trends in groups of countries. Hence, and given that the data derived from content analysis of newspapers and that other kinds of data, which would allow drawing conclusions on the existence of pluralism as a value orientation in these newspapers, have not been taken into account here, the subsequent analyses are explicitly focused on the empirical fact of plurality (Karppinen, 2013) and on the study of diversity.

The newspapers' coverage of the euro crisis

Six European countries were analysed: Germany, France, the UK, Spain, Greece, and Italy. This sample of countries provides a varied perspective into different interests and involvements in the euro crisis. These six countries are also some of the most important players in the euro crisis and from this research project's initial sample of ten countries the ones that devoted more newspaper coverage to the euro crisis in the periods in analysis. Despite not being a eurozone member, the inclusion of the United Kingdom is explained, on the one hand, by the importance of its voice within the EU's economic and financial affairs (London is currently Europe's centre of finance) and, on the other hand, by the importance its printed press gave to the euro crisis, mainly the *Financial Times* coverage, deemed to have generally an influential role.

We looked at six different topics of coverage to provide a more comprehensive analysis. Some issues per se might induce higher levels of consonance than others (for instance, who suffers more with the crisis), so it was important to examine a varied selection of topics to have the clearest picture possible of the newspapers' content diversity. The topics that were analysed focus first on the main causes behind the crisis and the responsibility to solve it, then on the type of answers the authorities should give to the crisis, and finally on the victims and beneficiaries of the crisis.

On the subject of the euro crisis's causes, the possibilities for coding included the structure of the euro system and the ECB's policies, national economic structure and policies, global economic problems, the behaviour of private banks and financial institutions, and political deficiencies (national and European), for example. Regarding the responsibilities for addressing the crisis, the options were: the struggling countries themselves, countries without sovereign debt problems, eurozone countries, EU institutions and the ECB, IMF, and World Bank, or private debt holders. As to the short-term solutions to the crisis, the alternatives comprised loans from other countries and institutions, ECB loans and bond purchases, abatement of existing loan provisions (extension, reduced rates, haircut), reduction of budget deficits through tax increases and austerity measures, fiscal stimulus and growth policies. Longer-term solutions to the crisis involved possibilities such as nations (weak or strong economies) dropping the euro, more EU power over national budgets, national structural reforms in nations with problems, or the breaking up of the eurozone. The beneficiaries and the victims of the euro crisis may include specific countries and regions, population groups, EU political and financial institutions, or private economic actors, for instance. Some of these issues were addressed in Chapter 2, but we consider them in a different way.

The analysis that follows is intended to determine the levels of diversity in the newspapers' content regarding these topics. The measurement of diversity points to overall moderate levels of diversity in the newspapers' coverage of the euro crisis: it is possible to see that regarding the first four topics (victims and beneficiaries of the crisis are included only at a later stage of the analysis) in the six countries there is an average of internal plurality of 0.66. This means that if we randomly take two news stories from one newspaper, there is a 66% probability of finding diverse approaches to the crisis and therefore 34% probability of finding the same type of approaches (Table 6.1).

Table 6.1 also shows the results of the average internal plurality of the four newspapers within each country. Overall, the French press shows the lowest average of diversity within its four newspapers (0.59) and presents the lowest levels of diversity in the debates on the responsibility to solve the crisis and on the measures to fight the crisis. On the opposite side, Spanish newspapers show the highest average level of internal plurality (0.70), closely followed by Italian and Greek newspapers.

The diversity of positions on the causes of the euro crisis is also higher in Spanish and Italian papers that discussed this issue, bringing more perspectives to debate. Very likely due to Angela Merkel and Germany's central role in tackling the crisis, German newspapers were more concerned in debating different perspectives on which institution/ country should bear the responsibility for solving the crisis. Greek and British newspapers displayed more diversity in coverage when their focus was on the short-term solutions to solve the crisis, while in the case of

Table 6.1 Analysis of the average internal plurality within national newspapers

	Germany	France	UK	Spain	Greece	Italy	Six countries	Standard deviation
Causes	0.69	0.73	0.71	0.78	0.72	0.77	0.73	0.03
Responsibility	0.73	0.50	0.55	0.66	0.61	0.66	0.62	0.08
Short-term solutions	0.61	0.57	0.74	0.71	0.75	0.64	0.67	0.07
Long-term solutions	0.60	0.57	0.63	0.66	0.63	0.71	0.64	0.04
Four topics	0.66	0.59	0.66	0.70	0.68	0.69	0.66	0.04

Note: Values are the average D_ws of the four newspapers in each country.

Italian newspapers it was the long-term solutions to the crisis that caused a more diverse expression of perspectives.

It is also interesting to note that southern European newspapers show overall higher levels of internal plurality when compared with their northern counterparts. It should be noted however, especially in the cases where diversity is lower, that single newspapers' results may push down average internal diversity. In addition, in the cases when single newspapers show low levels of internal diversity, it may still be possible to find high external plurality if all newspapers are different from each other and approach the crisis issues differently. If different newspapers incorporate varied views in their news treatment, it is still possible to find different perspectives on causes, responsibility, and solutions in the national media system and in the overall debate on the euro crisis. In this case, diversity within the media system would be higher than diversity within each newspaper. This is measured through levels of diversity among newspapers (D_b), instead of within newspapers (D_w). Therefore, a high level of newspapers' D_b indicates high external plurality.

Table 6.2 shows that diversity increases in the average of external plurality (D_b) when compared to the average of internal plurality (D_w) in all countries. However, in general, there are only low increases (only more expressive in the UK) from the single newspaper approach to when all newspapers are considered together. In fact, average D_b values show in most cases only a 1–3% increase over the D_w values. To put it simply: on average

Table 6.2 Differences between internal and external plurality in the six countries

	Germany	France	UK	Spain	Greece	Italy	Six countries
Causes	2	2	11	1	2	2	3
Responsibility	1	2	9	1	2	1	3
Short-term solutions	2	1	2	2	1	1	2
Long-term solutions	1	2	3	4	3	2	2
Four topics	2	2	6	2	2	2	3

Note: Values are percentages, calculated as differences between average D_b and average D_w in the different countries.

and taking all countries and all four topics into account, there is only a 3% average increase in external plurality when compared to newspapers' internal plurality. This suggests a relatively high consonance of all newspapers and therefore a low effect of external pluralism within each country.

The UK case provides the most noted exception to this tendency. It shows higher levels of external plurality, especially in regard to the debates on the causes of the crisis (11% more diverse) and on the responsibility to solve the crisis (plus 9%). Taking a closer look at the data, it is possible to see that in the news coverage of the euro crisis's causes, the *Financial Times* stressed the behaviour of private financial actors (mainly private banks and other private financial institutions) as the determinant factor causing the euro crisis, while *The Times* and *The Guardian* mostly pointed the finger at the structure of the euro system. The few articles published in *The Sun* that addressed this topic highlighted as the reason for the crisis the national economic structure and policies of the countries with more difficulties. Concerning the topic of the responsibility to solve the crisis, the difference between internal and external plurality is explained by the overall low internal plurality of *The Times* and especially of *The Sun*, which strongly emphasised the idea that the responsibility to solve the problems lay only in the EU institutions and in the eurozone countries, thus freeing the UK of any direct burden and responsibility.

In the case of Spain, it is the long-term solutions for the crisis that explain the main differences between external and internal plurality (4%). While *El Mundo* and *El País* firmly underlined the need for more EU power over national budgets, the newspapers *Expansion* and *ABC* displayed different solutions in their news articles and stressed mainly the need for national structural reforms in the nations with problems.

Given the relatively high degree of consonance in newspapers within most of these six countries, the next step is to develop cross-country comparisons, checking the levels of diversity in the news coverage of the euro crisis among countries. This type of analysis may be relevant for those who monitor the levels of overall pluralism in Europe, such as researchers, journalists, policy makers, politicians, and so on. In addition, it provides insight into the existing variety of national standpoints regarding the issues under consideration and an opportunity to investigate further possible cross-country trends.

Cross-country diversity may mean the existence of a variety of national perspectives on the euro crisis's causes, the actors' accountability and the possible solutions to overcome the problems. Furthermore, the presence of a high diversity of positions on issues across Europe could imply that, even if different perspectives are not fully debated nationally, they may still have a representation in the overall euro crisis debate and therefore they could potentially be taken into account if journalists cite their international colleagues' work or if a decision-maker is looking for a diverse range of information on an issue.

Countries were grouped into two sets of three for this part of the analysis: on the one hand, some of the countries targeted as having sovereign debt problems and that were in the spotlight during the timeframe of this analysis (Greece, Italy, and Spain), and on the other hand, the countries portrayed as not having such meaningful problems (France,[27] Germany, and the UK). Table 6.3 thus shows the overall results for all six countries, as well as the differences between the two groups of countries. It is possible to observe that there is more average country diversity in media content both in each of the topics considered and in general in the group that includes the southern countries with sovereign debt problems (0.70) than in the other group of countries (0.66).

Regarding diversity at the country level, it should be noted that a positive percentage increase of D_b over D_w indicates that cross-country diversity is higher than the level of diversity within countries. Analysing the average of all four topics (multivariate D) in all the six countries, there is a 5% increase of diversity, while in the four topics separately the increase varies between 3% and 6%, both indicating more cross-country than country plurality.

The within-group differences are more pronounced in the group that includes France, Germany, and the UK, which is mainly explained by the views on the long-term response to the euro crisis (13%) and the positions on the causes of the crisis (8%). Focusing more closely on the details of the news coverage, it is possible to find tangible reasons for this difference: Germany and France display more similar positions on most of the foregoing topics than the UK, and the UK is in some cases very different from Germany (especially in the discussions related to the causes of the crisis) and in other cases very different from France (especially in the possible long-term solutions to the crisis, where the need for national structural reforms in the countries with problems was strongly emphasised by British newspapers).

Given these somehow mixed trends it is worthwhile to explore further some of the results concerning not only the cross-country differences, but also the levels of diversity found in each country and in the sets of

Table 6.3   Country and cross-country plurality

	Average country plurality	Average cross-country plurality	Difference (%)
Causes			
France, Germany, UK	0.73	0.78	8
Greece, Italy, Spain	0.77	0.80	4
All six countries	0.75	0.79	6
Responsibility			
France, Germany, UK	0.63	0.66	4
Greece, Italy, Spain	0.65	0.66	2
All six countries	0.64	0.66	4
Short-term solutions			
France, Germany, UK	0.66	0.69	5
Greece, Italy, Spain	0.71	0.73	3
All six countries	0.68	0.71	3
Long-term solutions			
France, Germany, UK	0.61	0.69	13
Greece, Italy, Spain	0.68	0.70	2
All six countries	0.65	0.69	6
All four topics			
France, Germany, UK	0.66	0.71	8
Greece, Italy, Spain	0.70	0.72	3
All six countries	0.68	0.71	5

Note: Average country plurality is measured by the average of the D_ws of the different countries and the average cross-country plurality is measured by the average of D_bs of all pairs of countries. In other words, the average country D_w and the average of pairs of D_b for the several topics, including the average of all topics (multivariate D) for groups of countries and of all the six countries taken together. Data based on the total news coverage in the different countries, aggregated over all four newspapers. The objective here is to examine national differences and not the difference between each newspaper within countries as in Table 6.2.

Table 6.4 Comparative analysis of overall country and cross-country diversity

	France	Germany	Greece	Italy	Spain	UK
France	**0.61**	0.69	0.69	0.69	0.70	0.71
Germany	0.69	**0.67**	0.72	0.70	0.71	0.72
Greece	0.69	0.72	**0.69**	0.73	0.72	0.75
Italy	0.69	0.70	0.73	**0.70**	0.72	0.72
Spain	0.70	0.71	0.72	0.72	**0.72**	0.73
UK	0.71	0.72	0.75	0.72	0.73	**0.69**

Note: All four topics were considered in this analysis. Values on the diagonal of the table represent the country plurality and are measured by D_w. Values outside the diagonal refer to cross-country plurality, which is measured by the D_b of all groups of two countries. The objective is mostly to examine the existence of differences. Taking the four topics, both average D_w (values on the diagonal of the table) and D_b (values outside the diagonal) are measured. The highest D_b on one column indicates the highest diversity between two countries.

two countries independently of their geographical position in Europe (Table 6.4). The most different from each other are the UK and Greece (0.75), the UK and Spain, but also more surprisingly Italy and Greece (0.73). A possible explanation for the latter case is a more sceptical view of the Italian press towards the future prospects of the euro.

There are thus no clear northern and southern perspectives depicted in the press, influencing the diversity levels of news coverage. Instead, there are mainly national perspectives, which may vary from topic to topic and are in some cases notably consonant. From the six cases, France is the country with least diversity in its news coverage of the euro crisis (0.61) and Spain the country that included more diverse perspectives (0.72) (see diagonal values in Table 6.4). In general, the southern countries are more plural (Italy 0.70; Greece 0.69) and the remaining countries are similar (UK 0.69) or slightly less plural (Germany 0.67), which is a similar result to the one achieved in the analysis of internal plurality of newspapers in these countries.

This study allowed a closer look at the evolution of content diversity over time. Given that the research included 11 periods of analysis over three years (2010–12), it is possible to investigate if there was an upward or a downward trend in the diversity of perspectives on the euro crisis represented in newspapers. Table 6.5 shows a comparison between the first four and the last four of the 11 periods of analysis included in the

Table 6.5 Evolution of diversity over time (2010–12)

	Changes in country plurality	Changes in difference between cross-country and country plurality
Causes		
France, Germany, UK	7	−4.4
Greece, Italy, Spain	2	−3.6
All six countries	4	−3.6
Responsibility		
France, Germany, UK	8	−4.8
Greece, Italy, Spain	4	−0.8
All six countries	6	−3.2
Short-term solutions		
France, Germany, UK	17	1.5
Greece, Italy, Spain	8	2.7
All six countries	12	0.8
Long-term solutions		
France, Germany, UK	22	−8.5
Greece, Italy, Spain	29	−6.2
All six countries	26	−6.2

Notes: Values are percentages. The first column is calculated by the change of the average D_w of countries between the two periods in consideration (the first four and the last four time periods). The second column also looks at the change between the two time periods but applied to the difference between the average D_b and the average D_w of the various groups of countries. For more information on the time periods, see Appendix 1.

research by calculating the changes of the indices between these two periods. This analysis points to an overall increase of diversity over time in the average of all countries and for all topics. However, the increase is particularly striking in the short-term (12%) and especially in the long-term possible solutions for the crisis (26%). These values point to increasing breadth in the coverage of these issues, which means exploring more options and bringing new positions to the table, as the euro crisis progressed.

In addition, it should also be noted that the relative cross-national differences became narrower over time in some of the issues. The largest decrease in cross-national diversity occurred in the debate on the long-term solutions for the crisis. Therefore, it seems that, as time went on, new positions on this issue started being included and discussed in all countries. Conversely, in the short-term solutions coverage, the passing of time had the precise opposite effect, with cross-country diversity increasing slightly. This can be explained by the growing importance that was progressively attributed to growth measures versus the already prevalent position asking for austerity, reduction of budget deficits, and bailouts in the countries with more acute debt problems. It may also be related to the observation of the austerity measures' effects in some countries. This means that although cross-country overall consensus has grown over time, there was no convergence in the national perspectives on how to solve the crisis.

Finally, there is still space to analyse if the press coverage represents the same actors and countries as beneficiaries and victims of the crisis, or if there is diversity in these assessments. In this respect, it should first be noted that the discussion on the beneficiaries of the crisis is practically absent from the coverage. The number of news stories on this topic in our sample was so small that it ruled out meaningful comparisons between countries, which would have resulted in artificial differences, partly dominated by one or two articles (see Chapter 2 for details on the number of news stories). The journalists' lack of interest in this matter was obvious. Different countries and parties (such as private economic and financial actors, speculators, or specific groups of the population) may, in fact, have taken advantage of the euro crisis; however, this is hardly discussed in the newspapers. What can be actually inferred from this almost total absence from newspapers is that there are some issues, such as this one, that simply are not discussed and covered by the press. In this way, this absence also provides interesting information on the levels of diversity in the media coverage.

Although without constant levels of attention in the press, the victims of the crisis are a more assiduous presence in the coverage, especially when it comes to specific countries. This discussion reveals an opposite trend in relation to the levels of diversity when compared to the previous topics. In this case, it is the southern press that displays higher levels of consonance both in general and within each country. In each of these cases, newspapers usually point to their own countries as the main victims of the euro crisis. There is thus low internal and external plurality, with Greece slightly ahead in the group presenting the lowest levels of diversity (0.61).

Although there is also usually a strong national perspective of the own country as sufferer in the press (see Chapter 2), diversity in the news coverage of the victims of the crisis is moderately higher in France, Germany, and the UK. The following examples illustrate this tendency well. In the case of France, *Le Parisien* puts a strong focus on Greece's suffering (43%), whilst the other newspapers tend to address this issue by pointing to the eurozone countries and the EU countries in general as the main sufferers of the crisis. The German newspapers show a more diversified picture, except in the case of the *Bild*, which is more focused on Germany (42%) than on Greece (20%). As for the UK, most newspapers point to the European countries in general, but *The Sun* also pays a particular attention to the UK itself as one of the victims of the crisis (25%).

Consonance and plurality in the coverage: Is there balance?

Any crisis situation is perceived differently according to the country or group experiencing it and this perception is directly dependent on the type and degree of the national involvement in the crisis. Countries with debt problems have experienced the euro crisis very differently from the other countries; they were the target of speculation, harsh criticism, and finally had to apply severe austerity measures that affected their middle classes due to the substantial increase of taxes and their poorest citizens because of the decrease of subsidies for their subsistence. All this caused significant social and political tensions in these countries, as well as distrust among citizens of the various European countries.

Against this background, it was reasonable to expect to find very different journalistic approaches to the crisis – if nothing else, at least denoting the existence of cleavages between countries with critical problems and countries without critical problems.

Furthermore, as noted previously, different narratives about the crisis may also mean the inclusion of various positions and perspectives, reflecting the different possible interests behind discourses and decisions. Ultimately, this richness of perspectives represents inclusion in developed societies and may, in some situations, be transposed to fairer and more effective policies.

What is mainly reflected in the news coverage of the euro crisis is that the crisis is one thing and sometimes how it is perceived is something else. The literature documents the media's potential to influence our perceptions of issues and therefore the way we think about things (see the agenda-setting, framing, and priming theories, for instance). Overall, this analysis of the euro crisis's news coverage points to the existence of considerable levels of consonance, especially at the beginning of the crisis, a crucial moment for building contexts and creating a specific climate of opinion, and controlling interpretations and judgements about the crisis.

Even though with mixed results in some cases, there was more plurality in news coverage in the countries with debt problems than in the others. More precisely, when the topics had to do with causes, responsibility for solving the crisis, and possible solutions, there was more plurality in the countries with debt problems, but when the focus of coverage was related to the victims of the crisis there was more plurality in the other countries. Particularly, on the subject of the possible beneficiaries of the crisis, it is important to note that it received practically no newspaper coverage, which also provides interesting information on plurality, in this case the issues that are excluded. Overall, France was the country with least plurality and Spain the most pluralist in the news coverage of the euro crisis. In fact, there are usually differences between the French plurality levels and the levels of plurality in the other countries.

External plurality (four newspapers of each country) is in general only slightly higher (3 percentage points) than internal plurality (one newspaper), suggesting the existence of a considerable degree of consonance of all national newspapers, except in the UK case, which is the country that exhibits the highest levels of external plurality (11 and 9 percentage points, for instance). It should also be highlighted that, although there are no clear southern and northern approaches to the crisis reflected in the newspapers' coverage, it was possible to find higher levels of consonance regarding the solutions to the crisis in the countries without critical debt problems (Chapter 10 addresses the issues of media systems and journalistic cultures and the extent to which they reveal differences in coverage patterns). It was also possible to observe that generally there was more diversity between countries than within countries (Tables 6.2 and 6.3), which confirms, as expected, that the overall levels of diversity in Europe are higher than the levels of diversity within each country.

Over time, national diversity increased only very moderately and especially in the solutions for the crisis. A cross-national consensus has grown in the period of time under study regarding the causes and the responsibility to address the crisis, but not regarding the short-term solutions for the crisis. This may be explained by the growing space that the advocates of growth measures have begun to have in the media. Nevertheless, the data analysis also shows that alternatives to austerity were not intensively discussed, especially in the first phase, when most of the decisions on how to tackle the crisis were made. There was a prevalent perspective in the news coverage pointing to the need for bailouts followed by national structural reforms in the nations with problems, which was in turn supported by the dominant view on the causes of the crisis that stressed as the main problem of the euro the failures of some national economic structures and policies.

It is very likely these perspectives have contributed to reinforcing the dominant position promoted by the EU institutions and by the countries more directly involved in the decisions (see also Chapter 5). Other perspectives, when covered, were not as 'loud' in the press as these; for instance, something as fundamental as the structure of the euro system and its implications for the different national economies and their policies was not broadly discussed. Does it make sense to reduce dramatically the complexity of years of common policies and the implementation of a single currency in so many varying economies? However, simple explanations are usually the ones that most news media select. By drawing attention to some aspects at the expense of others, the media might contribute to the formation of certain judgements and evaluations, which will in turn legitimise certain courses of action. The only way to avoid these effects being even more powerful is to secure the presence of different perspectives in the news coverage. This highlights the importance of plurality and the dangers of consonance.

Based on the present analysis, it is not possible to form an explanation for this type of news coverage of the euro crisis. It could be the case that the coverage was mainly influenced by the rules of journalistic production or that the media were used as instruments by the political powers or by some interest groups (the 'markets' are often referred to as a major player) to influence perceptions and legitimise actions, or even both. In any of these cases, the quality of democracy is never best served by partial and uncritical contextualisation of issues and by moderate levels of plurality in media content, especially in times of enduring crisis and significant changes.

7

The Battle for the Euro: Metaphors and Frames in Euro Crisis News

Willem Joris, Liina Puustinen, Katarzyna Sobieraj, and Leen d'Haenens

Metaphors, figures of speech, create images in people's minds and facilitate the understanding of unfamiliar and complicated phenomena. Metaphors also convey deep implications, allowing us to see events in a certain way by accentuating certain aspects and disregarding others. They work as building blocks of our common imagery and consequently even influence our actions. Metaphors can have great rhetoric power, as they often become internalised, rendering their implications more natural and logical than they actually are. Therefore, by analysing metaphors, we can reveal some of the possible political implications behind the language use.

Metaphors are instrumental in the construction of frames in journalism (see also Millar and Beck, 2004) and are frequently used for explaining abstract and complicated social phenomena like climate change, healthcare (e.g. Schön, 1993) and economy (e.g. Williams, 2013). This chapter presents the dominant frames built upon metaphors of the economic crisis in Europe in the daily press across ten European countries.

The rise and fall of metaphorical language strongly relates to the evolution of a crisis. In crisis situations, both the amount and intensity of metaphors increase, while declining in calmer periods (De Landtsheer, 2009). The more often the same metaphors are repeated, the weaker their functionality, as their original meaning tends to disappear. As a consequence, highly conventionalised metaphors may lose their heuristic value without, however, losing their political power. They become taken for granted, to the degree where no alternatives can be imagined (Hellsten, 2003).

Metaphors, which are specific linguistic structures, can also be visual and are related to bodily and spatial experiences (Lakoff and Johnson, 1980). The focus of this chapter is on the linguistic metaphors used in the press coverage as well as on the choice of framing devices. Framing devices are clearly perceptible elements in a story, such as metaphors, lexical choices, catchphrases, or historical examples from which lessons can be learned (Gamson and Modigliani, 1989). Besides framing devices, our inventory also includes reasoning devices. The latter are the underlying, latent elements in a text, which can be discovered after careful reading: the definition of a problem, a causal interpretation, a moral evaluation, and treatment recommendations (e.g. Entman, 1993). Together, framing devices and a logical sequence of reasoning devices form an integrated structure, which is called a frame package (Reese, 2010; Van Gorp, 2007, 2010).

Studies on metaphors, economy, and crisis

Previous research has shown the pervasiveness of conceptual metaphors and their ability to powerfully structure how people gather information, and build up a way of talking and thinking about issues (Lakoff, 2008): 'Metaphor is often a serious figure of argument, not an ornament' (McCloskey, 1995: 215). The choice of metaphor is central to the development of thought, as it structures our perceptions of reality and actions in everyday life (Lakoff and Johnson, 1980; Lakoff and Turner, 1989). Moreover, as it is 'a structural mapping from one conceptual domain to another' (Lakoff, 1993: 418), a metaphor brings understanding and insight into new and unfamiliar situations by referring to other events or phenomena. Hence, metaphors are effective tools of communication as they can carry certain implications from one context to another (Hellsten, 2003; Hellsten and Nerlich, 2010). Metaphors' rhetorical power may impact people's behaviours as well as economic decisions by individuals or institutions (e.g. Williams, 2013; Williams et al., 2011).

Public metaphors are often initiated by politicians in their speeches; the news media reiterate and reinforce them and sometimes come up with new images. Therefore, people in power, such as political leaders, business leaders, and journalists, can impose metaphors on a particular situation that later become dominant views in the news media (Lakoff and Johnson, 1980: 157–60), which work as part of our social imaginary (Taylor, 2003).

Numerous studies have pointed out that the language of economics is highly metaphorical (e.g. Charteris-Black and Ennis, 2001; McCloskey, 1983, 1988; Richardt, 2005; Skorczynska and Deignan, 2006; Wang et al., 2013). Frequently used conceptual metaphors in economic language include seeing the economy as a machine, a construction, or a patient. A nation's economy and money are often visualised as liquid (swimming in money, need of liquidity) or as an orientation in space that may be up (more, positive) or down (less, negative); as activity, a nation's economy can be framed as a journey, sports, or a war (Richardt, 2005).

Medical metaphors have a long history in economics language and were used as early as the classic economic theory in the 1600s, with modern medicine developing at the same time (Miettinen, 2010). In newspaper language, the economy is often presented as a living organism or a human being suffering from various health conditions. In parallel, the economic crisis is defined as an illness or an ailment of the organism (Charteris-Black and Ennis, 2001; Horner, 2011; Wang et al., 2013), even as a communicable virus or a global contagion (Peckham, 2013). In this context, we can talk about the medicalisation of economy as the economic news is often dominated by medical metaphors (Miettinen, 2010: 211–12). Common metaphors used in covering an economic crisis also include war and natural phenomena such as weather changes or natural disasters (Charteris-Black and Ennis, 2001).

The findings of the studies on mediated metaphors of the recent economic crisis are fairly similar. Bounegru and Forceville (2011) studied the visual metaphors of the euro crisis in editorial cartoons and identified catastrophe/(natural) disaster, illness/death, and begging as the most frequent metaphors. Horner (2011) studied the metaphors used in public discourse of the US banking crisis in 2008 and found that the metaphors of illness, natural disasters, and mechanical failures were dominant. She pointed out that these metaphors eliminate the human element, portraying the response to the crisis as an emergency measure. Esager (2011) compared metaphors used about the 2008 credit crunch in English and Danish economic newspapers, and found the following metaphors: movement, liquid (e.g. in a container), living being, medical treatment, war or sports, machine, building, journey, object, and a natural phenomenon.

Metaphoric frames in the news

In a recent study, Joris et al. (2013) analysed the coverage of the euro crisis in Flemish newspapers through the identification of frame packages (Joris et al., 2014; Reese, 2010; Van Gorp, 2007, 2010). They identified three dominant metaphorical frames: combat, disease, and natural disaster. The combat frame referred to battles, fights, and conflicts between European leaders, financial markets, and/or citizens. The disease frame was constructed around the idea that the euro crisis is caused by a disorder or an illness of a country or a financial institution. The natural disaster frame was identified in news articles in which European countries or institutions are portrayed as hit by natural disasters or natural phenomena. The combat frame proved to be the most frequent (84.3%), followed by the disease frame (40.4%), and the natural disaster frame (19.2%).

We may raise the question of whether these three identified frames are either language/context-specific or actually universal in the coverage of the euro crisis. Therefore, in this study we widen our focus on the prevalence of these frames to nine more European countries.

The news coverage of the euro crisis was analysed through an in-depth content analysis of news stories. First, an inductive, qualitative analysis was conducted in order to recognise the dominant metaphors and news frames. Secondly, a deductive, quantitative analysis was executed to measure the prevalence of these frames.

The inductive analysis was initiated, making use of an open coding procedure. In each news story, the first two metaphors were identified. These metaphors were mainly found in the title, headline, or the leading paragraph, which usually summarises the content of the entire article. Next, the metaphors were clustered by axial coding. In an effort to construct the dominant frame packages, the metaphors were complemented by other framing and reasoning devices. After creating the frame matrix with the different frame packages (see Table 7.1), the authors coded the other news articles to verify that all metaphors of the euro crisis fitted with one of the frame packages. During this process no new frames were detected.

This inductive analysis was carried out in ten European countries. Finland, Germany, and the Netherlands represent the northern and economically stronger countries whereas Greece, Italy, and Spain comprise the southern European nations with major sovereign debt problems;

Table 7.1 Framing devices used in coverage of the euro crisis

Frame	Reasoning devices					Framing devices	
	Definition of the problem	Cause	Consequences	Possible solutions	Moral values	Metaphors	Catchphrases and lexical choices
War	*Conflict* between countries and/or financial markets concerning the euro	A *clash* of interests, visions, strategies and/or power	*Conflicts* and *rivalry* increases; *violence* and *war*	A *counterattack* to *defend*, or *peace* and *compromises*	Selfishness and egoism cause *conflict*, cooperation and unity is the best approach	Weapon, bazooka, attack, firepower, monster, blow, ghost, bullet, fight	In Portugal and Greece Europe has already won a few battles but the war will be decided in Italy. French president and his European colleagues have declared war on speculators.
Disease	Countries, financial markets and/or euro are sick	Countries/ banks with *acute or chronic* financial problems – the *disease* could touch anyone	Possible *contagion* for other countries or banks	*Remedy* to control the *illness* by *medicine* or *surgery*, adopting a proper *therapy*	The disease needs to be *cured* for a good *recovery*, and to stop the *contagion*	Contagion, virus, infection, pain killer, doctor, stress, allergic, addiction, junk	This crisis is like a cancer. If you don't do anything about it, it keeps on growing. Spain is devising a capital injection in its ailing savings banks.

(Continued)

Table 7.1 (Continued)

Frame	Reasoning devices				Framing devices	
	Definition of the problem	Cause	Consequences	Possible solutions	Moral values	Metaphors	Catchphrases and lexical choices
Natural disaster	Europe, countries and/or financial markets are confronted with a *natural disaster*	An unexpected and unpredictable event brought about by forces other than the acts of human beings	Much loss of life, much economic damage and panic	As soon as possible after the break out of the disaster a rescue plan needs to be prepared and applied. The plan is supposed to include prevention mechanisms for the future.	We need courage and constancy to handle the crisis	Storm, avalanche, tsunami, dam, apocalypse, dike, Armageddon, turbulences	Since the financial storm is not about to abate, even a safe haven could suffer damage. Without specific interventions the sovereign debt crisis is a rising hurricane threatening to blow down the European economy. We have now erected a solid firewall and we have given our fire brigade more effective equipment.

Frame	Reasoning devices					Framing devices	
	Definition of the problem	Cause	Consequences	Possible solutions	Moral values	Metaphors	Catchphrases and lexical choices
Construction	The euro/European project is an example of hubris, excessive optimism or wanting too much	The *architecture* or *construction* of the euro was too ambitious and not based on strong *foundations*	The *construction* or the society *collapses* and might cause much damage	The *construction* of the euro needs to be *repaired* or *renovated* to keep it stable	Hubris will be punished	Architecture, fall down, Titanic, life belt, domino, rotten, parachute, building of euro, EU motor, machineries, financial system	The eurozone is a house without strong foundations. The financial train will crash, if we don't repair the locomotive. The Cyprus debt crisis may result in a 'domino effect' across the eurozone.
Game	The euro crisis is like a *game*	*Players* are challenged to take part in a game	Sometimes you *win*, sometimes you *lose*	Try to do your best, so you may win as much as possible	The crisis is a game, sometimes you win, sometimes you lose	Arm wrestling, poker, soccer, race, betting, game rules, marathon	Merkel has begun her arm wrestling with Hollande. Draghi's bold move in euro chess game. He launched a bold gambit in the eurozone's game of chess with markets and elected leaders.

Belgium and France belong to the middle group; Poland and the UK are not members of the eurozone. This diversity of countries is especially interesting and valuable for conducting a cross-country comparison.

In each country, four newspapers were analysed: the leading financial business newspaper, two quality newspapers, and the leading tabloid. In case of absence of a tabloid or when access to archives was not possible, a centre-oriented leading daily was used. In total, 10,492 news articles were analysed.

As a result of the inductive analysis, we defined the five most frequently occurring mutually exclusive frame packages with a metaphor at the core of each frame: the war frame, the disease frame, the natural disaster frame, the construction frame, and the game and sports frame (see Table 7.1). Each metaphor of the euro crisis in the news articles fitted with one frame package only. Some articles proved to feature metaphors from different frame packages. Several frames may obviously occur together in a single article.

In order to find out whether these frames are universal, and to determine the relative occurrence of each of these frames with a view to a cross-country comparison, a deductive, quantitative analysis was required. Therefore, the coders in the country teams involved indicated whether or not a frame package was present in a given news story, based on the first two metaphors. In other words, in each news story, the coder identified the presence or absence of the five dominant frames, by a simple yes/no answer. In the following sections, we will present the results of both the inductive and the deductive analysis.

Frame packages of the inductive analysis

In the inductive analysis, the first two metaphors in the articles related to the euro crisis were identified. Metaphors related to the euro crisis were found in 33.7% of the articles; 11.9% of the articles had more than one metaphor referring to the debt crisis. The list of metaphors was extensive. However, most metaphors were found repeatedly. Therefore, metaphors, synonyms of metaphors, and similar metaphors were clustered into frame packages, resulting in five dominant frames: the war frame, the disease frame, the natural disaster frame, the construction frame, and the game and sports frame (see Table 7.1). Most metaphors identified could be positioned within one of those mutually exclusive frames.

However, it should be mentioned that, in addition to the five dominant frames, a few 'peripheral' metaphors appeared in the news, for example the euro crisis as a 'soap opera'. Since these metaphors occurred to a very limited extent and, consequently, the corresponding devices would not have a major impact on the public opinion, they were left out of the analysis. Furthermore, certain metaphors were too general for crisis situations, such as panic, chaos, or rescue. Depending on the context of the sentence or the article, the metaphor might be situated within a more specific frame package. In the next paragraphs, the five dominant frame packages are presented, and quotes will be used as illustrations.

War

> Europe has, since the Second World War, always been an economic and political battlefield, and the present battlefield is bloodier than ever before.
> (Het Financieele Dagblad, the Netherlands, 30 June 2012)

Terms referring to combats, battles, fights, and weapons are recurrently used in covering the euro crisis. Journalists frequently highlight conflicts between European leaders during summits, since national politicians mostly have opposing interests. Furthermore, the diverging interests of financial markets, such as rating agencies, and the political world are very often discussed. The financial actors are repeatedly portrayed as the enemy, so a counterattack by the European leaders is seen as appropriate. Therefore, the war frame that characterises a battle or clash between different actors is often used in reporting. The war frame can also be used for blaming others for being unwilling to compromise or judging the national governments for their inability to negotiate (see also Cammaerts, 2012). A clash of interests may increase the rivalry and violence between the different actors. Possible solutions in this frame package are counterattacks to defend a position, on the one hand, or peace and compromise, on the other.

War metaphors may highlight certain views and hide others. The metaphor generates a network of entailments: there is an 'enemy', a 'threat to the economic security', and 'weapons' are needed on the 'battle fronts' (see also Lakoff and Johnson, 1980: 156), such as 'a financial bazooka' (referring to a shoulder-fired missile developed by the Americans during the Second World War), illustrated in the following quotes from Belgian and Italian newspapers:

> *Observers expect a set of measures to be taken that speculators will not be able to cope with – measures which are referred to as a financial bazooka. (De Standaard, Belgium, 12 October 2011)*

> *The European Central Bank has one more weapon to use. (Il Sole 24 Ore, Italy, 17 December 2010)*

Sometimes the news stories refer to the global financial crisis as the enemy against which the European Union as a whole or the European Central Bank needs to fight. But, in other cases, the confrontation is seen to take place between the European states, some countries being weaker than the others, as in the following quotation from the British *Financial Times*:

> *Greece is expected on Monday to resist pressure for an immediate tightening of its current austerity package as it fights to win back the confidence of international financial markets and its eurozone neighbours. (Financial Times, UK, 14 February 2010)*

If the war frame is resorted to, the euro crisis is primarily viewed from the angle that the European leaders as well as the financial markets are mainly self-interested. In such a case, the news story is proposing that the reader favour a solution beneficial to the greater whole and support solidarity, so that the damage suffered may be kept to a minimum. The story implies that all the actors involved should assume their responsibility so that a new threat can be averted.

Disease

> *Fear of contagion: It is so similar to one of these flu outbreaks, which currently hardly anyone escapes. First the banks were sick and they infected the states. (Süddeutsche Zeitung, Germany, 25 October 2011)*

The euro crisis is often depicted as contagion caused by a virus. The disease frame is constructed around the idea that the crisis is affected by an illness of a country or of financial institutions. In many cases, the virus of bankruptcy is seen to spread from Greece and measures are needed 'to isolate the Greek virus from infecting the rest of the financial system of Europe', as it is expressed, for instance, in the Polish *Gazeta Wyborcza* (6 November 2011). It should not come as a surprise that news articles about the crisis refer to disease, since the word 'crisis' derives from the Greek word *krisis* and stands for a 'turning-point for better or worse in an acute disease or fever' (*Merriam-Webster's Collegiate Dictionary*, 2005). A crisis is an emergency situation in which a system or mechanism is seriously disturbed so that a remedy is required. This remedy will determine the future: either the disease will be cured, or complete chaos and even death of masses will follow. At the moment of truth, the patient is struck by discomfort, anxiety, and confusion (Millar and Beck, 2004). To cure the illness (appearing in various strengths, anything from an allergy, a virus, an infection, stress, to a cancer) and to prevent possible contagion of others, medicine, surgery or a proper therapy are recommended.

The use of the disease frame will create in the reader's mind the image of a problem requiring a correct remedy. If the disease is given an effective treatment, for example a financial injection or the removal of ailing parts (i.e. particular member states or so-called bad banks), full recovery may take place and further contagion may be avoided. But a disease can also attack a healthy person, totally unexpectedly and without anyone's fault, for example by means of an 'invisible' germ. In other words, if the disease frame is activated, the reader may be afraid that, even though healthy, he or she may suddenly come down with a chronic disease such as 'a serious heart condition' where 'you can't go on putting in new stents every day for in the end you will die', as mentioned in the Dutch *NRC Handelsblad* (25 May 2012) or like 'a patient haemorrhaging blood, cash had to be injected into a collapsed economy' as stated by the British *Guardian* (21 February 2012). The metaphor of haemorrhage is also used in a Belgian article:

> Yesterday the ECB merely applied a plaster to the wound, thus stopping the bleeding for a short while. But that's no more than first aid. To stop the haemorrhage once and for all, a more drastic intervention is required. The wound needs to be stitched, the sooner the better, and that is a job for the European heads of government. Otherwise the blood will soon begin to ooze through the plaster. (De Tijd, Belgium, 9 August 2011)

The economy is presented as a body, a living organism, and the countries most 'suffering' from the illness are described as 'patients', which is also found in other studies of metaphors of economic crisis (e.g. Horner, 2011; Peckham, 2013). In these scenarios, failure to act would possibly endanger the lives of the patients (Horner, 2011: 35). This is exemplified in a Polish newspaper which reports:

> *Concerns regarding the condition of patients are growing again – especially Spain and Italy, which will be prescribed new medicines. The question is whether they survive until the treatment starts to work.*
> *(Rzeczpospolita, Poland, 16 July 2013)*

Peckham (2013: 233) argues that the biological and economic risks have become intertwined after global viruses and economic shocks. The term 'Asian Flu' was used to describe the 1997 financial crisis and an outbreak of H5N1 avian flu in Hong Kong in 1997. 'The biologisation of the financial crisis, which is implicit in pervasive analogies of cascading financial shocks with "contagion", reclaims risk as a natural hazard or, at the least, as a form of "external risk"' (Peckham, 2013: 235–6).

Natural disaster

> *If the euro survives this storm, not just a rain shower, it means that it is more than strong. (Expansión, Spain, 27 October 2011)*

A third dominant frame in the coverage of the euro crisis is the natural disaster, which portrays European countries or institutions as suffering from a natural catastrophe or portrays the crisis in terms of natural phenomena. Here we find weather-related issues, for example heavy weather, storm, financial tsunami, or hurricane, but also turbulent seas or rivers, as illustrated, for instance, in a Dutch news article:

> *We have never sailed on tranquil waters. But in the last four years we have gone through heavy turbulence, real storms and unexpected hurricanes. (NRC Handelsblad, the Netherlands, 7 October 2011)*

An Italian newspaper *Il Sole 24 Ore* (12 July 2012) calls the economic crisis 'The perfect storm and the fear of the 2.0 crisis.' This is an intertextual reference to a Hollywood film called *The Perfect Storm* (2000). Borrowing metaphors from the domain of popular culture is common in newspaper language. Horner (2011: 37) writes that the US bailout in 2008 was also portrayed in the news as threatened by natural disaster. The 'bailout' was framed as a preventive measure in the face of a coming storm. The crisis was also referred to as 'the perfect financial storm of the century' and the term 'financial tsunami' was used in several contexts.

In our study material some articles also referred to an avalanche, earthquake, a quagmire, or a vortex, as exemplified in a quote from this Finnish newspaper:

> The rate of the euro falls and the breaking down of the European
> government bond markets will most probably snatch some of the
> weaker eurozone countries into the whirlpool.
> (Kauppalehti, Finland, 21 October 2011)

The frame of the natural disaster implies that Europe and the financial markets are threatened by a natural catastrophe, which is caused by an unexpected and unpredictable event brought about by forces of nature, forces other and bigger than the acts of human beings. Consequently, there could be much economic damage and many victims. A possible solution after the outbreak of the disaster is a rescue plan, which is also supposed to include prevention measures for potential upcoming catastrophes. The natural disaster frame presents the euro crisis as a problem arising totally unexpectedly, as it 'just happened' without anyone being responsible (see also Rantanen, 2012). If we show courage and determination to tackle the crisis, we will survive, the frame implies.

Construction

> Due to a lack of a captain, the euro has become a rudderless ship.
> (Le Figaro, France, 25 May 2012)

> The concrete of the European house is badly degraded: not only does the
> building need urgent repairs, it also needs a new architectural design.
> (NRC Handelsblad, the Netherlands, 25 June 2012)

The fourth dominant frame that often occurs in the coverage of the euro crisis is the frame of construction. It depicts the European economy or the economy of one of the countries as a building, vehicle, or other man-made construction. 'Construction' can refer to a house or shack that needs renovation or is in danger of collapse, but also to a train, a ship, an airplane, a motor, or a machine, having mechanical

137

failures, or whose forward motion is impeded (see also Horner, 2011: 36). A broken train metaphor is exemplified in quotes from this Belgian newspaper:

> *Initially the train could operate without major problems, but then it was hit by the crisis and the flaws in its construction became painfully obvious. (De Standaard, Belgium, 27 June 2012)*

The construction frame refers to the euro or the European project as an example of hubris, excessive optimism, or overreaching itself. The articles using this frame suggest that the design of the euro was too ambitious and that its foundations were not strong enough. Consequently, the system and even the society using it might collapse, causing much damage. The architecture needs to be reconsidered, repaired, or renovated to keep it steady. The construction frame is often used in the news coverage of the euro crisis mentioning a domino effect (in itself a game reference): if the weakest link of the construction collapses, the other parts are at risk of falling down too. This type of construction frame is illustrated in a quotation from a Polish newspaper:

> *Grexit would be remarkably expensive for the EU [...] Even worse, it would cause panic on the markets, which would increase the risk of the deadly domino effect in Portugal and Spain, and perhaps also in Ireland and Italy. (Gazeta Wyborcza, Poland, 17 May 2012)*

Overall, the use of the construction frame triggers the image that the construction of the euro or of Europe was already weak at the outset. Consequently, the former and the present European leaders are the ones to blame for the crisis. There are even some conspiracy theories of a 'Trojan horse' embedded in the construction frame (this example also borrows from the domain of war strategies):

> *The crisis aid of the stability fund would become a Trojan horse, which would bring the economic policy needs of the member states inside the walls of the central bank. (Helsingin Sanomat, Finland, 22 October 2011)*

The moral value of the construction frame is that 'hubris' will be punished: if the EU wants too much, and the project is not stable enough, it may result in a ruin.

Game and sports

The euro is like any game where Germany always wins.
(El País, Spain, 17 October 2011)

The rescue is like a race that politics cannot win.
(Sueddeutsche Zeitung, Germany, 14 November 2011)

The fifth frame package in the coverage of the euro crisis is the game and sports frame. In contrast with the war frame, the game and sports frame refers to a fairly friendly contest between players, who are challenged to participate in a game such as arm wrestling, soccer, or chess. All players do their best to win. However, if the game is lost, the result is not as fatal as when a war is lost: the game frame is less deadly than the war frame. Moreover, the players in a game or a sport have freedom and control; the participation is voluntary, not forced. Generally, the game frame looks at the crisis as something more 'normal' than the other frames of this study. As a result, the gravity of the crisis is downplayed. In the following example, the euro crisis is equated to a rugby game, implying a playful connotation with a twist of testosterone:

Italy vs. Germany is the match of the euro crisis. Rome relies on the short tackle, Berlin on extra time. (De Tijd, Belgium, 27 June 2012)

Soccer is also very popular all over Europe, and it is common for the journalists to look for metaphors in their own cultural contexts to communicate to national readerships (Kimmel, 2008). For instance, a Dutch paper *Het Financieele Dagblad* (30 July 2011) writes: 'The ball is now in the court of the European leaders, but I don't see them kicking it any time soon.'

Card games are popular metaphors also for political negotiations, strategies, and decision-making. 'Greece makes the stakes higher in the poker game', claims the Finnish *Ilta-Sanomat* (29 October 2011). The French *Le Monde* also refers to the European leaders playing a poker game that requires experience and tactics:

They should know when to lay their cards on the table. And this is not the moment. In the poker game with the markets, nothing requires European leaders to show their cards. (Le Monde, France, 21 December 2010)

Comparisons of the countries with deductive analysis

In order to determine the relative occurrence of each of these frames with a view to comparing the newspapers/countries concerned, a quantitative analysis was required. All five frame packages turned out to be present in the news articles examined. The number of metaphors differed between countries. This is partly caused by the variety of the coders in each country and their level of sensitivity in recognising metaphors. But studies in comparative linguistics (e.g. Esager, 2011) have also found differences in frequency of metaphor use in different languages. Consequently, the average occurrence of the frames by country was used to show the frequency of the five dominant frames. As only two metaphors per article were identified, this chapter should be considered as an explorative study, that will result in a more extensive analysis. In Belgium and the Netherlands, this step has already been taken. The intercoder reliability (Krippendorff's Alpha) of the frames was measured on a sample of 10% of the articles with very good results: war frame (α = .81), disease frame (α = .92), natural disaster frame (α = .90), construction frame (α = .72), and game frame (α = .72).

The war frame (9.4%) proved to be the most frequent frame in the sample as a whole, followed by the disease frame (7.7%), the natural disaster frame (5.2%), and the construction frame (4.0%). The game and sports frame (1.3%) was the least frequently used frame in the news stories under scrutiny.

The degree of occurrence (in percentages) of the five dominant frames was relatively low, because only the first two metaphors found in the title, the headline, or the lead of the article were identified. These percentages would have been higher had the full article been scanned for these dominant frames. Hence, we continue to work on the degree of occurrence in the news stories in which a dominant frame is spelled out. Since the number of identified metaphors differed between the countries (due to differences in training and expertise in recognising metaphors in news articles), the cross-country comparison only analyses the news articles containing a frame.

The war frame turned out to be the most frequently used frame in the coverage of the euro crisis. Consequently, the crisis is perceived as a problem caused by European leaders or by the financial markets, which are chiefly self-interested. This news coverage suggests a fear among readers that the crisis will escalate, and might end up in a war between nations. In contrast, the two other frequently used metaphors, disease (ranging from a minor allergy to a serious cancer) and natural disaster are framed in our culture as phenomena occurring without anyone's fault. Therefore, through the use of such metaphorical devices, it is suggested to the audience that no one is guilty of the crisis, as it came unexpectedly from nowhere and, like a disease, could touch anyone. Such metaphors have the political aim of distancing any claims for responsibility or blame, and they may also trigger collective distrust and fear (Rantanen, 2012). If the construction frame is resorted to, the journalist mentions a problem of instability of the European construction; some parts are too weak. Consequently, the reader may be afraid that the eurozone will collapse and the euro will disappear, in a domino effect. If the game frame is used in an article, the severity of the euro crisis is being normalised. Since this frame is the least frequently used frame, we may suggest that the crisis is chiefly covered as a threatening problem for European society.

When comparing the occurrence of the dominant frames of the euro crisis across the ten countries (see Table 7.2), the war frame was most often manifest in Greece, possibly because this country is most attacked by the financial markets or by other European countries. Also, in the other countries with major sovereign debt problems, Italy and Spain, the war frame was often used. In France, Belgium, and the Netherlands, the war frame also turned out to be the most popular frame in the coverage of the euro crisis. This might be explained by national cultures and the style of the national political actors. All three countries are faced with strong nationalist or extreme right parties, which are opposed to a further transfer of sovereignty towards the EU. France and the Netherlands both voted against the European Constitution in 2005. Furthermore, former French President Sarkozy is known for his rather 'aggressive' performances.

The war frame was less frequent in countries outside the eurozone (Poland and the UK) and in the economically strongest countries (Finland and Germany). One of the reasons for that might be that in Germany talking about war is still a taboo, which may affect the journalists' choice of metaphors. All countries that most used the war frame also portrayed the crisis as a disease. Some countries are already sick and are searching for a medicine; other countries are scared of being touched by a virus or illness. Strong countries like Finland and Germany are probably more 'immune' to the European virus. These strong countries covered the crisis as a natural disaster (mostly in Germany) or as a construction problem (mainly in Finland). The use of these metaphors framed the euro crisis either as a natural phenomenon that unexpectedly happened without

Table 7.2 Occurrences of frames across countries

Type of country	Country	War	Disease	Natural disaster	Construction	Game and Sports
Strong	Finland	13.4 (n = 32)	19.3 (n = 46)	**20.6** (**n = 49**)	**37.4** (**n = 89**)	9.2 (n = 22)
	Germany	**22.5** (**n = 9**)	17.5 (n = 7)	**35.0** (**n = 14**)	**22.5** (**n = 9**)	2.5 (n = 1)
Middle	Belgium	**43.4** (**n = 275**)	**29.8** (**n = 189**)	16.7 (n = 106)	7.7 (n = 49)	2.4 (n = 15)
	France	**44.6** (**n = 54**)	19.8 (n = 24)	18.2 (n = 22)	13.2 (n = 16)	4.1 (n = 5)
	Netherlands	**39.2** (**n = 143**)	**31.5** (**n = 115**)	13.2 (n = 48)	14.0 (n = 51)	2.2 (n = 8)
Weaker	Greece	**47.7** (**n = 94**)	**18.3** (**n = 36**)	13.7 (n = 27)	11.7 (n = 23)	8.6 (n = 17)
	Italy	22.2 (n = 47)	26.9 (n = 57)	**25.9** (**n = 55**)	18.9 (n = 40)	6.1 (n = 13)
	Spain	**32.5** (**n = 153**)	28.9 (n = 136)	19.5 (n = 92)	12.1 (n = 57)	7.0 (n = 33)
Non-eurozone	Poland	11.4 (n = 5)	29.5 (n = 13)	**43.2** (**n = 19**)	15.9 (n = 7)	0.0 (n = 0)
	UK	15.5 (n = 33)	36.2 (n = 77)	**27.7** (**n = 59**)	15.0 (n = 32)	5.6 (n = 12)

Note: Values are percentages. Variances in *n* are partly due to national differences in training and expertise in recognising metaphors. Bold type indicates higher scores in the countries that are more salient to the overall results.

any human blame or as a weak European construction that needs to be repaired before the whole structure collapses. The non-eurozone countries, Poland and the UK, framed the crisis predominantly as a natural disaster or a disease. These frames do not impose responsibilities on the political leaders or financial markets, and at the same time they portray the crisis as unpredictable and unexpected. The game frame was the least manifest frame in all countries under study. The game frame turned out to be used more often in Finland and Greece, but never appeared in the Polish newspaper sample.

The use of frames differed significantly between the European countries. However, between the types of newspapers the use of dominant frames hardly differed. The only significant difference was the more manifest use of the disease frame in popular newspapers $(F(2,2191) = 4.627; p < .05)$.

De Landtsheer (2009) identified that metaphors and frames are mostly used at the beginning of a crisis and during peak moments. A significant difference between 2010, 2011, and 2012 was found in our study $(F(2,10489) = 58,033; p < .001)$. The use of frames turned out to be high in 2010, when the crisis started, and it decreased in 2011 and 2012. A potential reason for that might be that the euro crisis was a new and complex situation in 2010 and journalists had to use more frames and metaphors to make connections with well-known situations in readers' minds. In 2011 and 2012, the citizen's knowledge about the euro crisis had improved, so interpretation and comparison was no longer necessary.

Our study focused on dominant frames of the euro crisis, based on the first two metaphors in the title, the lead, or the heading of each article. Although this generally summarises the content of the entire news article, the degree of occurrence of each dominant frame in this chapter was rather low. Consequently, we should be reticent to generalise our cross-country comparisons. In future research, it would be appropriate to code the full news articles, and to identify all frame packages, rather than only two metaphors.

Discussion: Why do metaphors matter?

This chapter examined the dominant frames in the coverage of the euro crisis. Five frames with a metaphor at their core were identified in the

143

European press: war, disease, natural disaster, construction, and game. Such metaphorical framing bears significant consequences for the conceptualisation of the responsibility in relation to the crisis.

The war frame was most frequently used in the overall data of ten countries. Picturing the euro crisis as war implies that the European leaders and financial markets are the 'bad guys'; they are chiefly the ones to blame for causing this crisis, or for not adequately addressing it, although very seldom were any direct accusations made in the news stories. As was found by Kepplinger, Köhler, and Post (Chapter 3), the most frequently mentioned actor responsible for solving the crisis in the news was a collective of eurozone members or supranational organisations. The eurozone members have to defend the countries with sovereign debt problems against the enemy, mostly the financial markets. Furthermore, many news articles mention the search for a counterattack, such as a 'bazooka'. Essentially, the war frame was used to dramatise the events, paint a picture of chaos, uncertainty, and as an alert to prepare for the worst. A war would lead to significant financial and human damage, which is in nobody's interest.

The metaphorical frames of war, construction, and game involve some kind of human engagement, a responsibility of some party being the aggressor or victim, someone having built the house, or participating in the game. But the metaphors of disease and natural disaster, which were the second most frequent, eliminate the human element. As confirmed by Hubé, Salgado, and Puustinen (Chapter 5), half of the news articles imply that the crisis was beyond anyone's responsibility. Moreover, the consequences of the disaster may lead to ill effects being experienced by everyone in the immediate environment (see Horner, 2011: 40). As Peckham (2013) points out, in the context of the US financial crisis in 2008, the definition of 'contagion' has been used vaguely and economists have expressed reservations about the appositeness of the term; yet 'communicable disease' is still an important theoretical framework for interpreting the transmission of financial crises. 'A tension underscores the conceptual equation of financial crisis with communicable disease, one that lies at the heart of the idea of the "risk society" developed by Beck (1992) and Giddens (1999), precisely at the moment when the risks posed by "emerging infections" and "financial crises" were coming into focus' (Peckham, 2013: 232–4).

The organic metaphors of economics hide the question of responsibility, as the metaphor directs the understanding of the recession as a 'natural' part of the operating system. This is, however, misleading as crisis situations usually result from the decisions of people in charge, such as faulty interest policy, over-leveraging of the private business sector, and insufficient control of the use of the new financial instruments (Miettinen, 2010). The intentional decisions made by the European politicians are, therefore, masked by the metaphors when the risks were allowed to grow too big. Peckham (2003) argues that conceptualising financial shock as a form of disease creates fear and expectations in the public and therefore influences policy making. 'There is a danger, as that fear displaces critical analysis.'

The implications of the metaphoric frames of the euro crisis news coverage leave us pondering: what is at stake when ideas of another domain such as warfare migrate to the field of economy? How does the language of war, disease, and natural disaster in economic news influence how people, politicians, and governments respond? How is the common imagery of economy shaped when it is seen in terms of a collapsing construction or a sinking ship? An experimental approach might answer these questions.

Part III

Influences on Coverage

8

Divergent Perspectives? Financial Newspapers and the General Interest Press

Ángel Arrese and Alfonso Vara

The financial and economic crisis that started in the US and Europe in 2008 is an important subject of study for further analysis of media economic discourse. There have been many studies that have addressed some of the dimensions of this media coverage of the crisis, both domestic and comparative analysis. One of the recurring ideas is that in the years before the crisis, news organisations were unable to warn of existing risks in the financial industry, about the housing bubbles, and so on (Arrese and Vara, 2012; Mercille, 2013a; Schiffrin, 2011; Starkman, 2014; Usher, 2012). Already in the middle of the economic crisis, the media is often criticised for its simplistic, acritical, or alarmist view of the economic and financial problems (Arlt and Storz, 2010; Fahy et al., 2010; Mercille, 2013b; Quiring and Weber, 2012; Titley, 2012; Tulloch, 2009; Uchitelle, 2011).

However, there are many new issues to examine and one of them is the role of different types of media when analysing certain aspects of the crisis. More specifically, given the economic and financial nature of the crisis, it is interesting to consider the peculiarities of specialised (in the business press) versus general coverage (in the general press). Is the crisis reported significantly differently to specialised audiences than to the general public? Do different sources carry similar weight in different types of newspapers? Is there a more pro-European or nationalistic attitude in the general press than in the specialised press? Do different political and economic actors have similar roles and prevalence in economic news? Does the elitist coverage dominate in all types of newspapers?

There are at least four characteristics of this crisis which make it particularly suitable to answer these questions. These features are:

- *Novelty and complexity.* As explained by Reinhart and Rogoff (2009), although this crisis shares many features with other financial crises throughout history, the truth is that it has been largely perceived as different. It was an unforeseen crisis, which has affected the real and financial economy, especially in richer countries, and whose interpretation has generated great debate and has captivated the attention of the public.
- *International and national.* There is no doubt that the 2008 crisis had an international character. However, at the same time, the considerably different impact that this crisis has had on each country in the world – for example, in the EU and the United States, or among different eurozone countries – is quite striking. Therefore, the interaction between global explanations of the crisis and the specific interpretations in each country is of special interest from the point of view of a comparative cross-national analysis.
- *Multifaceted and systemic.* The crisis that began as a financial crisis, triggered symbolically by the fall of Lehman Brothers, was soon taking on new dimensions, and ultimately affected all areas of economic activity (business, banking, employment, public finance, etc.). Of course, it also generated political crises, especially in Europe. Soon it was defined as a systemic crisis, an idea summed up very well by Rajan in his work, *Fault Lines* (Rajan, 2010).
- *Technical and popular.* Paradoxically, perhaps the most complex economic situation of the last century – as indeed in other crises – has been the one that has generated the greatest interest among the general public and in the media (Arrese, 2010). More than ever, the old tensions between journalism and economics (Arrese, 2000), between the rigour of expert analysis and the necessary simplification in information on current economic and financial events (Arrese, 2006) have emerged once again.

These four characteristics of the global crisis are also applicable to some of its more particular manifestations, such as the so-called crisis of the euro, which is the focus of this book. Sovereign debt problems of European states and insolvency of financial institutions, key to the crisis of the single currency, seamlessly share the aforementioned traits of the global crisis.

Moreover, in the case of the euro crisis, the tension between its European dimension and its particular impact on the national economies of the EU member states is at stake. From this perspective, the euro crisis is perhaps only comparable with the launch of the euro, which also generated broad interest from the media coverage standpoint (Vreese et al., 2001), or to other complex processes such as the enlargement of the Union (Vreese and Boomgaarden, 2006).

This chapter focuses on the last feature of the crisis already mentioned, on the tension between its technical and popular nature, which relates to the issue of media coverage of the crisis from more or less specialised approaches. We analyse the aspects and the extent to which the treatment of the euro crisis – a topic with obvious technical aspects, but also of great popular interest – differs among the most targeted media, directed to the elites, and the media appealing to the general population.[28] A priori, we expect to find very significant differences between the economic and financial press and the rest of the newspapers, and between the dailies from different countries, taking into account the very different circumstances of their national economies.

This general hypothesis makes sense in the context of the differences between the more conventional model of communication (*elite to mass*) and the model of communication between elites (*elite to elite*). It also conforms to the structural differences of economic media – especially economic and financial press – from other types of media. Both questions are discussed in the next section, and constitute the theoretical framework of the empirical analysis of this chapter.

Elite and public spheres in economic/financial coverage

The generic model of mass communication, which explains the relationship established between journalistic elites and society as a whole, has been supplemented in recent years by new analysis schemes that take into account more particular communication processes. One of these processes is the one that takes place in the communication between elites (*elite to elite communication*), which occurs in certain specialised areas of political, economic, scientific news, and so on. These are journalistic fields in which the media play a special role in mediating between the *decision-makers* (Kunelis and Reunanen, 2012; Strömbäck, 2008), a process that has not received much attention from researchers (Kepplinger, 2007).

Davis (2003) has proposed a 'critical elite theory alternative' centred on how the media affect the decisions of elites who promote certain public policies. In this alternative model, 'elites are simultaneously the main sources, main targets and some of the most influenced recipients of news' (2003: 673). As an almost perfect example of this model, Davis studied the characteristics of the communication process between elites in the case of financial information (Davis, 2000, 2003, 2005, 2006a, 2006b, 2007a), but later on, he extended these characteristics to the field of political communication (Davis, 2007b).

According to Davis, the way financial information is spread among specialised audiences – especially around particular markets such as the stock markets – produces a type of journalism which is 'captured' by expert sources (financial, corporate, etc.): 'elite sources dominate news production' (Davis, 2003: 672). This generates a journalism that follows the information agenda of business and markets, ignoring other interests (Davis, 2000: 285–6); a type of journalism with a coverage that is narrowly defined in its main content by the need to focus on information that can affect and move markets (Davis, 2005: 307), and which, in practice, excludes, rather than includes, the needs and interests of the general public (Davis, 2003: 684). As a result, 'financial and business news coverage reproduces the prevalent ideas, norms and values of those who work in these sectors' (Davis, 2011: 2). Davis (2006a) and Thompson (2009, 2013) have synthesised these peculiarities of financial information regarding the concept of 'reflexivity', according to which the specialised media are an essential part in the process of finding the necessary consensus for markets to work efficiently. In other words, 'they (financial media) are structurally predisposed to reinforce market consensus by focusing market attention on particular stories or frames, and providing the context for interpreting financial news' (Thompson, 2013: 222).

Although the world of financial information is, strictly speaking, an extreme case of analysis, the economic and financial press, and economic journalism in general, also participate in the circularity and reflexivity that occurs in the process of communication between elites. More specifically, research in economic journalism has emphasised five relevant features that constitute the specificity of the coverage of economic and financial issues with respect to other news beats, and as a way to differentiate between more or less specialised business publications. These five features, or coverage approaches as described here, will provide a framework for analysing the journalistic treatment of the euro crisis in the different types of newspapers under research.

Economistic approach

Economic journalism and more specifically, the media specialised in economics, business, and finance, have traditionally been labelled as 'economistic' from two perspectives. On the one hand, from the editorial point of view, it is said that the economic media reproduce, without much critique, the capitalist and neoliberal economic discourse (Chakravartty and Schiller, 2010; Doyle, 2006; Lewis, 2010; Kantola, 2006; Kuzyk and McCluskey, 2006; Madrick, 2002; Merrill, 2012; Sandvoss, 2010); or, in other words, from less ideological positions, they support the logic of interpretation of current events from pro-business and pro-markets angles (Doyle, 2006; Kuzyk and McCluskey, 2006; Madrick, 2002; Merrill, 2012). On the other hand, this 'economicism' also translates into a more technical treatment of topics, as required by the complexity and high level of abstraction of economic phenomena (Arrese, 2006). In practical terms, the economistic approach means a much higher dependence on analysts and experts to interpret the news (Doyle, 2006), many more difficulties for making these issues understandable and attractive for general audiences, so as to bring them closer to citizens (Gavin, 1998; Parker, 1997; Schifferes and Coulter, 2012), and, as another example, the tendency to privilege frames of analysis not 'contaminated' by non-economic approaches (Durham, 2007).

Utilitarian approach

It is evident that in today's world, information is of great importance and, therefore, the media that reports the functioning of economies and markets is also quite significant (Parsons, 1989; Schuster, 2006). As early as 1892, in an article in the *Economic Journal*, Arthur Ellis commented that 'we might say that opinion governs the course of markets almost entirely' (Ellis, 1892: 109). So it is not surprising that the economic and financial information disseminated by the media has a clearly utilitarian vocation, and that news judgements based on usefulness of information for the audience – especially for economic agents and market operators – predominate over other news selection criteria (Doyle, 2006). News that moves markets, scoops on business operations, mergers and acquisitions, or exclusive expert analysis that may affect the opinion and decisions of political and economic elites: these contents constitute the backbone of economic and financial journalism, and the tension between 'markets service journalism' and 'watchdog journalism' (Starkman, 2012; Tambini, 2010).

Reflexive approach

The dominance of expert sources and the large presence of economic and business protagonists in this news beat are a central aspect of the idea of 'reflexivity'. Several studies have echoed this reality, both when analysing the coverage of this crisis (Project for Excellence in Journalism, 2009; Schiffrin and Fagan, 2012) and, more generally, when considering the use of diverse sources in the different sections of a newspaper, comparing the economic section with the rest (Reich, 2012). The expert and institutional sources, as well as *insiders*, carry a lot of weight in the news, producing complex processes of 'negotiation' between journalists and economic agents (Kjaer and Langer, 2003). As noted by Grünberg and Pallas (2013: 229), the result is a process of 'recursive mediation', by which news production is 'continuously reconstructed in highly organised interactions between interested actors'. One important consequence of this reflexivity, as evidenced by Manning (2012), is the inability of journalists to develop more holistic and critical perspectives for the coverage and interpretation of economic news events.

Exclusive approach

As a corollary of the ideas explained in the previous paragraphs, the general public, the ordinary citizen, is almost completely excluded from the process of production and dissemination of economic and financial news. As a source, the citizen's presence is very small (Reich, 2012; Schiffrin and Fagan, 2012), but what is more important, ordinary citizen interests mostly remain largely excluded (Schiffrin and Fagan, 2012: 164). This has been particularly true during the present crisis, as shown by an analysis of the early years of the crisis in the US (Project for Excellence in Journalism, 2009: 1). One could conclude that something very similar occurs in many other countries, and in many different journalistic contexts, as evidenced by Mylonas (2012) when analysing the coverage of the Greek crisis by the German newspaper *Bild*.

International approach

Economic and financial news is undoubtedly one of the most globalised journalistic beats, in line with the globalisation of economies and markets. Media such as the *Financial Times, Wall Street Journal, The Economist, Bloomberg,* and so on have been operating on a universal level for many years, and their influence is felt in every corner of the globe (Cano Jiménez, 2010; Corcoran and Fahy, 2009; Durham, 2007; Kantola, 2006; Machin and Niblock, 2011). However, this international approach is not a prerogative of these well-known brands. In almost every country, the local business press has often modelled its journalistic formula on them and their strong international orientation. This has occurred even where the political and economic context has not been the most appropriate, as in Russia after the fall of communism (Koikkalainen, 2007). The international focus is reflected not only in the geographical breadth of coverage, but also in the difference between the editorial views of the overly nationalistic positions and those of parochial positions. In this sense, it is understandable that, during the current crisis, despite differences in impact on different countries, specialised coverage has been quite similar, as shown in some comparative analyses (Schranz and Eisenegger, 2011; Strömbäck et al., 2010).

The coverage of the euro crisis in the press can be analysed from these five approaches in order to determine how different types of media follow or ignore the logic of specialised information. This is particularly relevant because the euro crisis – materialised in the 11 events under research – has a peculiar nature. On the one hand, the crisis has very clear technical dimensions, those associated with its economic and financial aspect (reporting on public finance, bailouts, single currency, banking, etc.). On the other hand, many events stand out for their political significance, as the euro crisis has evolved at the pace of European summits, changes of governments, national political disputes, and so on. Finally, the crisis has raised great interest among almost all citizens, as the different public and economic policy decisions have had enormous personal and social impact (wage cuts, unemployment, strikes, business bankruptcies, etc.).

A priori, it is expected that these three levels of the crisis would carry a different weight in the three types of newspapers under research: business dailies, quality newspapers, and tabloids or popular dailies. Hopefully, the financial press, in accordance with their focus on certain subjects and audiences (businessmen and decision-makers), would cover the first level, the economic one, much more and therefore, more clearly reflect the journalistic approaches described for specialised information. The quality press, with a more heterogeneous audience, though still a very elitist focus (Meyer, 2005; Veltri, 2012), quite coincidently with that of the business press, and with a broader range of thematic interests, would reasonably offer a more balanced coverage, less dependent on the economic perspective and with greater emphasis placed on the political dimensions. Finally, the tabloids, which should contribute to a sharper distinction between 'public sphere and elite sphere' (Entman, 2004), would clearly be a long way from the previous types, giving greater prominence to the social and personal dimensions of the crisis.

Divergences in euro crisis coverage: business, quality, and popular press

The study carried out in this chapter is based on the comparison of the results derived from the content analysis of three types of dailies (business, quality, and popular) selected in each of the ten countries under research. To undertake this analysis, not all of the variables from the general Euro Crisis Project have been used. We have selected only those that could be useful for illustrating the degree to which each type of newspaper reflects the described dimensions of elitist journalistic approaches. At the same time, we have transformed many of the original variables of the Euro Crisis Project in order to synthesise answers in broader and more generic categories. This recoding is explained at the end of this chapter.

As for statistical methodology, categorical variables have been compared between groups (types of newspapers) with a chi-square (χ^2) test for independence and a Cramér's V value for measuring the level of association between variables. In some cases, when the transformation of variables allowed us to work with new ratio values (as with multiple response variables such as 'Sources' of 'Specific Source quoted'), the Kruskal-Wallis test was used. We are aware of the limitations of chi-square tests when used with big sample sizes – as in this case, we must be cautious not to reach unclear conclusions derived from the data.

Table 8.1 shows the newspapers included in each group of publications under research, as well as the total number of articles analysed for each type of newspaper. The big difference between group sizes could be a problem for statistical analysis, but not for chi-square, as observed

Table 8.1 Groups/types of newspapers and number of articles under research

Type	Dailies	Number of articles	Percentage total
Business	*De Tijd, Kauppalehti, Les Echos, Financial Times, Les Echos, Handelsblatt, Il Sole 24 Ore, Het Financieele Dagblad, Expansión, Puls Biznesu*	4,351	31.7
Quality	*De Standaard, De Morgen, Kathimerini, To Bima, Ta Nea, El País, El Mundo, ABC, Helsingin Sanomat, Kaleva, The Times, The Guardian, NRC, De Volkskrant, FAZ, Süddeutsche Zeitung, Gazeta Wyborcza, Rzeczpospolita, Le Figaro, Le Monde, Corriere della Sera, La repubblica, Il Giornale*	8,536	62.3
Popular	*Het Laatste Nieuws, Ilta Sanomat, The Sun, De Telegraaf, Bild, Fakt, Le Parisien*	831	6.1

frequencies for each item are sufficiently large (at least 5), in all cases of our analysis.

Content analysis variables related to each journalistic approach, and its interpretation, are described in Table 8.2.

In the following pages, the main results of the comparative analysis are presented and discussed, summarising the differences and similarities of the behaviour of each group of variables between the different types of publications.

Economistic approach

The more technical approach of coverage by the business press, in contrast with that of the quality newspapers, and especially the popular press, is evidenced in the data shown in Figure 8.1. The publication of contributions by experts and the frequency of news appearances of non-political public officials and other economic actors undergo a clear gradation in these three types of publications. As expected, the contrast is significantly higher between the economic and the popular press. This more technical perspective could possibly be translated in a more balanced and less extremist treatment of certain sensitive topics. For example, references to possible drop outs from the euro on the part of the countries with debt

Table 8.2   Correspondence between variable values and elitist journalistic approaches

Approach	Variable	Description
Economistic	V8. Story writers	Higher presence of expert writers
	V14. Crisis roots	More weight for economic and financial factors
	V17. Short-term Response	More importance of austerity measures and approaches
	V13. Specific sources quoted	More non-political actors
	V25. Consequences of rescues	More positive for the future of the eurozone and the markets
Utilitarian	V5. Genre	More interpretative (opinion) and analytical
	V7. Story impetus	More actions and decisions than events and declarations
	V20a. Benefits of crisis	More attention to effects for private actors
	V18a. Benefits of euro currency	More attention to effects in economic terms
Reflexive	V12. Type of sources used	More economic and technical than political and other type of sources
	V15. Responsibility to solve	Higher role for economic and financial institutions
	V24. Portrayal ECB	More attention to the role of the ECB
Exclusive	V12. Type of sources used	Lower presence of society representatives as sources
	V20a. Benefits from the crisis	Less attention to the benefits of the crisis in the population
	V21a. Suffers from the crisis	Less attention to the harmful effects of the crisis in the population
	V10. Sections	Less news outside the 'business or finance' section
International	V8. Story writers	More foreign-based staff writers
	V10. Sections	Less news in the domestic/national section
	V22. Geopolitical frame	Less national/domestic geopolitical frame
	V.24. Portrayal of EU institutions	Better portrayal of European institutions

Figure 8.1 Percentage of articles for 'economistic' variables

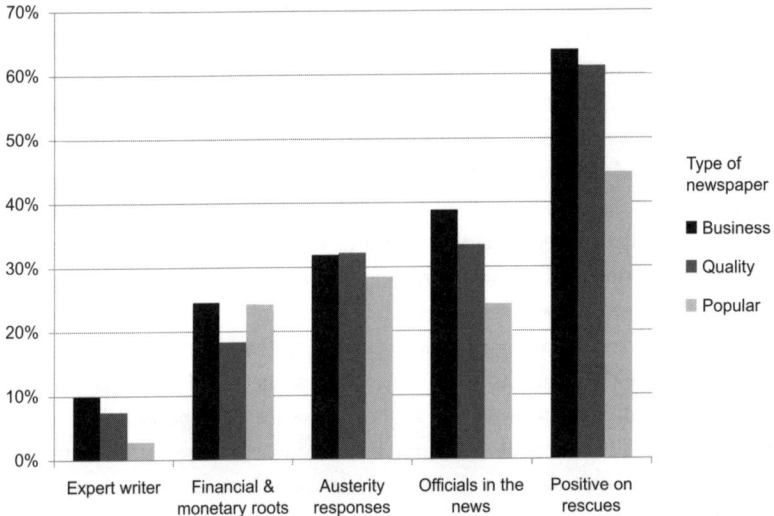

Note: The variable 'Type of newspaper (business, quality, popular)' is statistically significant for differences between groups in the variables under research, although with levels of association (Cramér's *V*) negligible or really weak (Story source: χ^2 (20, $N = 13,718$) = 481.391, $p < .000$, Cramér's $V = .132$; Crisis roots: χ^2 (4, $N = 3,899$) = 26.639, $p < .000$, Cramér's $V = .058$; Short-term response: χ^2 (4, $N = 6,557$) = 16,881, $p < .000$, Cramér's $V = .036$; Consequences of rescues: χ^2 (2, $N = 3,802$) = 24.966, $p < .000$, Cramér's $V = .081$). For the variable 'Specific sources quoted', the number of different types of actors (politicians or officials) quoted in each article (up to 5) has been counted. The Kruskal-Wallis test was used to assess statistical significance: Politicians (χ^2 (2, $N = 13,718$) = 134.150, $p < .000$); Officials (χ^2 (2, $N = 13,718$) = 62.357, $p < .000$).

problems carry much more weight in specialised titles than in general ones (almost 60% of the mentions in the popular press regarding the possible departure of a country from the euro focus on Greece, while in the case of specialised publications, Greece represents 40% of the cases).

On a more ideological level, it is noteworthy that differences between newspapers are reduced when considering the coverage of issues related to austerity measures. One would expect a clearer distinction in this subject, along with the idea that the business press would favour the consensus prevalent among the political powers, officials, and experts regarding the benefits of this approach, linked to more neoliberal economic views. However, perhaps the real contrast is in the treatment of austerity, such as that which is related to the financial rescue processes. In this case, the business press coverage is much more optimistic than that in the tabloids with regard to the potential future benefits of the austerity policies for a stronger eurozone.

Moreover, it is also significant that references to financial institutions being one of the main causes of the crisis carry virtually the same weight in the financial newspapers as in the popular press. This time, the type of media less focused on the role of financial institutions is the quality press.

The study of these variables allows us to perceive the varying degrees of economism present in these three types of dailies. However, it also raises the question of whether or not these differences are sufficiently important – beyond their statistical significance – given the enormous gap that exists between some publications, in so far as their subject and audience profiles are concerned. In fact, only the higher presence of experts and a more positive view of the rescue measures for the eurozone are variables with a sufficient, although weak, statistical association (Cramér's V) with the type of newspaper variable.

Utilitarian approach

The questions in this section reveal quite clearly the more utilitarian approach of the business press, but only in the case of two variables: news genre (more interpretative and opinionated as we move from the popular press to more elitist papers) and the impetus for the news (based more on decisions and market data than on events and statements) (see Figure 8.2).

In fact, the variable that most strongly distinguishes the different types of publications is the latter, especially if you consider one of its items: news caused by the movements of markets (bond market spreads, evolution of Stock Exchange prices, new macroeconomic data, etc.). For the business press, 27.8% of the news has this origin, compared with 19.9% in the quality papers and 17.7% in the tabloids.

Another sign of a more or less utilitarian approach could be the reference to winners and losers because of the single currency and the sovereign debt crisis. Although there are few direct mentions of beneficiaries of the euro or its crisis, one would expect the references to be significantly different in the three types of papers. However, this is not the case, and the economic consequences, especially for the private sector, are featured in almost identical proportion in all the newspapers, at the expense, for example, of other social actors and the population.

Figure 8.2   Percentage of articles for 'utilitarian' variables

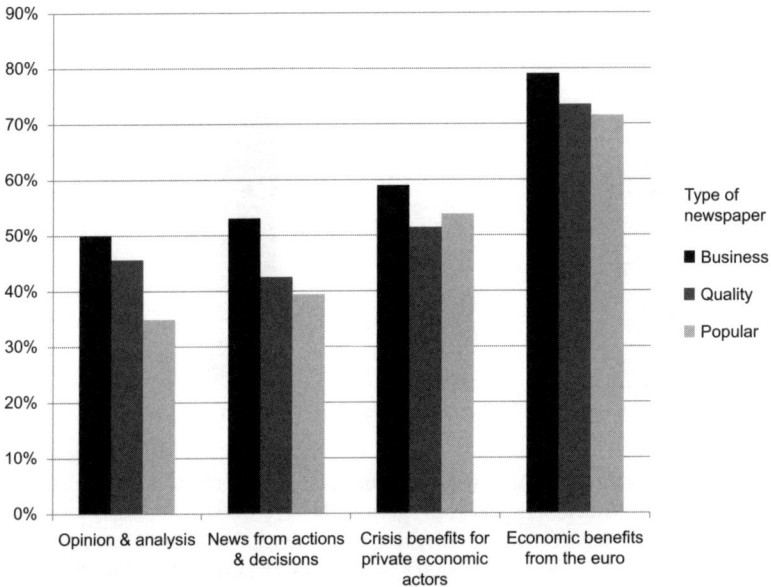

Note: The variable 'Type of newspaper (business, quality, popular)' is statistically significant for differences between groups in two of the variables under research, although with levels of association (Cramér's *V*) negligible or really weak (Genre: χ^2 (6, *N* = 13,613) = 92.018, *p* < .000, Cramér's *V* = .056; Impetus for the news: χ^2 (2, *N* = 10,362) = 106.717, *p* < .000, Cramér's *V* = .101). It is not statistically significant in the other two cases: Benefits from the crisis: χ^2 (6, *N* = 1,234) = 12.305, *p* = .056); Benefits from the euro: χ^2 (4, *N* = 675) = 5.733, *p* < .220). However, in these last two variables *N* (valid answers) is less than 10% of the total articles under research.

Reflexive approach

The reflexivity of economic information is particularly evident in the use of sources, as shown in Figure 8.3. The business press clearly prioritises technical sources (European officials, economists, analysts, etc.) over sources from political and other spheres of society. In this case, the contrast is evident not only with the popular press, but also with quality papers.

The other two variables (the responsibility of financial institutions to solve the crisis, and the role of the European Central Bank) which assume a prominent role in the crisis for the financial sector – in which

Figure 8.3 Percentage of articles for 'reflexive' variables

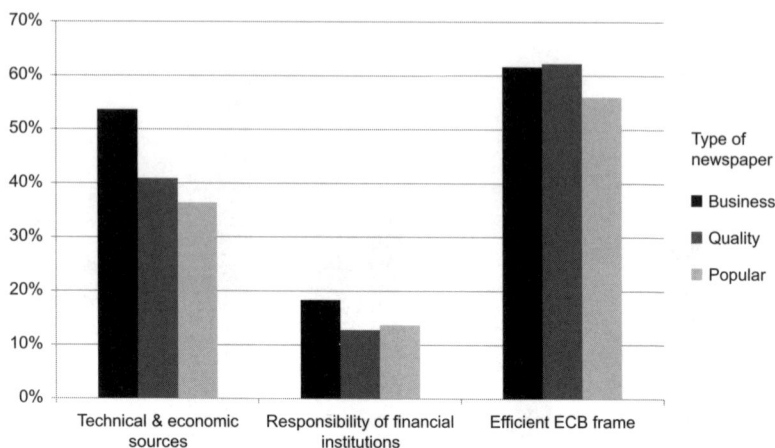

Note: The variable 'Type of newspaper (business, quality, popular)' is statistically significant for differences between groups in the variables under research, although with levels of association (Cramér's *V*) negligible or really weak (Crisis Responsibility: χ^2 (4, *N* = 3,899) = 26.639, *p* < .000, Cramér's *V* = .036; Portrayal for ECB: χ^2 (4, *N* = 3,607) = 24.013, *p* < .000, Cramér's *V* = .058. For the variable 'News Sources', the number of different types of sources (Technical & Economic or Political & Society) quoted in each article (up to 5) has been counted. The Kruskal-Wallis test was used to assess statistical significance: Technical & Economical (χ^2 (2, *N* = 13,718) = 167.217, *p* < .000); Political & Society (χ^2 (2, *N* = 13,718) = 140.666, *p* < .000).

many sources and some of the most influential readers of the business press work – do not show very significant differences between the types of dailies. In the case of the responsibility of financial institutions, the positive or negative views expressed in the different newspapers may differ, but with regard to the attention given to their role, the coverage is quite similar. Clearer still is the consensus in the references to the centrality of the ECB during the crisis, in the proportion of the news as well as in viewing it as a very efficient institution. This coincides well with the findings in Chapter 4.

Exclusive approach

The media coverage of different issues regarding the euro crisis in non-economic sections, the search for more diverse news sources, instead of the official ones, and greater attention to the beneficial or harmful consequences of the debt crisis for the general population could be signs of a more multifaceted and holistic press coverage, a coverage that is more appealing to the diverse interests of citizens; the alternative would mean leaving citizens on the sidelines, at the expense of the concerns of the elites, especially the economic elites. Figure 8.4 shows the differences in these variables, especially significant in the cases of news published in non-economic sections, and the level of attention to the harmful consequences of the crisis on the population. Caution must be exercised regarding the first of these differences – much more news in different sections in the popular press – because

Figure 8.4 Percentage of articles for 'exclusive' variables

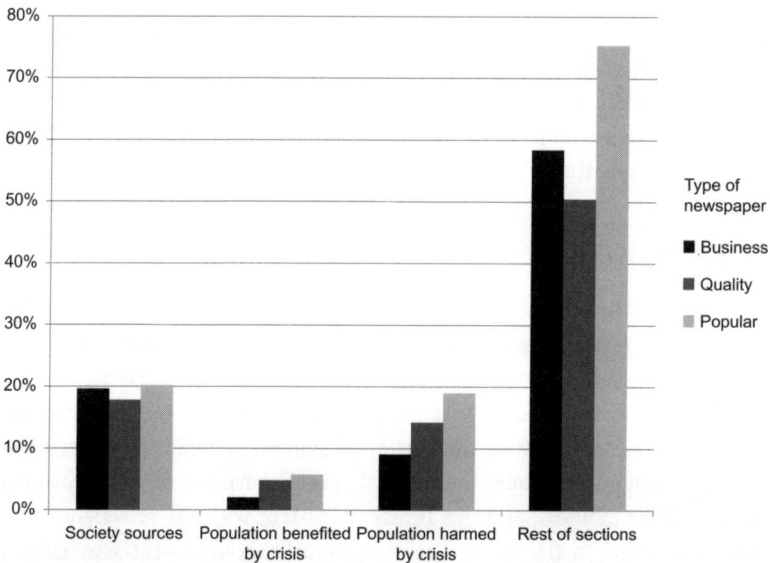

Note: The variable 'Type of newspaper (business, quality, popular)' is statistically significant for differences between groups in two of the variables under research, although with levels of association (Cramér's V) negligible or really weak (harmful consequences from the crisis: χ^2 (6, $N = 7{,}677$) = 107.163, $p < .000$, Cramér's $V = .084$ and Section (with the categories 'Business/Financial Section, and Rest of Sections'): χ^2 (2, $N = 9{,}370$) = 129.617, $p < .000$, Cramér's $V = .118$). The relationship is not significant for the variable Benefits from the crisis: χ^2 (6, $N = 1{,}234$) = 12.305, $p < .056$). For 'sources', the Kruskal-Wallis test was used to assess statistical significance: Technical & Economic (χ^2 (2, $N = 13{,}718$) = 167.217, $p < .000$); Political & Society (χ^2 (2, $N = 13{,}718$) = 140.666, $p < .000$).

the distribution of sections in the business press is often quite different from the rest, and there are more subsections on specific areas of economic and financial activities.

As for the coverage of positive and negative effects of the crisis in the population, considering the variety of events covered during the 11 periods under study, many of them very institutional, a clear distinction between the economic and the popular press is observed. However, it is noteworthy that in all cases, the coverage of these issues is very low (below 20%).

As a matter of fact, one would expect more sources of 'society' (citizens, unions, consumer associations, NGOs, etc.) to be used by the popular press to interpret the consequences of the euro crisis regarding the lives of ordinary people, as well as to report what the big events that took place in Europe between 2010 and 2012 had meant on a more personal level. However, this is not reflected in the data. The use of these sources is low (around 20%), and almost identical in the different types of journals. The idea that the interpretation of the great milestones of the euro crisis is left to political and technical sources, to be in some way 'captured' by them and their elitist and exclusive view, is confirmed by these data and has implications for the idea of the public sphere that will be discussed in Chapter 11.

International focus

The more international perspective of the crisis is the journalistic trait where the contrast between different types of media is clearer. As can be observed in Figure 8.5, in regard to the weight that the texts written by correspondents carry, as well as the percentage of news published in the national/domestic section, there is a substantial difference between the three types of publications. The contrast is very sharp between the business press and the tabloids, and this is also consistent with the prevalence of a domestic frame in the latter. The most significant statistical associations are given in the first two variables (correspondent contents and news in national sections), especially between the economic and the popular press.

As explained in the next paragraph, the greater attention given to the international view on the part of the business press could be related to a more homogeneous representation of the crisis among these newspapers, in contrast with more parochial interpretations, conditioned by the domestic situation, in the general interest press.

While it is true that the differences are also statistically significant in the case of a more or less positive frame of the European institutions, the

Figure 8.5   Percentage of articles for 'international' variables

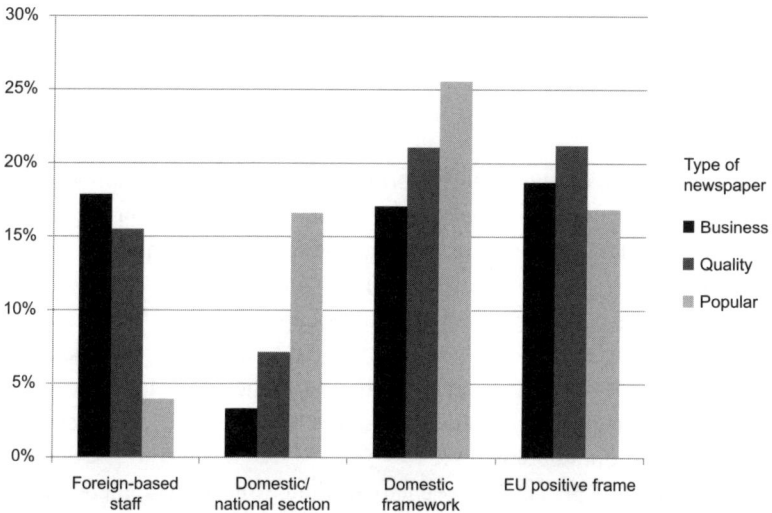

Note: The variable 'Type of newspaper (business, quality, popular)' is statistically significant for differences between groups in all the variables under research, although with levels of association (Cramér's V) negligible or really weak (Story Source: χ^2 (20, $N = 13{,}718$) = 481.391, $p < .000$, Cramér's $V = .132$; Section: χ^2 (18, $N = 13{,}718$) = 184.781, $p < .000$, Cramér's $V = .118$; Geopolitical framework: χ^2 (8, $N = 13{,}718$) = 133.631, $p < .000$, Cramér's $V = .070$; EU Portrayal: χ^2 (2, $N = 5{,}324$) = 10.031, $p < .007$, Cramér's $V = .043$).

association between variables is not. Moreover, it is surprising that, in this respect, the financial press and the popular newspapers share, in contrast with the quality dailies, a higher coverage of more negative aspects.

Now that the analysis of the coverage of the euro crisis by different types of newspapers has been carried out, we proceed to highlight some peculiarities of economic newspapers according to the country, taking into account the very divergent economic outlook for each of them during the period under study.

Business press across countries

Beyond the informative profile of the business press as a homogeneous group in contrast with other types of publications, there are interesting differences among business dailies across countries. Perhaps the most important of them, as regards the interpretation of the crisis, are between newspapers in countries with sovereign debt problems (Greece, Italy, and Spain) and those without.

Crisis coverage

The differences in the editorial positioning on the crisis among the specialised press, grouped by 'countries with (or without) debt problems', are less marked than those among the general newspapers, when classified under the same criteria. For example, Table 8.3 clearly shows the percentage differences between the groups of dailies, based on the coverage of key questions regarding the crisis. Almost all variables and items diverge more among general interest dailies than in the case of business newspapers, which could mean that the latter are less affected by the national economic situation.

Despite this greater homogeneity of the business press, there clearly are aspects of the crisis in which there is more or less discrepancy among individual newspapers. A clear example of diversity in coverage is the frame on the performance of the European institutions during the crisis (see Figure 8.6). In some dailies, news references to their inability or inefficiency clearly dominate (*Financial Times, Les Echos,* and *Il Sole,* for example), while others pay much more attention to their central and decisive role (*Kauppalehti, Handelsblatt,* or *Naftemporiki*).

There is, by contrast, more similarity in the coverage of the efficient frame of the ECB, with the only exceptions being *Il Sole 24 Ore* and the *Financial Times*. These big financial newspapers offer a more balanced coverage of issues regarding the efficiency or inefficiency of this financial institution. In general, however, as expected in the case of financial publications, there is more agreement on the performance of technical (ECB) than political institutions (European institutions as a whole).

Something quite similar to the consensus on the ECB emerges from the coverage of topics regarding the crisis solutions. On the one hand, all the newspapers devote more attention to austerity measures than to growth policies. On the other hand, there is a considerable contrast between some of them. Once again the *Financial Times* and *Il Sole 24 Ore* offer a more balanced coverage, and *Naftemporiki* offers the most extreme coverage; this is understandable considering the situation of Greece during the period under analysis.

Table 8.3 Dailies in sovereign or non-sovereign debt countries: business and general interest press

Variables	Category	Business Press[1]			General Interest Press[2]		
		Countries with debt problems	Countries without debt problems	Dif. |x|	Countries with debt problems	Countries without debt problems	Dif. |x|
Responsibility for the crisis	Countries	27.8	22.3	5.5	38.3	24.1	14.2
	EU institutions	54.6	58.8	4.2	50.4	61.8	11.4
	Financial institutions	17.6	18.9	1.3	11.3	14.1	2.8
Short-term measures	Loans	54.2	55.9	1.7	46.5	61.9	15.4
	Austerity	31.4	32.2	0.8	35.9	29.1	6.8
	Growth	14.4	11.9	2.5	17.7	9.0	8.7
EU frame	Inefficient	51.4	48.3	3.1	49.8	45.1	4.7
	Efficient	48.6	51.7	3.1	50.2	54.9	4.7

(Continued)

Table 8.3 (Continued)

Variables	Category	Business Press[1]			General Interest Press[2]		
		Countries with debt problems	Countries without debt problems	Dif. |x|	Countries with debt problems	Countries without debt problems	Dif. |x|
ECB frame	Inefficient	33.3	27.1	6.2	28.8	27.4	1.4
	Efficient	61.0	62.0	1.0	65.4	58.2	7.2
	Legal	5.7	10.9	5.2	5.8	14.4	8.6

Notes: Values are percentages. To calculate percentages of answers, the categories 98 = Other and 99 = None have been excluded from this analysis. 1. *Business Press*: The variable 'Countries with (or without) debt problems' is statistically significant for differences between groups in the variables (ECB Framing: χ^2 (2, $N = 1,265$) = 13.134, $p < .001$ and Responsibility for the crisis: χ^2 (2, $N = 1,265$) = 13.134, $p < .001$), but not significant for variables (EU Frame: χ^2 (1, $N = 1,621$) = 1.568, $p < .211$ and Short-term measures: χ^2 (2, $N = 2,014$) = 2.692, $p < .260$). 2. *General Interest Press*: The variable 'Countries with (or without) debt problems' is statistically significant for all the variables of the table: (Responsibility for the crisis: χ^2 (2, $N = 5,041$) = 118.472, $p < .000$), (Short-term measures: χ^2 (2, $N = 3,703$) = 7.972, $p < .005$) and (ECB Framing: χ^2 (1, $N = 4,543$) = 129.310, $p < .000$), (EU Frame: χ^2 (2, $N = 2,342$) = 49.198, $p < .000$).

Figure 8.6 EU efficient versus EU inefficient: business newspapers
(percentage of articles)

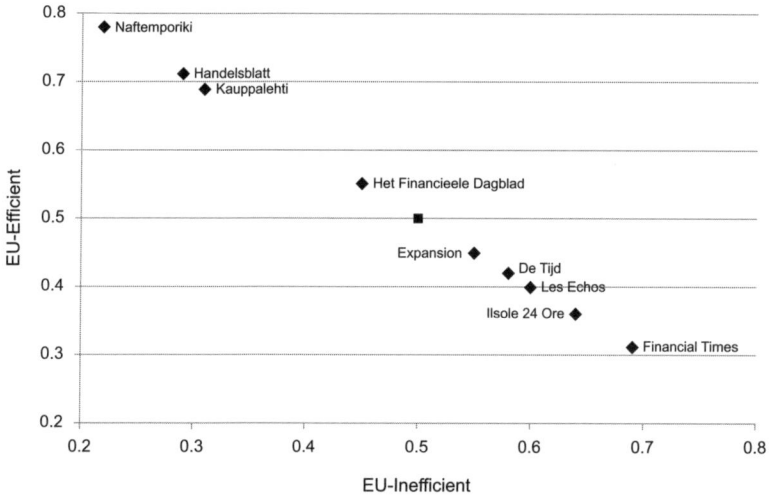

Note: The square-point represents the average business newspaper.

However, an intense coverage of austerity measures and policies does not necessarily mean a positive view is given. This can be examined by analysing the optimism or pessimism in the news regarding the success of the financial rescues, which are directly linked to the adoption of austerity programmes. It has already been mentioned that positive aspects of rescues are generally covered more than negative ones, at least if we interpret it from the standpoint of the impact of financial rescues on the future of the eurozone. Figure 8.7 shows how all newspapers from countries with serious debt problems (*Naftemporiki, Expansión,* and *Il Sole 24 Ore*) have a lower percentage of news with an optimistic view regarding the success of rescue policies.

The percentages of news coverage discussed in this section do not take into account the editorial view of newspapers, their opinion in favour of or against certain policies or institutions. These percentages simply highlight how much attention was paid to policies and institutions in the newspapers throughout the period analysed. It may be, as surely happens in some cases – see, for example, the intense coverage of austerity measures in dailies such as *Handelsblatt* (Germany) or *Naftemporiki* (Greece) – that the editorial positions of newspapers

Figure 8.7 Successful rescue versus failed rescue: business newspapers (percentage of articles)

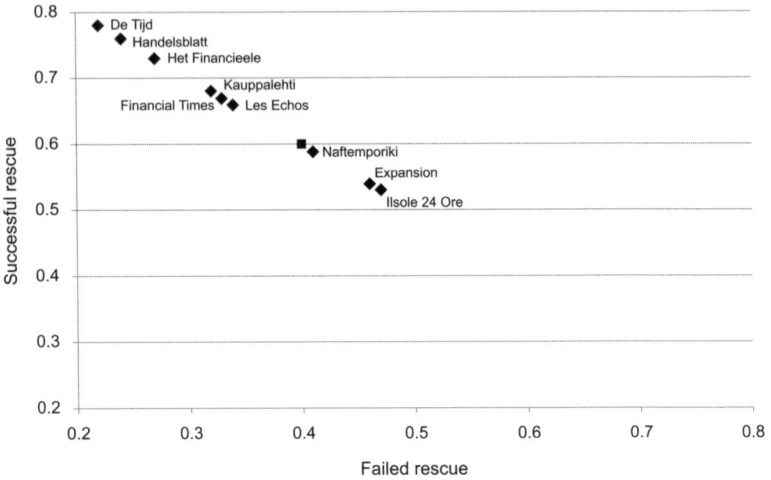

Note: The square-point represents the average business newspaper.

with the same level of coverage on a particular issue were very different, even clearly opposed.

Discussion

This chapter has examined how the distinction between three different types of newspapers – business, quality, and popular – is significant when explaining differences in news coverage reporting about the euro crisis. Overall, all differences, analysed from the perspective of the five elitist approaches to economic and financial information explained in the first part of this chapter – economism, utilitarian, reflexive, exclusive, and international – allow discussion about different patterns of coverage among the elite press (business and quality dailies, with minor differences between them) and the popular press (tabloids). There are some central variables in the formation of these different patterns, such as: participation of experts writing for the paper, use of more technical sources, concentration on certain events (decisions, market movements, etc.) as main triggers for news, a more positive view of bailouts and austerity measures, much greater attention to the role of the ECB during the crisis, and, in general, a more balanced, homogeneous and international position in relation to key aspects of this crisis.

Overall, we have found strong support for our proposal to analyse the euro crisis coverage from the standpoint of the peculiarities of journalism and information in environments of communication between elites (*elite-to-elite communication*). We have also described a certain degree of gradation, which was expected, as regards the presence of these peculiarities in the three types of newspapers analysed. The main contrast observed in this analysis is that which exists between the business press and the tabloids.

With respect to the business press, after comparing the ten financial dailies included in this study, we found that the national particularities and differences are responsible for some interesting divergences in both euro crisis frames and in how the crisis was reported. On the other hand, it was found that the pattern of coverage of issues such as the role of the ECB, austerity policies, and optimism regarding the future of the eurozone is very similar in most titles. This similarity is greater than in the general press when considering the behaviour of both groups of newspapers under very different economic conditions, those in countries with big sovereign debt problems, and those without such problems. This could explain the special role that the business press plays in a greater transnationalisation of European issues, particularly economic issues, needed to set up the so-called 'elite European sphere' (Corcoran and Fahy, 2009).

However, beyond these initial findings, it is interesting to consider one issue that was raised in this work: the 'gradation' in the adoption of a more or less elitist perspective among the three types of newspapers studied. Although the effect of a big sample size of articles facilitates statistically significant relationships between most of the variables, meaning that gradation is supported, the fact is that, as observed in the different sections of the analysis, many of these relationships have a very low degree of association/correlation. Arguably, many of the differences among the three types of newspapers are not relevant enough, especially considering the huge gap between them – particularly between business papers and tabloids – with respect to their thematic focus and target audience.

Focusing on the extreme types of publications (business and tabloids), one wonders whether the little differentiation in the coverage of the euro crisis is due to the relaxation of the usual elite news patterns of the business press, or, by contrast, to the inability of the popular press to get rid of these patterns, which are very dominant in complex economic issues such as this one. Based on the results of the present research, one could more likely defend the latter, which coincides with research conducted in specific cases, such as the coverage of the crisis in Irish mainstream media (Fahy et al., 2010; Mercille, 2013a; Titley, 2012) or the Greek crisis in a tabloid such as the German *Bild* (Mylonas, 2012). Therefore, we could argue that in the case of the euro crisis, the press discourse – almost without distinction by formats – has also been 'captured' by the logic of elite-to-elite communication, the dominant logic of news in high politics, economics, and finance. This finding is consistent with some of the conclusions of other chapters in this book (see especially Chapters 3 and 5, on the prominent role of institutional responsibilities and actors; Chapter 9, on the coverage of the crisis away from the interests of the 'man of the street'; and Chapter 11, on the dominance of elite rationalities when explaining the crisis. However, further research is needed in order to test these ideas, perhaps with studies regarding economic and financial events that are not as complex and systemic as the euro crisis.

We should not forget that the multidimensional character of the European sovereign debt crisis, with its multiple political, economic, and social ramifications, is a big challenge for a research study such as this one. As with other episodes of the great economic crisis that began in 2008, in this case, there has been a cross-over of all of these dimensions, and every paper has had to adapt to this reality, often with enormous difficulty (Guerrera, 2009). Economic journalism has had to become more political, and political journalism has had to become more economical. As pointed out by Schifferes, the continuing split between the specialist and generalist functions of financial journalism has had a temporary but brief coming together during the financial crisis (Schifferes, 2011).

There is little doubt that after experiences such as the coverage of the euro crisis, one of the general challenges of journalism, and of every media outlet in particular, will be to find the correct way to address issues such as these, in accordance with the demands of their audiences and more clearly adapted to their own distinctive journalistic formula.

Regrouping of original categories in the codebook used in this chapter

In order to avoid going into too much detail, for the purposes of this chapter we have aggregated the codes provided by the codebook (see Appendix 3) in a meaningful way according to the issues to be discussed.

The numbers in this section refer to the numbers of the codes in Appendix 3: Codebook. These codes define the categories that are used in this chapter.

5. Genre

1. **News** (Includes: 01. News story)
2. **Interpretation and analysis** (Includes: 02. News analysis and background story; 04. Editorial; 05. Opinion/commentary)
3. **Features and interview** (Includes: 03. Feature story; 06. Interview)

7. Story impetus

1. **Actions and decisions** (Includes: 02. Request-based; 03. Decision-based; 05. Market development based)
2. **Declarations and events** (Includes: 01. Event-based; 04. Statement/pronouncement based; 06. Reports in other media)

12. Type of sources quoted

1. **Technical and economic** (Includes: 100. Officials (non-elected) and subtypes 101 to 106; 400. Bankers/Financiers and subtypes 401 to 406; 500. Economists and subtypes 501 and 502)
2. **Political and society** (Includes: 200. National Government Leaders and subtypes 201 to 204; 300. National Political Leaders and subtypes 301 to 304; 600. Society representatives and subtypes 601 to 610)

13. Specific sources quoted

1. **Politicians** (Includes: 01. Berlusconi; 03. Cameron; 05. Hollande; 08. Merkel; 09. Monti; 10. Papademos; 11. Papandreou; 12. Rajoy; 15. Sarkozy; 18. Zapatero)
2. **Officials** (Includes: 02. Barroso; 04. Draghi; 06. Juncker; 07. Lagardere; 13. Van Rompuy; 14. Rehn; 16. Strauss-Kahn; 17. Trichet)

14. Fundamental root/cause of the crisis

1. **Political** (10. Starting conditions of euro and subtypes 11 to 13; 50. Political roots and subtypes 51 to 54; 60. Maastricht treaty and subtypes 61 and 62)
2. **Economic** (20. National industrial policies and developments and subtypes 21 to 25; 30. National fiscal and social policies and subtypes 31 to 36; 80. General economic roots and subtypes 81 and 82)
3. **Financial** (40. Banks' and financial institutions' policies and subtypes 41 to 46; 70. European Central Bank (ECB) and subtypes 71 to 73)

15. Main responsibility to solve the problems

1. **Countries** (01. Countries with sovereign debt; 02. Countries without sovereign debt)
2. **EU institutions** (03. eurozone; 04. The European Union)
3. **Financial institutions** (05. European Central Bank; 06. IMF and World Bank; 07. Banks, investors and other lenders)

16. Main short-term response to the crisis

1. **Loans** (01. Loans from other countries without supervision; 02. Loans from other countries with supervision; 03. European Central Bank loans)
2. **Austerity** (04. Abatement of existing bank provisions (haircuts); 05. Reduction of budget deficits and austerity measures)
3. **Growth** (06. Fiscal stimulus; 07. Growth policies)

17. Main long-term response to the crisis

1. **EU empowerment** (01. More EU power over national budgets)
2. **Broken eurozone** (02. Nations with weak economies dropping out; 03. Nations with strong economies dropping; 05. Breaking up the eurozone)
3. **National reforms** (04. National structural reforms in countries with problems)

18a. and 19a. Benefits (and harmful consequences) from the existence of the euro currency

1. **Economical** (10. Beneficial/harmful consequences for national economies and subtypes 11 to 15; 20. Beneficial/harmful consequences for the European Economy and subtypes 21 to 25)
2. **Political** (30. Beneficial/harmful national political consequences and subtypes 31 to 34; 40. Beneficial/harmful European political consequences and subtypes 41 to 45)

3. **Social** (50. Beneficial/harmful national social consequences and subtypes 51 and 52; 60. Beneficial/harmful European social consequences and subtypes 61 to 63)

23. Portrayal of EU Institutions
1. **Inefficient** (01. Insignificant in addressing the crisis; 02. Lacking capabilities to address the crisis; 03. Ineffectual or confused in addressing the crisis)
2. **Efficient** (04. Central to addressing the crisis; 05. Strong and determined in addressing the crisis)

24. Portrayal of the ECB
1. **Inefficient** (01. Insignificant in addressing the crisis; 02. Lacking capabilities to address the crisis; 03. Ineffectual or confused in addressing the crisis)
2. **Efficient** (04. Central to addressing the crisis; 05. Strong and determined in addressing the crisis)
3. **Legal** (06. Acting within its legal framework; 07. Acting at the border or outside of its legal framework)

25. Forecast of the consequences of the rescue measures
1. **Positive and non-problematic for the eurozone. Successful rescue** (01. Deeper integration; 02. Stronger and more stable euro; 03. Success/eurozone preserved)
2. **Negative and problematic for the eurozone. Failed rescue** (04. Breakup of the eurozone; 05. Failure/countries with debt problems drop the euro; 06. Enduring transfer system to countries with sovereign debt problems: 07. Europe-wide inflation)

9

Countries Still Matter

Paolo Mancini and Marco Mazzoni

Even in the face of the dramatic crisis that Europe has passed through in recent years, and that is still influencing it today, a widely shared European representation of this crisis does not exist. As we will show in this chapter, national identities and interests still matter and these remain stronger than the idea of European identity itself. National identities also seem to overcome potential differences among different types of newspaper, as shown in a number of chapters of this volume. Although similarities among European countries on the coverage of the euro crisis emerge, we show differences remain important and undermine efforts to construct a widely accepted European public sphere.

Our data show that what affects the coverage of euro crisis is not the difference between, say, tabloid and elite newspapers or between liberal and conservative newspapers, even if these differences have some importance as we shall see later on. But rather what matters mostly is the national belonging of the news media outlet that covers the euro crisis. 'Parochialism' is the word that has been used in previous studies as to European public sphere and identity to stress how matters concerning Europe are treated essentially in relation to more limited national interests (Bee and Bozzini, 2010; Gripsrud and Weibull, 2010). Another word has been 'domestication' (or 'nationalisation') (AIM, 2007; Cornia, 2010; Gleissner and Vreese, 2005; Morgan, 1995; Ornebring, 2009; Semetko et al., 2000) while the idea of 'segmented Europeanisation' indicates the fragmentation of a unique European public sphere in many different discursive areas. As Kleinen-von Königslöw has written, there exists 'a European public sphere where each country increases its surveillance of Brussels, but a shared European discourse among the European community of nations fails to develop' (Kleinen-von Königslöw, 2012: 444).

All these words explain our results well. Newspapers cover the euro crisis from the point of view and from the perspective of their own countries (see Chapter 2). In this sense the specific topic of the euro crisis presents many similarities with the more general coverage of Europe, its institutions, and decisions. It confirms the most diffused interpretations as to the existence (better non-existence) of a truly European public sphere (EPS), a topic that will be directly addressed in Chapter 11. Indeed, many studies have stressed the absence or, at least, the weakness of a public sphere that goes beyond national borders and that indicates a public debate that involves readers as European citizens and not as Germans, Italians, Greeks, and so on (Machill et al., 2006). The absence of a true EPS or its weakness goes together with the disaffection that European people have clearly expressed towards the EU through several failed referenda on the constitutional treaty and the Lisbon treaty. And, more dramatically, this weakness is also demonstrated by the opposition against Europe and European integration that has emerged in many countries in recent years.

For Habermas, surely one of the most important scholars discussing the issue of European identity, and his followers (Downey and Koenig, 2006; Koopmans and Erbe, 2004; Trenz, 2004), European identity could be fostered through either the progress of the so-called 'Europeanisation of the national media' (Habermas, 2009) or 'through the rise of common/ similar ways of referring to and interpreting specifically European occurrences across those media' (Krzyzanowski, 2009: 19).

Our study shows exactly the opposite: the euro crisis is represented in the news media depending essentially on national belonging. The lack of Europeanisation of the national media is directly connected to the absence or weakness of a unique EPS (Baisnée, 2007; Brüggemann et al., 2009; Pfetsch et al., 2008; Schlesinger, 2007).

The data from the 'Euro Crisis, Media Coverage and Perceptions of Europe within [the] EU' project that demonstrate this interpretation in a clear manner are shown in Figures 9.1 and 9.2. From these figures, we understand that what makes the difference among the observed newspapers as to the portrayal of the EU (Figure 9.1) and the main focus of the article (Figure 9.2) is mainly national belonging. Indeed, newspapers are grouped in our figures essentially (there are few exceptions) depending on nationality, while the political affiliation and the specific kind of the news outlet (elite, business, tabloid) do not seem to represent dimensions that gather newspapers together. As to the portrayal of the European institutions, which was addressed in Chapter 4, Italian newspapers, together

Figure 9.1   Portrayal of the EU

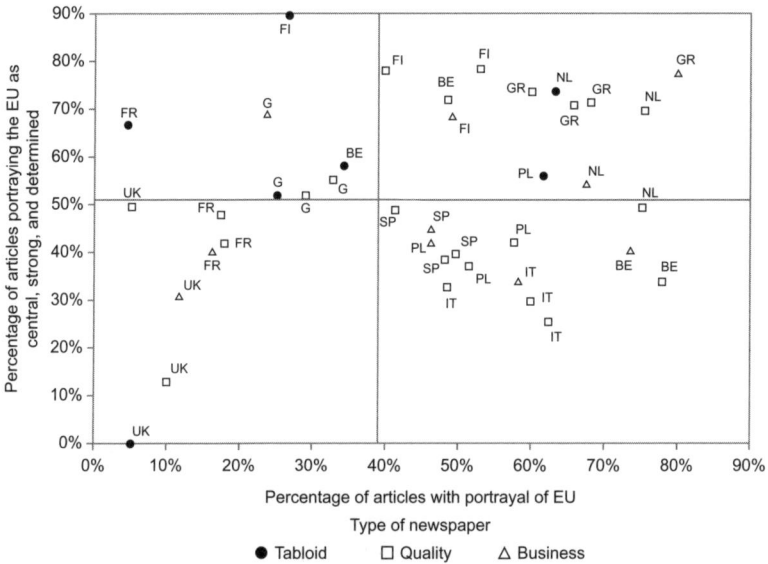

Note: Figure represents the coding of 'What is the main portrayal of the EU Commission/EU, European Institutions'. The x-axis represents the percentage of articles 'containing whatever portrayal of the EU'; the y-axis represents the percentage of these articles that portrayed the EU with respect to the crisis as 'central, strong, and determined'. The lines in the figure show the means of the variables.

with the Polish, Spanish, and Belgian, diffuse a prevalently weak image of them (being mainly grouped in quarter four) while the Greek ones together with the Finnish depict them as chiefly strong (quarter two).

All Greek papers (Figure 9.2) have a main domestic frame, like the Italian papers (they are in quarter two). German press outlets too cover the euro crisis with a strong domestic point of view and so do the Spanish ones.[29] The domestic frame is less pronounced in France, Finland, Belgium, the Netherlands, and Poland. The United Kingdom represents a specific case with three papers that propose a major European frame in their coverage (this is particularly evident as to the *Financial Times*) while, on the other side, *The Sun* covers the euro crisis mainly from a very domestic point of view. Even if with some differences among them, all the papers of each single country seem to be associated by very similar decisions on which image to offer of the European institutions and from which perspective to cover the events. This common attitude emerges regarding many other topics of our study.

Figure 9.2 Domestic geopolitical frame by country and type of newspaper

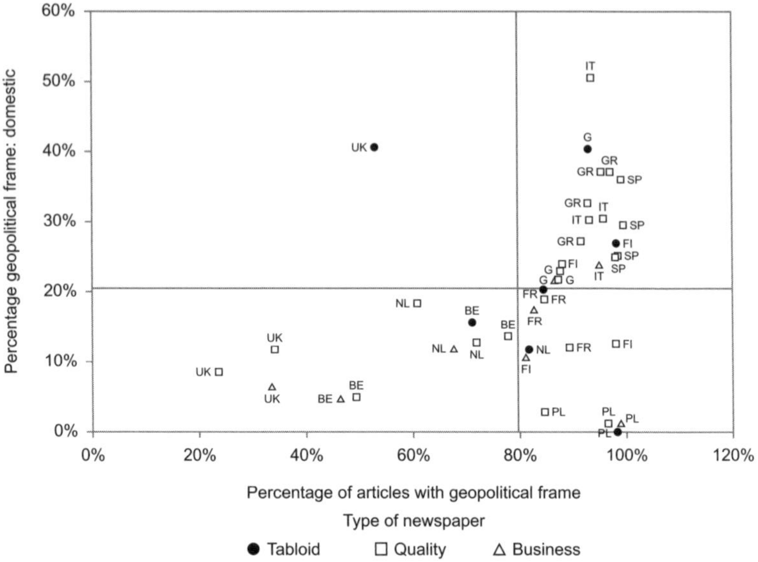

Note: Figure represents the coding of 'Identify the main geopolitical frame of the article'. The x-axis represents the percentage of articles containing whatever geopolitical frame; the y-axis represents the percentage of these articles containing 'domestic frame'. The lines in the figure show the means of the variables.

Our data point out that the representation of the euro crisis depends on contextual and incidental features that explain the interpretive frame chosen from our observed newspapers: these frames are essentially of national character. Just some examples: Greek newspapers perceive European institutions as very powerful; indeed the Greek government has imposed on Greek citizens very strict measures that are now determining a situation of dramatic crisis. A clear domestic interpretive frame prevails: Greek newspapers look at the consequences within their own country, they look at ongoing strikes and street demonstrations against the imposed measures. This kind of coverage may be connected to the idea of 'vertical Europeanisation' (Kleinen-von Königslöw, 2012): a public sphere that extends its focus to include an increasing observation of EU institutions exists but it has a clear and strong domestic geopolitical frame.

The idea of 'vertical Europeanisation' assumes different characters in Italy: first of all Italy, together with Germany, France, and the UK, is the country devoting larger attention to the euro crisis but EU institutions are portrayed as weaker if compared with the representation of the Greek press. The coverage is strongly 'domesticated' (Gleissner and Vreese, 2005; Ornebring, 2009), as shown in Figures 9.1 and 9.2, as the newspapers seem to have a common 'national' attitude towards the euro crisis – but the main persons quoted in the articles are especially a foreign prime minister (Chancellor Merkel), a foreign head of state (Sarkozy), and European officials (Draghi, Barroso). In other words, domestication exists but the discussion within the national public sphere is deeply affected by foreign actors and their decisions.

The UK looks at the crisis from a completely different point of view: this country is not part of the euro and therefore British newspapers are discussing the crisis 'from abroad'. 'The European framework' prevails in the articles in which the euro crisis is represented as a problem that regards mainly 'those Europeans on the other side of the channel', as opposed to the UK. There is an important exception, *The Sun*. This tabloid paper clearly confirms what is already known of the popular press more generally: when covering Europe, the popular press, especially the British popular press, has a very clear domestic focus (Marini, 2003). News about Europe is reported if it involves the UK in some way or may be subject to comparison with British situation and features. These are short articles that mainly report hard news and devote no space at all to commentary and opinion (Table 9.1). Stories about the euro crisis are not an exception: what are the consequences of the ongoing euro crisis for Great Britain and its citizens? This is the more general framework within which news about the euro crisis is inserted into the British popular press.

Table 9.1 Articles by type of newspaper and genre

	News	Opinion	Feature, interview, and other	Total
Business	1,892	2,151	308	4,351
	43.5%	49.4%	7.1%	100.0%
Elite	3,831	3,863	842	8,536
	44.9%	45.3%	9.9%	100.0%
Tabloid	456	290	85	831
	54.9%	34.9%	10.2%	100.0%
Total	6,179	6,304	1,235	13,718
	45.0%	46.0%	9.0%	100.0%

As is well known, the German government and public opinion are in favour of strong EU policies to impose on countries with high debts the necessary measures without affecting German national banks that are deeply involved with rooted habits of loans towards countries in crisis. Indeed, as shown in Figure 9.2, the Finnish press presents a very similar attitude. Like the UK, the Polish press covers the euro crisis 'from abroad', not being part of the eurozone and not suffering such a dramatic economic crisis as many other European countries. The French press too displays a frame 'from abroad', together with a weak representation of the EU. As others have pointed out, this result may highlight that France perceives European integration as an important vehicle for its national ambition; in fact, 'France is the country that has been most efficient in putting its mark on European-level debates, a tradition that does not seem to have abated under the presidency of Nicolas Sarkozy' (Koopmans et al., 2010: 67).

All papers in these countries are therefore inserted within a common 'national' attitude that is affected by local contingencies and situations that go beyond the specific kind of newspaper and beyond the specific political orientation of the paper.

A full European public sphere is not clearly evident or it is very weak. Indeed, as shown in Figures 9.1 and 9.2, newspaper choices and discourses are not organised along the lines of political, ideological, and economical orientations: such divisions do not exist because a unique, European decision process is not in operation, is rather weak, or has a main 'technical' dimension as is the case with the European Commission (see Baisnée, 2007). National interests and needs seem to prevail, in the euro crisis case and in other cases as well.

In the same way, what is more important for the news media in general is not their segmented readership but their national audience: in most cases, newspapers know that they are not talking to their own niche readership. Rather they are talking, as to Europe and its problems, to a national readership.

The market nature of Europe versus 'the man in the street' Europe?

In spite of what we have written so far, some differences do emerge between types of newspapers, essentially as to the structures of their articles, their thematic choices, and assumed readers. These differences do confirm many already existing hypotheses. It may appear obvious but business newspapers devote more attention to the euro crisis. Table 9.2 clearly shows how, if related to the total number of articles written by type of newspaper,[30] business papers devote the largest coverage to the euro crisis. As said, for many aspects this is obvious as we are dealing with a matter that, first of all, has important economic and business implications. At the same time, this confirms that Europe has a major 'market nature'. Many authors have underlined this and our data confirm their hypotheses (Kaitatzi-Whitlock, 2005; Koopmans and Statham, 2010; Trenz, 2004); in particular, Kaitatzi-Whitlock (2005: 75) writes: 'The adoption of the central premises of the Internal Market, as applicable to this factor, [...] was primarily due to the political immaturity and extremely economistic nature of the Community.'

There are several aspects to the attention devoted to the euro crisis by business papers, as shown in Figure 9.3. *Le Monde* (not a business paper) publishes most articles on our topic (*Le Monde* was already the race leader in Kleinen-von Königslöw's study on the Europeanisation of national public spheres), but close behind we find four financial newspapers (*Il Sole 24 Ore, Financial Times, Les Echos,* and *Handelsblatt*). Their attention varies considerably depending on the country: it is much higher in the UK, Germany, France, and Italy, while it is much lower in Spanish, Greek, and Polish papers. The dimension of the national economy seems to affect the amount of euro crisis coverage in the business papers. Those countries with stronger economies (the UK, France, Germany) devote more attention to the events in other European countries and to opinions and statements of actors from these countries, as these can have consequences for their own economy (cf. Koopmans et al., 2010).

German and French financial papers focus on the euro crisis because very often the 'tandem Sarkozy Merkel' has played a considerable role in

Table 9.2 Percentage of euro crisis articles by type of newspaper

Type of newspaper	Percentage
Business	47.0
Quality	40.1
Tabloid/popular	12.8
Total	100.0

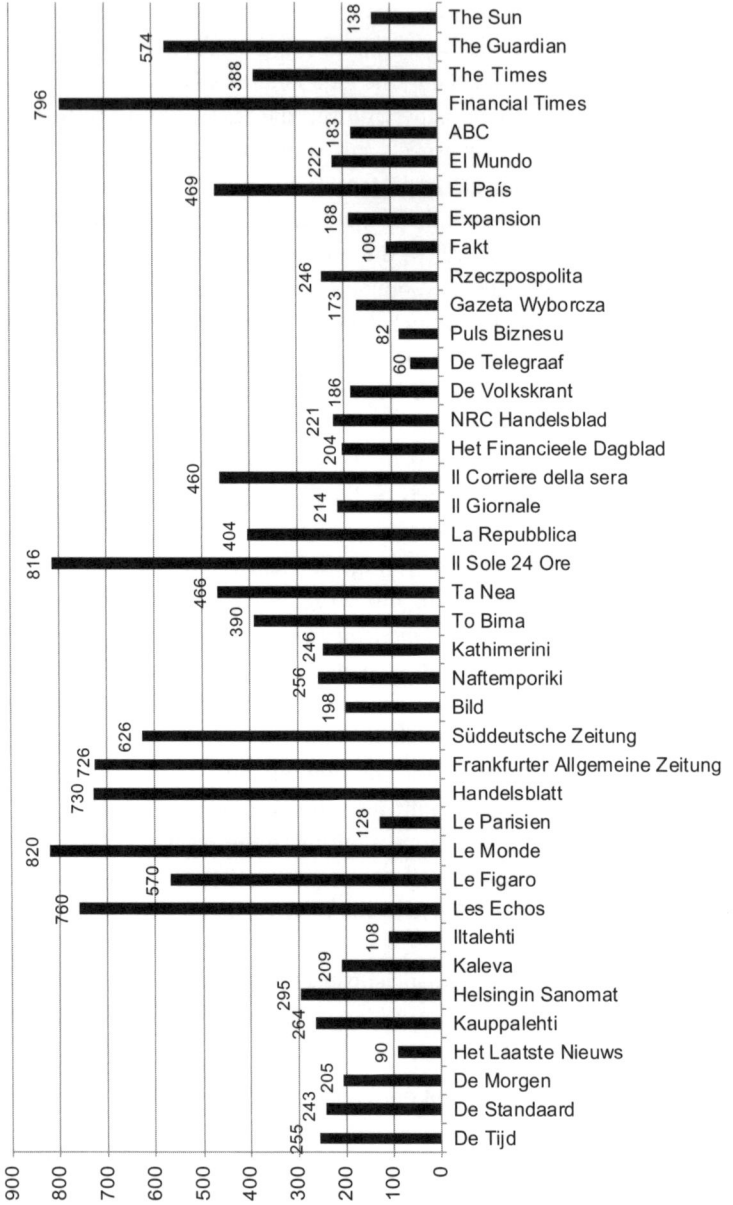

Figure 9.3 Number of euro crisis articles by newspaper

The Sun	138
The Guardian	574
The Times	388
Financial Times	796
ABC	183
El Mundo	222
El País	469
Expansion	188
Fakt	109
Rzeczpospolita	246
Gazeta Wyborcza	173
Puls Biznesu	82
De Telegraaf	60
De Volkskrant	186
NRC Handelsblad	221
Het Financieele Dagblad	204
Il Corriere della sera	460
Il Giornale	214
La Repubblica	404
Il Sole 24 Ore	816
Ta Nea	466
To Bima	390
Kathimerini	246
Naftemporiki	256
Bild	198
Süddeutsche Zeitung	626
Frankfurter Allgemeine Zeitung	726
Handelsblatt	730
Le Parisien	128
Le Monde	820
Le Figaro	570
Les Echos	760
Iltalehti	108
Kaleva	209
Helsingin Sanomat	295
Kauppalehti	264
Het Laatste Nieuws	90
De Morgen	205
De Standaard	243
De Tijd	255

looking for an economic and strategic solution, as can be seen from many articles collected for this research. As to Italy, *Il Sole 24 Ore* (the major national business paper) has always extensively covered European matters. Moreover, Italy is one of the major European economies and suffering the effects of the euro crisis.

Articles published in business papers are mostly long articles dealing with opinions and commentaries (Table 9.1): this confirms that these papers address a very specific readership that requires in-depth information to better understand and decode what is going on and to better take its decisions. It is not by chance that what we defined as 'expert' sources (economists, university professors, other business sources, etc.) have a major place in business papers (Table 9.3). Indeed, these 'experts' are able to offer insight – they may suggest interpretations, possible causes, and future developments of the present situation: these are pieces of information that may be very useful for those who are acting in the economic field. Obviously, the main topic of business papers is the market, as shown in Chapter 8. Table 9.4 reveals they supply hard news on its evolution (exchange rates, bonds, and shares market, etc.) but they also give all the necessary background information on these in their longer articles.

Business papers have a major foreign and European focus (much more than the other kinds of newspapers that depend greatly upon international and foreign sources, as shown in Chapter 3). The economy today clearly extends beyond national borders, including a global dimension and even more clearly a European dimension. Markets are definitely covered, stressing their transnational dimension. This is coherent with what is stressed in Chapter 8.

Table 9.3   Articles by type of newspaper and source quoted (the first five persons quoted in the story)

	Politician	Civil society	Expert	Other	Total
Business	4,020	853	3,565	590	9,028
	44.5%	9.4%	39.5%	6.5%	
Elite	10,523	1,523	4,632	1,181	17,859
	58.9%	8.5%	25.9%	6.6%	
Tabloid/ popular	775	168	390	51	1,384
	56.0%	12.1%	28.2%	3.7%	
Total	15,318	2,544	8,587	1,822	28,271

Table 9.4   Articles by type of newspaper and story impetus

	Market	General	Event-based	Statement and decision	Total
Business	1,208	1,159	1,003	981	4,351
	27.8%	26.6%	23.1%	22.5%	100.0%
Elite	1,696	2,347	2,324	2,169	8,536
	19.9%	27.5%	27.2%	25.4%	100.0%
Tabloid/popular	147	207	265	212	831
	17.7%	24.9%	31.9%	25.5%	100.0%
Total	3,051	3,713	3,592	3,362	13,718
	22.2%	27.1%	26.2%	24.5%	100.0%

These findings could also be interpreted as an indication of the business papers' sensibility towards the construction of what Olausson has defined as the 'frame of certainty' (Olausson, 2010: 145) that legitimises the strategic role of the EU in the eyes of political and financial elites, offering precise, hard news that seems to be aimed at legitimising the role of EU institutions. At the same time, our data confirm that business papers stress the existence of a sort of unique European public sphere particularly devoted to economic markets.

The coverage of the euro crisis by the tabloid press presents very different features. First of all, the popular press devotes little attention to the euro crisis, much less than the other types of paper (12.8%, see Table 9.2). This finding confirms a tendency that other scholars have noted: the tabloids do not give room to the euro crisis because in these newspapers 'EU politics as the main focus of an article seems to be a lost cause' (Kleinen-von Königslöw, 2012: 452). By contrast, this seems to reinforce the idea of the 'market nature' of Europe spread by quality and business papers. Journalists of the tabloid press know, or they assume to know, that the 'man in the street', the usual addressee of the popular press, is not interested in the euro crisis, and, we would add, in Europe in general. Therefore, they put few stories about the euro crisis in their papers, covering it through short articles that just describe what happened (hard news) without offering any particular insight or in-depth analysis.

Moreover, the tabloid press offers a very specific view of Europe: as already said, its coverage is mostly organised around a domestic frame

Table 9.5   Articles by type of newspaper and geopolitical frame

	Domestic	Foreign	European	Other	Total
Business	742	1,077	1,413	47	3,279
	22.6%	32.8%	43.1%	1.4%	100.0%
Elite	1,797	1,961	3,114	138	7,010
	25.6%	28.0%	44.4%	2.0%	100.0%
Tabloid/ popular	212	167	301	11	691
	30.7%	24.2%	43.6%	1.6%	100.0%
Total	2,751	3,205	4,828	196	10,980
	25.1%	29.2%	44.0%	1.8%	100.0%

(Table 9.5): Europe, in our case the euro crisis, reaches the pages of popular papers when it can be treated in connection to problems, situations, and news that are close to national citizens and have or may have some direct and immediate consequences for them. 'Parochialism' or 'domestication' are the words already used to characterise this kind of coverage and it seems to feature mostly in the choices of popular papers on the euro crisis.

The domestic frame depends also on the fact that popular press is close to what Walter Lippman (1922: 227) defined 'the printed diary of the home town': in this case what matters is what happens close to 'home town', and this is reinforced also by sources from civil society playing a more important role in the tabloid press than in other kinds of newspapers (Table 9.3).

In the popular press, the euro crisis is seen through the eyes of the 'man in the street': it becomes news when it touches the citizen in a more direct and immediate way and therefore it has a main 'regional' focus. In the tabloid press, other 'men in the street' (civil society and not experts or politicians) are the sources of the news more than in other newspapers. As to the euro crisis, the popular press seem to be strongly in favour of an easier and, so to speak, painless solution: loans from other countries (Table 9.6). 'Let's make it easy: let's borrow money from richer countries': this is the solution fostered by tabloid press.

Looking at this kind of coverage, one could not say that a European public sphere exists: there is news that refers to and debates about an economic and political entity, Europe. This entity appears strong and important to the citizens (in Figure 9.1, almost all tabloid papers are placed in the upper quarters that look at European institutions as central, strong, and determinant) but this representation essentially depends on regional needs and interests.

Table 9.6   Articles by type of newspaper and main (short-term) response to the crisis

	Loans	Austerity	Growth	Other	Total
Business	1,112	642	260	286	2,300
	48.3%	27.9%	11.3%	12.4%	100.0%
Elite	2,275	1,341	543	548	4,707
	48.3%	28.5%	11.5%	11.6%	100.0%
Tabloid/ popular	247	109	28	33	417
	59.2%	26.1%	6.7%	7.9%	100.0%
Total	3,634	2,092	831	867	7,424
	48.9%	28.2%	11.2%	11.7%	100.0%

Does political orientation matter?

There are differences also in connection to the political affiliation of the newspaper. As said previously, these differences appear minor if compared with the nationality of the paper.

Table 9.7 shows that liberal newspapers[31] pay more attention to the euro crisis than conservative and neutral newspapers; more than other papers they support a solution based on growth. On the opposite side, conservative papers seem to indicate that the solution has to be found by national governments. In short, our data suggest that the conservative press is boosting trust in the national governments' capability to solve the euro crisis: this attitude is probably linked to the fact that in many European countries, at the time of our research, conservative leaders were in charge (Berlusconi, Sarkozy, Merkel, Cameron, etc.), and the conservative press seems to have supported their actions.

Table 9.7   Percentage of articles devoted to the euro crisis by orientation of newspaper

Orientation	Percentage
Conservative	29.2
Liberal	37.2
Neutral	33.6
Total	100.0

Data related to the choices of single newspapers do not confirm the diffused interpretations that conservative papers are more 'Euro-sceptic' and the liberal papers more 'pro-European' (Marini, 2003).

Indeed, as shown in Figure 9.3, *La Repubblica* (liberal paper) in Italy depicts the EU as more insignificant than *Il Giornale* (conservative) does; it is similar to the situation in France where *Le Monde* (liberal) covers the EU institutions as weaker than *Le Figaro* (conservative); this discrepancy is even more evident in Belgium where *De Morgen* (liberal) covers the EU as ineffectual or confused through twice as many articles as in *De Standaard* (conservative), and in the Netherlands where *De Volkskrant* (liberal) pays more attention than *De Telegraaf* (tabloid) to the weaknesses of the EU. By contrast, in Poland, *Rzeczpospolita* (conservative) covers the EU as weaker institutions than *Gazeta Wyborcza* (centre-left), and in Germany *FAZ* (centre-right) depicts the EU as more effective than *Süddeutsche Zeitung* (centre-left).

Even if quantitative differences in this regard are not so relevant, our results seem to stress that the liberal press in general has a more European attitude than the conservative press which is more focused on internal politics and solutions. At the same time the liberal press, because of its high expectations regarding European institutions, does not spare criticism of the poor performance of these institutions when they do not seem to be able to deal with a crisis that is undermining the process of integration.

Which countries lead the dance?

We have already talked about parochialism: there exists a more general attitude in which the choices of newspapers are mostly related to national conditions and realities. Rather than assuming a general European interest, newspapers are still linked to the countries within Europe (Figures 9.1 and 9.2): in particular, this is the attitude of tabloid papers. Another indicator of this is the fact that there are countries in which the coverage of the euro crisis is more relevant and countries where this is much less relevant. From our data (Figure 9.4), we understand that, even with exceptions, the biggest countries, France, Italy, Germany, and the UK, devote more attention to the euro crisis while smaller countries, Finland, the Netherlands, and Belgium, seem to pay less attention to the euro crisis. In some way this is unexpected because the two countries that

Figure 9.4 Number of euro crisis articles by country

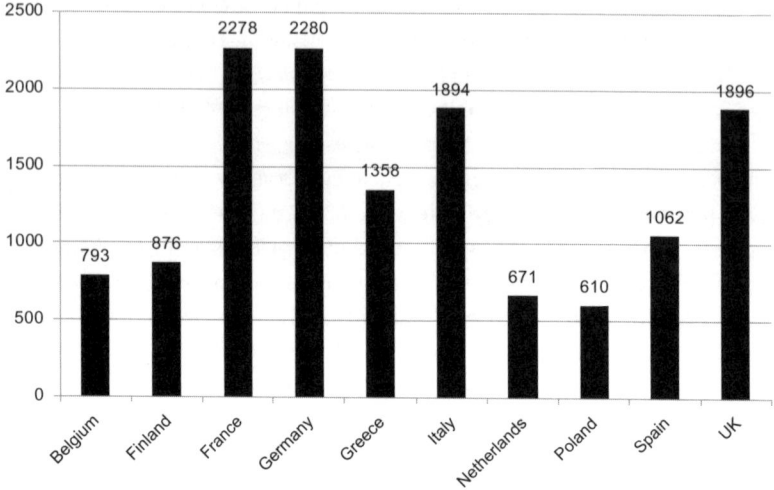

the Eurobarometer shows as more pro-European (the Netherlands and Belgium) have strongly under-represented, at least in comparison with other countries of our study, the euro crisis debate.

There are several possible explanations for this difference: obviously the largest countries have a major role in the euro crisis as they have the largest economies and therefore, on the one hand, they may risk the major negative consequences. On the other hand, they may also benefit in larger measure from the crisis.

Other more incidental reasons may play a role in the different attention devoted to the euro crisis, including journalistic culture, newspapers' resources, newspaper format, or direct involvement of national leaders. France and Germany, for instance, and more specifically their leaders Angela Merkel and Nicolas Sarkozy, have been very active in trying to find a solution to the euro crisis. In this sense, the attention of German and French papers to the euro crisis is also an attention devoted to their own national leaders; it has important internal political implications.

Traditionally, Italy has always devoted great attention to European matters (Bellucci and Conti, 2012; Machill et al., 2006). Beyond this Italy is the 'largest' country in crisis and its failure may have very dramatic consequences for the entire eurozone.

The attention devoted by British newspapers can be explained by the major role of the *Financial Times*: as is well known, for several years the

FT has become a sort of official source for many reporters and officials in Brussels and in other major European centres. The *FT* is the newspaper of the business elites in Europe and elsewhere. It devotes much attention to the euro crisis not just because this is an economic and financial crisis but also because it regards the eurozone as a region about which the *FT* is the major information provider. In a way, the *FT* is the only paper that depicts some sort of unique European public sphere.

In spite of being a small country, Greece devotes great attention to the euro crisis as it is the country that in some way brought the crisis to its highest point and is suffering more dramatically its consequences.

Discussion

In general, the coverage of the euro crisis does not appear to be very different from what many other studies have shown to be the representation of Europe within the news media. It shows that a truly European public sphere, where citizens and means of communication of different orientation meet and discuss without national distinction, does not exist. Very likely it cannot exist within the specific conditions and the specific decision-making processes that regulate European integration today. The representative institution of European citizens (the European Parliament) has very little power and is not perceived as the place where the decisions are taken; therefore, there is little interest in affecting its decision-making process through the news media (Cornia, 2010). The other institutions (the Commission and the Council of Europe) are not representative ones: they have a mainly technical character and they are not directly exposed to the influences of public opinion outside the national domain.

The most dramatic crisis that the eurozone has passed through since its creation is treated mostly through national interests, needs, and attitudes. Nevertheless, our data show that national public spheres are deeply affected by the events that take place in Europe and also by the decisions and actions of European actors, among which a major role is played by prime ministers/ heads of state (Merkel, Sarkozy), European officials (Barroso, Draghi), and business people. They are important figures beyond national borders and who affect public debate essentially among European elites.

There is a major interest in European matters on the part of business newspapers (see Table 9.2): this would confirm the economic nature of

European unification that is also reflected in business news outlets. It seems possible to state that major limits to Europeanisation are found in the lack of interest by ordinary people towards Europe, as demonstrated by the scarce interest in the euro crisis shown by the tabloid press. While the Habermas normative concept of the EPS depicts it as a realm of 'pure' public interest, free from private or nationalist interests, our empirical evidence shows quite a different picture from this ideal standard: the development of a truly democratic and transnational EPS is impeded by lack of popular interest in European matters. As Lauristin (2007: 401) notes: 'European debate is believed to be of interest only to narrow groups of Europeanised elites, who comprise the audiences of the influential quality press and also dominate the voices speaking about European matters in the media as whole.' The findings confirm that the business papers are those that highlight a major European vocation while, on the opposite side, tabloid papers seem to show little attention towards the euro crisis and refer essentially to national contexts and situations.

Data deriving from the analysis of tabloid papers corroborate these interpretations: Europe, and its crisis, is perceived as far from the interests of 'the man in the street', the assumed reader of tabloid press. Extrapolating from this, it could be said that two different 'Europes' do emerge: the Europe of the market and the Europe of citizens. The latter is already a matter of discussion and debate in the news media, envisaging, in the business and elite papers, some sort of sketchy European public sphere. The former looks at Europe from the point of view of Italians, Germans, Greeks, and so on. 'The Europe of citizens' seems to perfectly fit into the idea of 'segmented Europeanisation': public opinion exercises control over European institutions but mainly, if not only, from a national perspective.

Political orientation seems to be less important in addressing the way in which the newspapers cover the euro crisis but some differences do seem to emerge: the liberal press presents a major European focus while in the conservative press a more domestic focus prevails. Because of its higher expectations, the liberal press has shown a more critical attitude towards the performances of European institutions in general. From our study it emerges that the most important variable that affects the coverage of the euro crisis is the country, quite independently of the political affiliation and editorial line of the newspapers.

Another explanation for this result may be suggested: Europe (and its crisis) is a complex topic. We can guess that, because of its complexity, the euro crisis pushes professional journalists of the same country to share the same sources, the same news values, and perhaps to consult each other before writing their articles. This could be another way through which national belonging guides the euro crisis coverage. The idea of 'segmented Europeanisation' seems to explain our results well. News media exercise some kind of control over European institutions but this is done essentially through taking into account national attitudes, interests, and feelings. And this also applies to the euro crisis. In other words, it could be said that a European public sphere is just at its outset.

In spite of the strong domestication of the news on the euro crisis, some similarities among the observed news outlets do emerge: first of all a common theme of discussion exists. There is one main problem that national public spheres face, and similar solutions to this problem are discussed. A sort of initial prototype of a European public sphere seems to emerge: all through the observed countries newspapers of the same kind point out similar attitudes, as other chapters in this volume have shown. But the data we have investigated also demonstrates that national belonging is more important than the emerging similarities, confirming the results of many other studies beyond ours. Indeed, as to several issues we have investigated in this chapter, newspapers seem to show editorial choices that are rooted within the framework of national interests, perceptions, and needs.

10

European Journalism or Many Journalisms? Influences of Media Systems and Journalistic Cultures

Robert G. Picard and Susana Salgado

It has long been recognised that practices of journalism differ among nations and that the roles of media in society and their relationships with power and authority affect the values, norms, and techniques employed in news and production. Although there are some underlying commonalities – a focus on contemporary events and developments, attempts to verify information, and to provide fair coverage – the journalistic techniques employed and the methods used to present news and information differ among countries.

This chapter attempts to establish how news coverage differs in countries and the extent to which those differences align with existing models in comparative media and journalism research. Evidences of some fundamental journalistic practices were measured in this study and they are used to explore the extent to which differences are present in coverage of the euro crisis and whether those differences support existing claims about journalism and media practice.

Indicators of journalistic practices

Specific indicators useful in comparing techniques and presentation include: genre (type of story), story impetus (what induced the article), prominence (page and section placement), size of article, type of sources quoted, and geopolitical frames presented.

The number of stories and different genres would be expected to vary depending upon accepted journalistic practice in a paper or a country. These include news stories and interviews that tend to be more straightforward presentations of facts and information, news analysis/background stories that involve more judgement and subjective interpretation on the part of journalists, feature stories that tend to explain developments through the lens of those various participants or those affected by events, interviews that elicit explanation or justification from major figures involved in the events, and editorials and opinion/commentary stories that present the writer's or newspaper's view on developments.

The factors that led to a story about the euro crisis being published, story impetus, also vary. Some were caused by events (meetings, summits); some by requests (applications, request for aid); some by decisions made by governments, government entities, or political party/ies; some by statement/pronouncements of officials; some by market developments; and others by reports in other media. Consequently, the importance of political or market developments and the perceived significance of various activities can vary depending upon the news values, agenda-setting, and techniques of coverage in a country (among other factors).

Prominence of display of stories, evidenced by the pages on which they were published or the sections in which they were published, provided an indication of papers' perceptions of the news value of stories about the euro crisis. This value could vary by newspaper, country, or relation to the issues of the crisis.

Size of article also provided a measure of journalistic practice because of differences in practices regarding short-form and long-form journalism. The former generally are short, quickly read pieces of news and the latter are longer explorations of the news and its context.

Finally, the geopolitical frame is useful because it provides an indicator of whether the journalistic practice is to localise issues, report them as foreign issues, or to present them as Europe-wide issues.

Theoretical explanations of media systems and cultures

Understanding how media systems and journalistic cultures shape news coverage of politics and events in general has been on the agenda of social observers and researchers for some decades. This topic remains of great interest to scholars because more comparative research in different contexts and focused on different subjects is still needed to advance knowledge about the nature and consequences of these relationships.

The existing literature points in sometimes divergent – although not always conflicting – directions. Some emphasise that globalisation of news seems to have led to a great similarity in the content of news and in the daily news agendas (Shoemaker and Cohen, 2006); others stress that national differences remain and still count for a great deal, especially at times of global crisis and tension (McQuail, 2013).

Donsbach and Patterson (2004) draw attention to the underlying complexity of this type of research and its impact on conclusions explaining if and how national media system characteristics and journalistic cultures influence the coverage of issues and events. In their view, journalists in Western democratic societies operate under similar conditions (legal, political, economic, and cultural) and have relatively easy access to different types of political information and to those in power. However, journalists simultaneously operate in societies that have different press histories and that are not identical in their media and political structures. Donsbach and Patterson identify these dissimilarities as potential causes for differences in the way that journalists perceive and do their jobs (2004: 251).

It theoretically makes sense to assume that national media systems shape national journalistic culture and that both affect the practice of journalism, but it is much more challenging to empirically support this expectation.[32] Some scholars have tried to offer theories and approaches to explain the links between media systems, journalistic cultures, and structures of news coverage by establishing patterns that ultimately cluster several countries with similar tendencies. Because the objective of this chapter is not to analyse and provide in-depth details of all these studies, we focus only on a few notable comparative systematic studies that stand out for the comprehensiveness of their approaches and for the attention that they have received.

Our goal is to consider the euro crisis news coverage in the light of these theoretical proposals to determine if their theoretical arguments can be empirically established with the coverage. Although the euro crisis could be considered a special situation, with the peculiarities caused by the additional economic, political, and social challenges to Europe, it offers a unique opportunity to test the theories/approaches because the financial and economic issues concerned all European countries even if not in an equal manner.

The objective is therefore to study how the news coverage of the euro crisis in different European countries might have been influenced by national media systems, journalistic cultures, and the differing levels of involvement countries had in the crisis. We explore the effects of these differences on the news stories' format and content and, more precisely, we analyse the elements of journalistic practice that were actually affected by dissimilarities amongst countries. These include factors explained earlier, such as the genre of articles selected to inform the public about the crisis, the impetus of stories (what – if anything – induced the coverage), the page placement of articles, their length, the types of information sources used to inform about the crisis, and the geopolitical frames employed in addressing the crisis. If journalism choices and practices are significantly influenced by national differences, the differences should be apparent in these indicators. By focusing on news coverage characteristics, we can explore the extent to which national influences and the expectations raised by the existing theoretical frameworks are evident in the coverage of the euro crisis. The chapter thus investigates the extent to which systemic and cultural factors are as important as national interests in the European currency and European integration in determining patterns of media coverage.

Media and journalism in a comparative perspective

News content and news format are influenced by a wide range of elements, including the availability of information and sources of information and the time pressure to report events (acceleration of news cycles), which is much more acute now that the internet and other digital platforms are directly influencing journalistic work practices. Depending on the context, some factors assume particular relevance and tend to affect other elements.

Based on comparative media theory, we can assume that the content and format of news can be seen as a reflection of the characteristics of national media systems, as well as being a reflection of journalistic cultures. How the media system is structured and the dominant journalism culture in a country would be expected to deeply affect how journalism is practised, the emphasis given to news stories, the amount of effort put into them, and journalists' attitudes towards facts, events, and sources of information – factors such as whether they challenge government and elites or primarily rely on them for information, whether news stories result from events or investigations are influenced by national factors.

The leading contemporary research about journalism culture has been conducted by Hanitzsch (2007, 2011) and colleagues (2011). It has examined previous studies on the topic and suggested how to look at the 'diversity of journalistic practices and orientations' (Hanitzsch et al., 2011: 273). The main idea behind these studies is that the way news is produced varies by country and therefore journalism is strongly linked to the culture within which it operates. After proposing a theoretical foundation on which to sustain future systematic and comparative research on journalism cultures (2007), Hanitzsch and his colleagues mapped different national journalistic cultures with the 'Worlds of Journalism', a collaborative effort that involved researchers from 18 countries (Hanitzsch et al., 2011).

Hanitzsch (2007) proposed a conceptualisation of journalism culture that consists of three essential constituents (institutional roles, epistemologies, and ethical ideologies), further divided into seven principal dimensions: interventionism, power distance, market orientation (institutional roles); objectivism, empiricism (epistemological dimensions); relativism, idealism (ethical ideologies). The empirical investigation is on how journalists perceive journalism's institutional roles, epistemological underpinnings, and ethical standards, and these three domains are seen as basic elements of difference between journalism's cultures.

Hanitzsch et al. (2011) tried to distinguish possible broader groupings of journalism cultures. Based on the assumption that there are different groups of journalists who share similar understandings of the profession, a cluster analysis led Hanitzsch (2011) to identify four broad milieux of journalists as representatives of different national contexts: 'populist disseminator', 'detached watchdog', 'critical agent change', and 'opportunist facilitator'. Hanitzsch primarily found the first two of these patterns in the European countries included in his study. The detached watchdog pattern dominates in Germany, Austria, and Switzerland, while journalists in Spain, Romania, Bulgaria, and Russia were aligned more with the populist disseminator pattern.

Spain may not be the only Western European democracy to deviate from the detached watchdog pattern. Kuhn (2014), using a completely different research instrument, found important differences between the French and the Anglo-American journalism. French journalists tend to be less distant and less autonomous and show more deference towards elite politicians than Anglo-American journalists, who follow more clearly a journalistic tradition of critical watchdog and 'fourth estate' thinking. In France, there is very often close cooperation or even connivance between journalists and elite politicians. To support this view, Kuhn cites Halimi, a radical-left commentator, who sees the French style of political journalism as 'uncritical and reverential' (Kuhn, 2014: 37). This is expected to have implications for the types of stories produced and the sources quoted in stories, for instance.

Contrary to Hanitzsch's expectations about German journalism, Pfetsch (1999) asserts that the German culture is distinct from the British and American models in a number of important aspects. These authors consider that German journalists' attitudes towards political institutions are mixed: journalists tend to be obedient to state institutions and to the government, but they also often take sides instead of adopting a distant and neutral mode of reporting. German journalists believe that 'it is legitimate that they advocate their own political views and ideas, side openly with one of the political parties, or infuse their convictions in the political debate' (Pfetsch, 1999: 27–8). Thus one would expect to find a greater mixing of opinion in news and analysis stories than in Anglo-American journalism.

The relationship between politicians and journalists has been an important component of analysis when the objective is to analyse journalistic cultures and the journalist's institutional role, and different studies that have focused on these debates could be described in these pages; however, the objective here is just to provide some context, not an exhaustive report. A precursor to research on this topic was advanced by Blumler and Gurevitch (1975, 1995). These authors proposed a theoretical framing to identify the type of relationship between journalists and political sources and news. In their proposal, they divided the orientations of journalists between 'sacerdotal' and 'pragmatic' according to the importance of political news and sources for media outlets. When journalists have a sacerdotal approach, political news is considered newsworthy in itself and their attitude towards politicians is reactive and respectful. If, on the contrary, a pragmatic journalistic approach is more common, political news is examined in relation to the rest of the events of current news value through news selection criteria and is only included in the news report if it is deemed newsworthy taking into consideration the other available news and audience preferences. If in the first case, political events and statements by politicians have guaranteed media coverage despite their intrinsic value; in the second case, they have to compete with other news stories for journalistic attention and coverage space. Blumler and Gurevitch relate this pragmatic orientation to the 'agenda-setting' role of the media, in which journalists have an active role and try to set their own agenda, selecting issues and perspectives that may not already be on the politicians' agenda, whereas an 'agenda-sending' stance is more closely related with the sacerdotal orientation, because the journalists' role is mainly to cover the political agenda.

Although illustrative of how different journalistic attitudes may influence news content and useful to include in discussions on the political role of journalists and their contribution to democracy and to citizens' critical understanding of democratic mechanisms, these last theoretical propositions are mostly country-focused or based on conceptual frameworks. Therefore, they are distinct from the work of Hanitzsch and his colleagues which represents empirical systematic attempts to study various countries comparatively.

Hallin and Mancini's well-known contribution on how to *compare media systems* (2004) represents a milestone in this field of studies and is an important attempt to cluster different countries around similar trends. It has stimulated numerous comparative reflections about these issues and several attempts to apply both the proposed models and theoretical framework to media systems around the globe (see, for instance, Gross, 2008; Hallin and Mancini, 2011; Jakubowicz, 2008; Nord, 2008; Salgado, 2014b; just to mention a few). It also has highlighted the idea that the characteristics of media systems impact on media coverage of reality. Elements such as the degree of journalistic professionalisation, the role of the state, the structure of media markets (media outlets and audiences), and even the levels of political parallelism influence media content and format. Political parallelism means the connections between media and politics; it refers to the political tendencies of media outlets and more broadly to the extent to which the different political ideologies and political parties of a given political system are reflected in the media system.

Based on the differences found in European countries, Hallin and Mancini proposed three models in which countries could be categorised. The Liberal model includes the UK and Ireland, the Democratic Corporatist model includes the northern/central European countries, and the Polarised Pluralist model the southern European countries and France. We would thus anticipate differences in the content and format of news coverage in these different groups of European countries.

Theory and practice: expectations raised and the coverage of the crisis

Expectations raised

The differences in structure of media systems and journalistic cultures would be expected to be reflected in the national news coverage of events and the countries' different levels of involvement in the euro crisis would also motivate different journalistic approaches to the crisis's events and actors. We would expect that countries more directly involved in the crisis, either through their direct influence in decisions (Germany and France, for instance) or through their request for financial assistance (Greece and Spain, for instance), would have a news coverage reflecting the greatest importance of the crisis to their national contexts. Conversely, countries less involved, either because they did not join the single currency (the UK and Poland) or simply due to their peripheral position regarding the crisis (Belgium, the Netherlands, or Finland) would be expected to give less importance to the news coverage of the crisis. It would thus be expected that the more distant from the heart of the crisis, the less attention would be given to this issue, which would be reflected in the publication of fewer articles and less discussion on the beneficiaries and the sufferers of the euro and the euro crisis. This would also be expected to lead to less negative impact of the crisis or support for the European Union in general, and a clearer European geopolitical frame in articles and opinions when compared to the other countries.

Given Hallin and Mancini's media systems models and Blumler and Gurevitch's proposals on the relationships between journalists and political news and sources, it is straightforward to assume that a 'sacerdotal' attitude will be more a characteristic of Democratic Corporatist or Polarised Pluralist models than of Liberal model countries (Strömbäck and Kaid, 2008). As Hallin and Mancini argue, although commercial newspapers have become more and more important all over Europe ('convergence toward the Liberal model', 2004: 76), Democratic Corporatist countries also have a history of a strong political press that still shapes media systems of northern and central Europe (2004: 160). In the case of the Polarised Pluralist model countries, there is a strong role of both the state and the political parties and a history of strong political parallelism.

In countries belonging to the Polarised Pluralist model, there is a considerable presence of the state in the media system and journalists tend to exhibit more frequently a 'sacerdotal' attitude towards politicians and political news in general, as well as an 'agenda-sending' posture of the information politicians want to convey. According to Hallin and Mancini, the professionalisation of journalists is not as strong as in the other models and the autonomy of journalists is usually limited. Political parallelism tends to be high in these countries and the press is marked by a strong focus on the political life and with a tradition of commentary. Instrumentalisation of the media by the government, political parties, or people with political ties is also common. This model is also characterised by an elite-oriented press with relatively small circulation, in which freedom of the press and the development of commercial media generally arrived late. Many newspapers struggle to survive financially and subsidies may be available to media outlets, which tends to aggravate their limited autonomy from political power.

The countries that fall into the Democratic Corporatist model would display a mix of 'sacerdotal' and 'pragmatic' approaches and of commercial and public interest orientations in the media. This happens because, as Hallin and Mancini note, these countries are marked by the coexistence of political parallelism and journalism professionalisation, as well as by strong welfare state policies and other forms of active state intervention.

The Liberal model countries are mainly commercially oriented and therefore journalists tend to develop and employ more 'pragmatic' and 'agenda-setting' approaches, adjusting their work to what they believe are the preferences of their audiences. Hallin and Mancini posit that these are countries with a strong development of media markets and professionalism.

Expectations of countries in the Polarised Pluralist model

Following these observations and considering the euro crisis media coverage, we would expect that news in media systems with a more prominent presence of the state would reflect more the public authorities' perspectives and journalists would have a more 'sacerdotal' approach towards national and European politics. Hence, newspapers would generally give more attention to the euro crisis, perceptible in the number of stories, and more front-page, medium and long articles instead of short news stories with little or no prominence. This type of journalistic approach to the euro crisis implies that coverage is mostly reactive, consisting predominantly in reports of events, decisions, and statements, as well as a high percentage of commentaries and opinion articles on those events, decisions, and statements. In terms of the sources of information quoted, a greater presence of EU and national government sources would be expected, including more interviews to authorities. In short, a reactive coverage reflecting mainly the authorities' positions, without an 'agenda-setting' posture in the sense of initiating coverage of issues and events not previously defined by political actors would be the norm. As a consequence of this type of coverage, a European perspective would be expected to be more salient as a geopolitical frame.

Expectations of countries in the Liberal model

Given the complex nature of the crisis and its strong business and financial facets, more commercially oriented newspapers would be expected to provide fewer front-page news stories, and to report the crisis mainly through short stories. An expected feature of this type of journalistic coverage would be the publication of more analysis and feature articles, an approach to journalism that looks for an angle to report with more drama and conflict and provides a more analytical approach to the crisis. There would be expected to be a strong concern in looking for and giving priority to what is saleable behind these coverage characteristics.

This would be expected to produce more proactive coverage, inclusive of themes and issues that may not be on the established political agenda, reflecting a strong 'agenda-setting' posture in the sense of initiating news coverage. Consequently, the euro crisis coverage in this context would be expected to be marked by a higher presence of news stories not tied to events and a larger number of market development news stories, for example evolution of euro currency exchange prices, perspectives of European economic growth, and so on. We would also expect the inclusion of varied types of sources, such as citizens and society representatives, financiers, and experts in general, as well as national and European leaders. Finally, in this type of coverage, the European perspective would be expected to be overshadowed by national and foreign perspectives due to perceptions of audiences' interests.

Expectations of countries in the Democratic Corporatist model

Euro crisis news coverage in countries that belong to the Democratic Corporatist model would be expected to reflect a mix of the features of the two previous models. The strong position of the state in the media system should be translated into high levels of attention to the governments and European officials' agenda and statements; however, solid journalistic professionalisation could also mean that there is a concern to go beyond the established political agenda. It would also be expected that the euro crisis issue would be considered by national journalists as an important issue per se and receive attention and coverage. A blend of all types and sizes of news stories without clear predominance of one in particular should also define news coverage in the newspapers of countries pertaining to this model of media system.

Journalistic culture expectations

If we apply Hanitzsch and colleagues' proposals to the media coverage of the euro crisis, our expectations about the coverage in European countries changes significantly. These authors' conclusions and the resultant clustering of countries around similar journalistic cultures and behaviours point in somewhat different directions. According to them, within the four global professional milieux of journalists, there are relevant patterns that point to the existence of two distinct professional milieux in Western European journalism. 'The milieu of the detached watchdog clearly dominates the journalistic field in all western countries with the exception of Spain' (Hanitzsch, 2011: 486). This type of journalism is also characterised by scepticism towards the political and business elites, which is substantiated in a belief that journalists should monitor all political processes. 'The milieu of the populist disseminator dominates the journalistic field in Spain, Romania, Bulgaria, and Israel' (2011: 487). Although with some similarities to the detached watchdog milieu in the sense that journalists also see their role as 'objective and detached disseminators of news', what clearly distinguishes this milieu is the priority given to the production of interesting information, which should attract the widest audience possible. Moreover, the watchdog function is practically absent in this milieu.

Expectations of countries with the populist disseminator approach

Journalists in the populist disseminator milieu are therefore strongly oriented towards the audience; their main objective is to provide interesting information, which may not be critical of the government and the politicians' decisions in general.

Thus, following Hanitzsch's directions of what characterises journalism in this journalistic milieu, we expect to find in the euro crisis coverage in these countries' newspapers shorter stories, but also feature articles with human-interest elements. It will also be a reactive coverage, tied to events, with little background and contextualisation, and mainly focused on domestic leaders and officials and less on experts as sources of information.

Expectations of countries with the detached watchdog approach

In countries where journalistic culture is mainly oriented towards the idea of the 'detached watchdog', journalists cultivate a critical approach towards the political and business elites, which they believe should always be monitored for the sake of democracy. There is a strong belief in the journalistic role of providing the audience with political information that is suited for making informed political decisions. However, according to Hanitzsch, these journalists are also less interventionist than their colleagues in other professional milieux: 'they are least likely to advocate for social change, influence public opinion and set the agenda [...] And are also most opposed to the idea that they should support official policies' (2011: 485).

The European countries that are part of Hanitzsch and colleagues' study and that are presented as representative of this milieu are Germany, Austria, and Switzerland. Of these three countries, only Germany is both in our euro crisis news coverage study and in Hanitzsch and colleagues' project. However, analysing and following the main characteristics of the four possible milieux, it becomes more or less clear that, in addition to Germany, the UK, Belgium, the Netherlands, and probably also Finland could be included in the same group.

Under the logic of the 'detached watchdog' milieu, we expect that journalists in these countries would provide longer stories about the euro crisis, but also more analysis and background information aimed at helping audiences understand what is behind developments and what the future implications of certain policy decisions may be. Given the objective of providing the most suitable information possible for supporting citizens' informed decision-making processes, these journalists would be expected to rely on a wider variety of sources of information, which in turn could lead to a more varied balance in news stories regarding the geopolitical frame. In addition, more diversity in journalistic genres and impetus of news stories is also expected in this type of media coverage of the crisis.

Expectations of what the newspaper coverage should be in each European country following these different authors' framework proposals points to some inconsistencies in the clustering of countries. For instance, the UK would follow the Liberal model features and therefore be commercially oriented with journalists adjusting their news coverage to audience preferences under Hallin and Mancini's countries configuration of media systems. However, the Hanitzsch and colleagues' division of countries by professional milieux, and the description of the distinctive characteristics of different milieux, suggests the insertion of the UK in the 'detached watchdog' milieu and not in the 'populist disseminator' milieu which is primarily described by its key concern in attracting the widest audience possible. Although included in these different studies, Spain illustrates a similar situation, with some ambiguities. Hallin and Mancini place Spain in the Polarised Pluralist model, suggesting, among other things, the existence of political parallelism, a strong media focus on politics, and high possibility of instrumentalisation of the media by politicians. These characteristics point to a very close relationship between the media and the political system, which should be perceptible in news coverage. Hanitzsch and colleagues, however, use this country as an example of the 'populist disseminator' milieu, which is distinguished from the other milieux by its primordial goal of pleasing the audience.

Before considering other possible inconsistencies or even conflicts between the existing models used in clustering countries, it is important to see how the theories hold in practice with regards to the euro crisis. We will therefore turn to the results of the European newspapers' coverage analysis before coming back to the broader discussion.

Table 10.1 shows coverage expectations from the theories. Germany and Spain were included in both the journalistic culture and media system research approaches and produce clear expectations regarding news coverage if the comparative media and journalism theories/approaches hold true. Expectations are less clear for the other countries because they were either not included in both approaches or did not fall into the archetypes of the theories.

Table 10.1   Expectations of national coverage given comparative journalism theories

Country	Journalistic culture and media system alignment	Expectation of news coverage
Belgium	Elements of both Populist Disseminator and Detached Watchdog cultures; Democratic Corporatist	Range of story size; event oriented but with some analysis/features; domestic leader focus, but with wider variety of sources; balanced geopolitical framework
Finland	Elements of both Populist Disseminator and Detached Watchdog cultures; Democratic Corporatist	Range of story size; event oriented but with some analysis/features; domestic leader focus, but with wider variety of sources; balanced geopolitical framework
France	Elements of both Populist Disseminator and Detached Watchdog cultures; Polarised Pluralist	Range of story size; event oriented but with some analysis; domestic leader focus, with focus on political leaders; much opinion and commentary; balanced geopolitical framework
Germany	Detached Watchdog; Democratic Corporatist	Longer story size; more analysis/features; greater source variety; balanced geopolitical framework
Greece	Elements of both Populist Disseminator and Detached Watchdog cultures; Polarised Pluralist	Range of story size; event oriented but with some analysis; domestic leader focus, with focus on political leaders; much opinion and commentary; balanced geopolitical framework
Italy	Elements of both Populist Disseminator and Detached Watchdog cultures; Polarised Pluralist	Range of story size; event oriented but with some analysis; domestic leader focus, with focus on political leaders; much opinion and commentary; balanced geopolitical framework
Netherlands	Elements of both Populist Disseminator and Detached Watchdog cultures; Democratic Corporatist	Range of story size; event oriented, but with some analysis; domestic leader focus, but with wider variety of sources; balanced geopolitical framework

Table 10.1   *(Continued)*

Country	Journalistic culture and media system alignment	Expectation of news coverage
Poland	Elements of both Populist Disseminator and Detached Watchdog cultures	Range of story size; event oriented but with some analysis; domestic leader focus, but with wider variety of sources; balanced geopolitical framework
Spain	Populist Disseminator; Polarised Pluralist	Shorter stories; feature stories; event oriented; domestic leader source focus; much opinion and commentary; domestic geopolitical frame
United Kingdom	Elements of both Populist Disseminator and Detached Watchdog cultures; Liberal	Range of story size; event oriented but with some analysis; more features/analysis; more proactive coverage; domestic leader focus, with focus on political leaders, but with wider variety of sources; balanced geopolitical framework

Newspaper coverage of the euro crisis

This section addresses the following questions: whether models on media systems and journalistic cultures are evident in the euro crisis news coverage; if there are patterns of media coverage that are not anticipated and explained by the existing theoretical models; if there are clear clusters of countries, what is behind the formation of these possible clusters; and if crisis content and format of media coverage are better explained by other factors.

We analysed both content and format variables in different types of newspapers from European countries that experienced different types of involvement in the euro crisis and represent different journalistic cultures and media systems.

Impetus for coverage

One of the elements included in this analysis has to do with the impetus of each news story. With this variable we were interested in understanding the motivation behind the publication of euro crisis articles. Do journalists have a more reactive approach to events and news publishing because meetings or summits happen, decisions were made, countries requested assistance, national or European leaders made statements, or simply because another media outlet published or broadcast something on the crisis? Or do journalists reveal a proactive approach to the crisis going beyond the event/action-oriented agenda and publishing articles not tied to a specific event of development of the crisis?

News coverage was more proactive (i.e. news stories not tied to events) in the Netherlands and the UK (42 and 41%, respectively). Belgium and Finland present very similar results (28 and 29%), while Poland (23%) is between this group and that of Spain and France (15%) and Germany (12%). The country with the fewest news stories not tied to events was Greece (only 5%). The impetus variable results underscore the mainly reactive nature of news media in most countries. Journalists wait for something to happen and then report on it and most of this coverage is based on governmental actions and banking and market developments.

To some degree, the analysis of this variable seems to point to some elements of the Hallin and Mancini models. The UK pertaining to the Liberal model embodies a more proactive approach in the euro crisis coverage; however, the variable also positions Spain, France, and Germany very close and none of the existing models provides an explanation for this. A possible reason could be their greater involvement in the crisis, but the data do not show a higher interest of their newspapers in understanding the crisis context beyond the established agenda, as would make sense.

Genre of stories

The second element of our analysis concerns the journalistic genre selected to inform the public about the crisis. As explained elsewhere (Salgado, 2014a), there are important differences between various journalistic genres regarding the degree of political and journalistic control. Some genres are more controlled by journalists (they select, rearrange, frame, evaluate, and in some cases provide interpretation and opinion) and others give more freedom to politicians (and other actors) to convey their messages.

The most common genre is the news story in all countries, except the Netherlands where more analysis articles were published (48%) than news stories (25%). Finland reveals a balanced distribution between analysis articles (30%) and news stories (31%). The second most common genre in most countries is analysis. The publication of this type of articles was relatively important in Belgium (37%), Italy (30%), the UK and Poland (29%), and Greece (26%), but less important in Spain (20%), Germany (18%), and France (17%).

Although the UK and Italy also show expressive values (23 and 22%), the publication of opinion (commentary, editorials, and opinion articles) was more important in Spain (29%) and Finland (26%). In the Netherlands, the number was roughly 20% while in German and Polish newspapers 19% of the articles published on the euro crisis had explicit opinion. Belgium and Germany showed lower presence of opinion (18 and 16%), but surprisingly it was the Greek newspapers that published the least explicit opinion, only 13%. Regarding editorials, which means the direct expression of the newspaper's position and opinions on the euro crisis, the presence of this type of article was in general very low, with numbers ranging between 1 and 5% in all countries, except in Belgium and Finland (8 and 13%, respectively).

In the ten European countries analysed and during the time periods included in this study, only about 5% of the coverage was interviews, and feature stories were also relegated to the bottom, except in Greece, where 8% of articles on the euro crisis contained human-interest elements. In the other countries, the percentage of articles ranged between 1% (the UK and Poland), 2% (Spain and France), 3% (Germany and the Netherlands), and 4% (Italy, Belgium, and Finland).

Taking into consideration the first two variables, the Netherlands seems to follow the Liberal model guidelines: a proactive coverage and a high percentage of journalistic analysis about the crisis. The Liberal model is marked by professionalism and a type of journalism that looks for a different angle to 'tell the story', as a way to attract more audience. However, we would also expect to find a higher presence of feature stories in these countries, but what we see from the analysis is that the presence of feature stories is very low overall, including in the Liberal model countries. Regarding opinion and commentaries, we would expect to find more presence of this genre in the Polarised Pluralist model countries. We see that Spain seems to fit well, but Greece does not.

Prominence and size of stories

The next variables concerning page placement and size of news stories refer to elements that can also be used to evaluate the importance attributed to

211

the euro crisis issue in each country.[33] Regarding the presence of the euro crisis in front-page headlines, the higher percentage was found in Italy (15%), but it was not followed by other southern European countries as Greece and Spain, in this regard. The Netherlands had 11% and Germany 9% of newspapers' front pages with the euro crisis. Surprisingly, and given that our sample includes periods of time when extremely important events related to the crisis happened, newspapers do not seem to attribute much importance in terms of headlines to the crisis. In general, the presence of the crisis on front pages is low and there is no visible pattern in terms of clusters of countries.

A different way of evaluating the importance of the euro crisis for European newspapers is through the size of their articles, and therefore is related to the space that is reserved for this issue in the newspaper pages. We considered a short article if it had less than 500 words, a medium article if it had between 500 and 999 words, and a long article in the case of 1000 words of more. All countries, except Finland (where the majority of articles published about the euro crisis were short, 86%), show a similar pattern in the size of articles and similar percentages of medium and long news stories. So, it seems, at least at first sight, that space is not used as an element of differentiation in newspapers. Based on normal distribution, we would expect more mid-sized stories than small or long stories, but the fact that most articles are skewed upwards in size tends to run counter to the prevailing wisdom that news stories are getting shorter overall. It could be the wisdom is wrong or that the nature of the euro crisis led to different behaviours, which could make sense due to the complexity of the issues covered.

News sources relied upon

The type of sources quoted in news stories can also convey important information about the news coverage. This analysis showed, above all, that very high percentages of articles (overall near 80%; see Chapter 5 for more details on news sources) were published without any quotes from sources in all countries. Bankers, financiers, and especially economists were privileged sources for journalists, who also cited European officials and government leaders. The most absent source seems to be the public, since less than 5% of articles in all countries included quotes from the represented society, businesses, unions, civil society, social organisations, and so on. Differences among countries in this regard are not instructive, but Polish and Italian journalists generally made the greatest use of this type of sources, whereas Belgium, Germany, and the UK are among the countries that consulted economists the most.

Geopolitical frame of stories

Finally, with the geopolitical frame, we expect to gather information not only on differences and similarities between European countries according to their position in Europe and in the crisis, but also on how the euro crisis was perceived nationally. Articles were coded as having a 'domestic frame' if they addressed the crisis mainly as an internal issue within the newspaper's country; the 'foreign country frame' was used if the article addressed the crisis as an issue internal to another country, portraying this other country as separate from the country in which the article was published (they/them); it was considered that the article conveyed a 'European frame' if the crisis was presented as a European issue, portraying Europe and Europeans as 'us/we/our'; finally, it was also signalled when there was no clear frame in the article.

The first important conclusion to note is that the UK did not portray any geopolitical frame in two-thirds of its entire coverage. This could be partly explained by historical British scepticism towards the EU and the single currency and possibly because of the influence of the *Financial Times* coverage, which tends to see markets and market-related issues as global. When there was a geopolitical frame in British articles, it was predominantly foreign, but the presence of the foreign frame in the Netherlands was even more significant (42%). These two countries also had the lowest percentage of articles with a European frame, 5% in the UK and 12% in the Netherlands. The European frame was strongly portrayed in Poland (65%), Finland (64%), Spain (55%), France (43%), and Germany (40%). Greece was the country with more domestic frame articles (34%), but there is no great difference between these and the articles with a foreign frame perspective (31%).

It should also be noted that the overall result of articles with a European frame is surprising (34%). One important argument used in discussions about Europe and the EU construction has been that the news media are too national and do not express the European perspective of issues very often. These data seem to indicate that, at least in the euro crisis news coverage, it is not always the case. With this sample focused on the euro crisis, it is impossible to answer the question of whether other European issues are reported the same way, but in this case, clearly newspapers are presenting the European perspective more than conventional wisdom and previous debates seem to suggest, a finding that has implications for the idea of the European public sphere that will be discussed more fully in Chapter 11.

When considered in aggregate, the overall results versus expectation are revealed in Table 10.2. However, as noted above, full expectations existed only for Germany and Spain and the expectations for the other countries were less clear and supported by theory because they were

Table 10.2 Expectations of national coverage versus notable findings

Country	Expectation of news coverage	Findings of news coverage
Belgium	Range of story size; event oriented but with some analysis/features; domestic leader focus, but with wider variety of sources; balanced geopolitical framework	More analysis Less opinion More features/interviews
Finland	Range of story size; event oriented but with some analysis/features; domestic leader focus, but with wider variety of sources; balanced geopolitical framework	Less analysis More opinion More features/interviews More short stories More stories with European geopolitical frames
France	Range of story size; event oriented but with some analysis; domestic leader focus, with focus on political leaders; much opinion and commentary; balanced geopolitical framework	Less proactive More stories with European geopolitical frames
Germany	Longer story size; more analysis/features; greater source variety; balanced geopolitical framework	Less proactive Less analysis Less opinion More stories with European geopolitical frames
Greece	Range of story size; event oriented but with some analysis; domestic leader focus, with focus on political leaders; much opinion and commentary; balanced geopolitical framework	Less proactive More analysis Less opinion More features/interviews

Table 10.2 *(Continued)*

Country	Expectation of news coverage	Findings of news coverage
Italy	Range of story size; event oriented but with some analysis; domestic leader focus, with focus on political leaders; much opinion and commentary; balanced geopolitical framework	More analysis More features/interviews Less prominence
Netherlands	Range of story size; event oriented, but with some analysis; domestic leader focus, but with wider variety of sources; balanced geopolitical framework	More proactive More analysis Less prominence More stories with foreign geopolitical frames Less stories with European geopolitical frames
Poland	Range of story size; event oriented but with some analysis; domestic leader focus, but with wider variety of sources; balanced geopolitical framework	More analysis Less features/interviews More stories with European geopolitical frames
Spain	Shorter stories; feature stories; event oriented; domestic leader source focus; much opinion and commentary; domestic geopolitical frame	Less proactive Less analysis More opinion More stories with European geopolitical frames
United Kingdom	Range of story size; event oriented but with some analysis; more features/analysis; more proactive coverage; domestic leader focus, with focus on political leaders, but with wider variety of sources; balanced geopolitical framework	More proactive Less features/interviews More stories without geopolitical frames Less stories with European geopolitical frames

either not included in both the journalistic culture and media systems approaches or did not fall into the archetypes of the theories.

Not all variables used in this research point to clear and relevant differences among countries or to the journalistic culture and media system explanations being sufficient to explain performance in the euro crisis coverage. This is the case, for instance, for placement and size of articles and the types of sources of information cited. The variables do not always point to the expected clusters of countries, given the proposed frameworks of both the Hallin and Mancini and Hanitzsch and colleagues for media systems and journalism cultures. The Hallin and Mancini models seem to make sense in some cases, but they do not fit in others, so it is not straightforward to use this framework to explain country differences in the euro crisis newspaper coverage. It is even more difficult to see the expected patterns if we use Hanitzsch and colleagues' work on journalism cultures. However, given that these authors' initial project does not study many of the countries included in the euro crisis news coverage analysis, our attempt to fill the voids may be the cause of the differences.

In general, the data analysis does not provide strong empirical support for any of the existing frameworks to study comparatively news media and journalism. However, a possible explanation could be that the euro crisis led to a different type of reporting.

Conclusions

This chapter has explored whether different media systems and different journalism cultures are clearly reflected in the way newspapers covered the euro crisis. We did not find significant support for that view. The existing theories showed some failures in providing predictability and explanation across variables and the theories sometimes conflicted with each other in application. Spain, for instance, is given as an example of a country where journalists assume the role of 'populist disseminators' with a market- and audience-oriented approach and therefore news coverage is expected to have more news stories designed to attract audiences. This implies a more proactive attitude in searching for interesting angles to cover the crisis, as well as a focus on feature stories and analysis articles. However, in our analysis, Spain is in the group of countries with less feature and analysis articles and is one of the countries where the presence of news stories not tied to events is lower, together with Italy, France, and Greece, but also Germany. If we include Spain in Hallin and Mancini's Polarised Populist model, the expectations for this country's news coverage are different. Spain should, in this case, predominantly display reactive news coverage (instead of proactive) because limited autonomy of journalism and a strong focus on the government agenda are strong features of this model.

How can the inconsistencies between the expectations raised by the existing theoretical frameworks and the empirical analysis be explained? The euro crisis news coverage showed that, in many cases,

Figure 10.1   Potential clusters based on eurozone participation

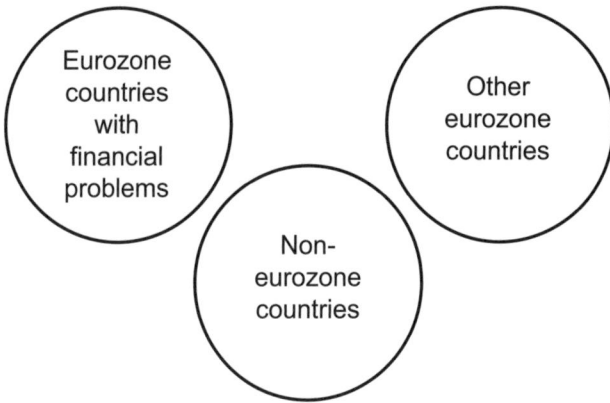

expected clusters of countries were not perceptible. So, where should we look for explanations? Germany, for instance, seems to share some patterns of coverage with the southern countries, and it also shares some similarities with the French coverage. This data analysis does not allow us to draw a consistent picture to posit possible new clusters based on the existing approaches.

A possible explanation for differences in news coverage could be given by the countries' different situation regarding the eurozone and their different involvement in the euro crisis. If we were to break up nations by their political and economic positions in the crisis, we would expect to find three different groups of countries (Figure 10.1). The first group includes Greece, Spain, and Italy – countries that have experienced more difficulties, have received financial assistance, or were singled out for needing economic reforms. A second group includes the remaining euro countries. It includes countries that have had prominent roles in decisions (France and Germany) and others that have been less involved (Belgium, Finland, and the Netherlands). A third group includes countries that have not adopted the single currency (the UK and Poland). Although offering some consistency in some situations, these groupings of countries also do not provide an effective explanation of the differences found in the news coverage among countries.

A different possibility would be to divide the countries based on the levels of their involvement in the crisis (Figure 10.2). This would place France, Germany, Greece, Spain, and Italy in one group, with Belgium,

Figure 10.2   Potential clusters based on crisis involvement

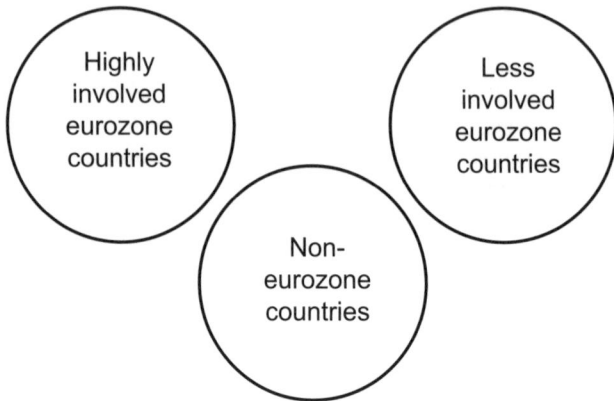

Finland, and the Netherlands in another, and the UK and Poland in a third group. However, when the data are reviewed, this grouping also does not provide a definitive explanation; the different levels of involvement in the crisis did not support any specific pattern in news coverage.

This study has shown more similarities in news coverage relative to impetus, size, focus, placement, and other underlying coverage characteristics than expected and produced some results that are difficult to explain. This differs from other chapters that have shown greater differences in *how* the crisis was covered within the stories themselves. Although our findings contribute to overall knowledge on how the euro crisis was reported in different European countries, they raise more questions than answers about the role of media systems and journalistic cultures on actual practices of journalism. Such conclusions challenge the existing models and the field of comparative journalism practice.

It must be noted, however, that creating such models is, in fact, extremely complex because it requires reductionism of economic, social, and political factors inherent in national practices. The results may end up being polarised archetypes that do not fully explain the hybridity that will be found in many countries. This present study plainly illustrates this major challenge and shows that when the objective of comparative studies is to create predictive and testable theory, empirical analysis of media coverage (the by-product of media systems and journalism cultures) will have to be included in comparative studies more frequently to test the assumptions and explanatory power of the models.

Part IV

Where is the Coverage Taking Europe?

11

Unity or Heterogeneity: The Promise of a European Public Sphere?

Juha Herkman and Timo Harjuniemi

Several analyses have demonstrated that historically, European integration has been a very elite-driven project where ordinary people have had little to say (see Beus, 2010: 16–24; Hooghe, 2003). Since the 1990s, the pressure towards a more open and democratic union has made the European institutions more transparent and the European Commission has become proactive in inventing strategies for public discussions (Beus, 2010: 26). In spite of these improvements, the support for the EU had declined radically at the beginning of the twenty-first century, even in those countries that only a decade earlier were at the forefront of integration – for example France, Germany, and the Benelux and Mediterranean countries (Taylor, 2008: 26–7). The reason for this, according to many commentators, has been the alleged democratic deficit deriving from the increasing gap between the ruling European elites, with a positive stand towards European integration and the more Euro-sceptic people in many European countries. As Simon Hix (2008: 64) concludes, the gap between the attitudes of the elites and masses cannot be resolved solely by the EU's public relations strategy.

The so-called European public sphere has been offered as a cure for the European Union's democracy deficit (see Beus, 2010; Koopmans and Statham, 2010). The discussion intensified especially after Jürgen Habermas, the father of the public sphere theory, declared that the European democracy deficit as well as the problems in European integration can be resolved only through the formation of a pan-European political public sphere, where the European public can deliberate and argue for various interests (Habermas, 2001: 65).

However, studies have repeatedly claimed that, because of the high diversity of languages and political cultures in European countries, the idea of a common European public sphere is inconceivable (see Lingenberg, 2009: 46–7; Trenz, 2008: 56). The construction of identities is still predominantly based on national public spaces, and there is no pan-European news agenda that would be a significant part of everyday lives and self-understanding of European peoples (Schlesinger, 1997, 1999). As Hans-Jörg Trenz (2008: 56) puts it, 'the research agenda has thus shifted from an encompassing European media sphere to the *Europeanization* of public and media communication' (Trenz, 2008: 56). Instead of a supra- or pan-national European public sphere, it has been argued that a more realistic goal is to pursue the Europeanisation of various national public spheres (see Koopmans and Statham, 2010: 36).

The euro crisis is an interesting case for the analysis of Europeanisation of public spheres. It is an overarching topic in European countries, and it has thorough effects on their communicative, political, and social activities. However, it can be assumed that public acts and debates vary nationally since the crisis has rather distinct national consequences. The crisis forms an intrinsic peephole to view the ideas and possibilities of a pan-European public sphere and Europeanisation of national public spheres. If we urge for a European public sphere or Europeanisation of national public spheres, the social imaginaries of European citizens should contain some traces of pan-European norms and identifications (see Heikkilä, 2007). The media can thus shape a reflective surface indicating the possibility or impossibility of an emerging European public sphere.

This chapter explores the possibilities of European-level public debates manifested in the media coverage of the euro crisis by analysing the frames and sources favoured in the national press of ten EU countries. It compares the framings and actors in the stories to find out whether the crisis has created possibilities for the emergence of pan-European deliberation or Europeanisation of the national public debates, or has rather fed the separation of distinct national publics.

The public sphere and the media

Habermas (1996: 360) has defined the public sphere 'as a network for communicating information and points of view', which in a communication process of deliberation are coalesced 'into bundles of topically specified *public opinions*'. In the ideal form of the public sphere, the deliberation between various public opinions leads to the crystallisation of the best argument that guides political decision-making (Habermas, 1989). For Habermas, the public sphere is an abstract universal norm that should be, for democracy's sake, aspired to by all means. It cannot be measured or 'reliably grasped in a solid empirical way' (Splichal, 2006: 710).

As a normative ideal, the public sphere is highly endorsed as a theoretical and political principle, but it has also many restrictions. First, as such it diminishes empirical analyses of social and political life important for the understanding of the concrete practices of power and identity formations. Second, it does not help to comprehend media's complex role in contemporary social and political life. Even if Habermas has more recently seriously considered the relationship between media and politics (Habermas, 2006), the main premise in his theory of the public sphere claims that the emergence of modern political institutions and media organisations led to the decline of the ideal (bourgeois) public sphere by 'colonising' and alienating the public debates in the late-nineteenth and early-twentieth centuries (Habermas, 1989).

However, many theorists have noticed that the media have been intensive and important players in the formations of modern democracies (e.g. Thompson, 1995). Today, the idea of public life is organically tied to various media. There has been a prolific discussion about the 'mediatisation' of politics and even of societies, cultures, and everyday life (see Hjarvard, 2013; Lundby, 2009). Even if the media are not everything, or might have a contradictory influence on political public sphere, it is necessary to analyse the media's role in public life both in national and transnational contexts for several reasons. First, politics have to be visible and meaningful through the media to become legitimised in public. Second, the people need the media to get information about political processes. Third, contemporary political actors must to some extent adapt to the requirements shaped by the media (Koopmans and Statham, 2010: 44–5). Therefore, 'media coverage is crucial for collective actors to gain political resonance and influence' (Koopmans and Statham, 2010: 45).

Indeed, the concept of a pan-European public sphere seems to appear more as a Habermasian normative ideal than realistic empirical entity. As Peter Golding (2008: 133) has reminded us, the nation states seem to remain the primary locus of identity formation and political action for most European citizens. According to Golding, this fact 'has led to a reconstruction of the notion of a European public sphere as an aggregation of national public spheres or an element of all of them, rather than as a novel and displacing form of consciousness which will rapidly supplant the nation states' (2008: 133). Therefore, many scholars have begun to study the Europeanisation of the national public spheres rather than the formation of some pan-national European public sphere (see Koopmans and Statham, 2010).

Ruud Koopmans and Jessica Erbe (2004) have introduced a model of three possible forms of Europeanisation that can be useful in empirical analysis. The first form in their model is the emergence of a *supranational European public sphere*, which refers to pan-European political interaction and development of European-wide media. The second form is *vertical Europeanisation*, consisting of communicative linkages between the national and the European actors, especially the institutions of the EU. The third form is *horizontal Europeanisation*, consisting of communicative linkages between different European countries (see also Koopmans and Statham, 2010: 38–41). The appearance of these forms of Europeanisation can be empirically analysed, for example, through various media coverage. We will next analyse the different forms of Europeanisation in the euro crisis press coverage in ten EU countries by comparing the framings and sources favoured in their newspapers.

Framing the euro crisis

In journalism studies, 'framing' refers to a pattern of organising information within journalism. This organisation includes the selection of some aspects of perceived reality and making them more salient than others in journalistic texts. By emphasising some aspects, frames also exclude others (Borah, 2011; Entman, 1993: 53; Gitlin, 1980: 7).

In our content analysis, a category of 'geopolitical frame' formed a general media frame exploring whether the stories framed the euro crisis in a European, national, or foreign context. This question is essential in terms of the social imaginary of the European public sphere. It illustrates whether the media encounter the crisis as something that happens to 'us' as a pan-European community or to 'us' as a separate nation. It might also be that the euro crisis is framed as something that happens to 'them' (to someone else, not to 'us'). Geopolitical framing is therefore central for media representations of national and European identities and forms a kind of issue-specific frame for the press coverage of the crisis (cf. Vreese et al., 2001: 109).

In general, the most popular geopolitical frame of our sample was the 'European frame' that covered approximately one-third (33.9%) of all articles. However, the 'foreign frame' (22.9%) and 'domestic frame' (19.2%) were also quite popular, both encompassing about one-fifth of the total amount of articles. The European frame was the most used especially in Spain, Finland, Germany, France, and Poland. The category of geopolitical frame was also very reliable since almost 80% of the articles contained one of the three frames above, and the inter-coder agreement percentages were also rather high. It is therefore justified to claim that the European press has most commonly framed the crisis as a common, pan-European event rather than emphasised the domestic or foreign framing or approach to the crisis.

However, it is quite obvious that the euro crisis is commonly framed geopolitically as a European crisis because it certainly is seen primarily as a European problem. The framing also varied quite significantly between the countries (see Figure 11.1). First, in two countries, namely in Belgium and in the UK, 'no geopolitical frame can be coded' was the most popular value. Especially in the UK press, the majority of the stories (66.8%) did not contain clear geopolitical framing; in Belgium the share of these kind of stories was a little smaller (40.5%) and in the Netherlands about one-third of all articles (31.6%). Second, excluding the 'none framings', the Belgian and British press framed the crisis most commonly as a foreign event. The same goes for the Dutch press. Third, the domestic frame was most common in the Mediterranean region (Greece, Italy, and Spain). The domestic framing was proportionally popular also in German and British papers.

It is therefore possible to classify the countries in three categories according to the geopolitical framing of the euro crisis in their press coverage: (1) the countries emphasising European framing, (2) the countries emphasising none and foreign framings, and (3) the countries with no clear emphases but yet relatively strong stressing of domestic framing. The first group contains such central and northern European countries as Germany and France, but also Finland and Poland as well as Spain. The second country group includes northern European countries such as Belgium, the Netherlands and the UK. France and Poland resemble this group in their higher emphasis on foreign than domestic framing. The

Figure 11.1   The amount of European, domestic, and foreign frames in different countries

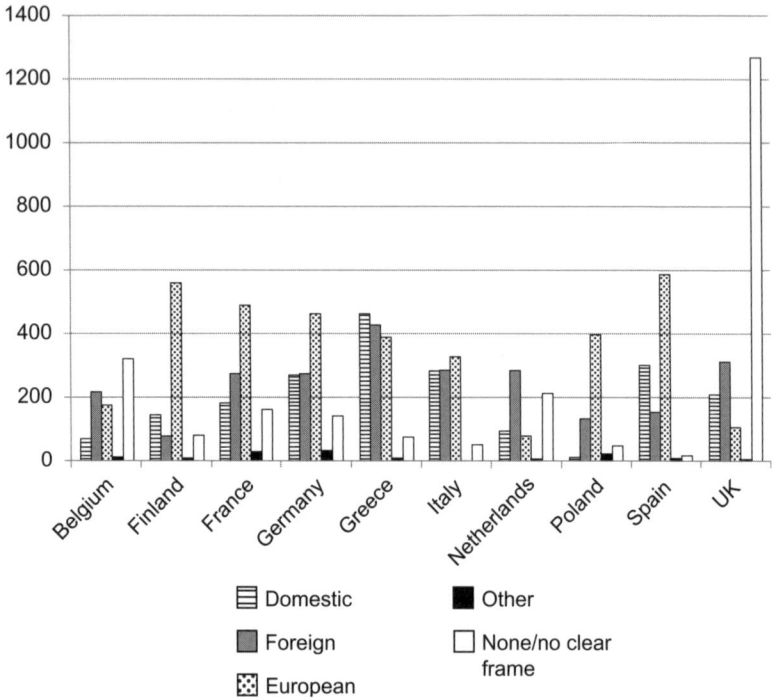

third country group is composed of 'Mediterranean countries' Greece and Italy. The strong domestic framing connects Spain to the Mediterranean camp as well.

In order to have an in-depth look at the Europeanisation of national public spheres in these three country groups, it is important to compare how reasons and causes as well as beneficiaries and sufferers of the euro crisis were represented by the press of respective countries (see Chapter 2). Because the repercussions of the crisis have varied vastly from country to country, it can be assumed that the attitudes towards the questions above differ nationally.

First, it has to be mentioned that more than two-thirds (69.0%) of the articles did not indicate any fundamental root for the euro crisis; in this respect the European press was not keen on blaming any specific event for the crisis. Papers emphasised the much repeated explanations of failures in national and overall fiscal and debt policies as well as the unsound starting conditions of the euro. For example, banks and financial speculations were blamed astonishingly seldom (mostly just in Germany and the UK). Also, political confrontations were seen as minor reasons for the crisis (mostly just in Greece and Spain). All in all, the European press echoed the dominant view of the European political and economic elites which emphasises the lack of fiscal discipline as the root of the euro crisis (see Chapter 8).

The papers were more active when it came to pointing out the ones responsible for solving the crisis, as in 55.1% of the stories responsible actors were mentioned. The European frame dominated this category as well, since in almost one-third of the articles (30.2%), the eurozone members as a group or the EU as an institution were seen as the actors mainly responsible for solving the crisis. Interestingly, in the countries with sovereign debt problems – Greece and Spain – the view that problem countries themselves should solve the crisis was both absolutely and relatively the most popular one.

Similar emphases can be found in the media representations concerning the ways of solving the crisis. In general, suggestions repeated the most legitimate impressions of the euro elite. Granting loans to problem countries (17.3%) and reducing budget deficits in euro countries (12.0%) were the most popular specific mechanisms for combating the acute crisis. National structural reforms (17.1%) and redistributing fiscal authority to EU institutions over national budgets (12.3%) were the most popular broader responses to the crisis. Breaking the eurozone or dropping weaker economies from the euro did not occur as real options in any country. Surprisingly again, in the Greek press the option of deficit reduction appeared to be a more popular response than receiving loans from fellow EMU countries. In addition, the Greek papers were most active in promoting the redistribution of fiscal authority to EU institutions. Only the Belgian, Dutch, and Finnish papers resembled the Greek press in this sense. However, it needs to be stated that austerity measures and deficit reductions have been de facto conditions of the bailout packages. Thus, these options – austerity measures and bailout loans – were not mutually exclusive.

No real beneficiaries of the crisis were indicated in the papers, as only 10% of the stories included a mention in this category. Large investors, financial speculators, and private business were noted in some German, Greece, and Italian articles, equally with Germany as a country benefiting from the crisis.

However, almost two-thirds of the articles indicated a view concerning the sufferer of the crisis. One country or region – namely Greece, EU countries in general, and southern EU countries – was named in 39.9% of the articles as by far the most common sufferer. In all countries, the national press also highlighted domestic problems caused by the crisis. This was also the case in the Netherlands, Belgium, Germany, and Finland – countries that had, in the period of sampling, escaped much of the crisis fallout. Two striking divergences could be found from the press coverage. First, in the Greek papers, the people were seen as the second most common sufferer from the crisis. Second, in German papers, private business and banks were thought to be significant sufferers.

The geopolitical framing of the crisis in three country groups can be roughly summarised as in Table 11.1. Even if European framing generally dominated the media coverage, in northern European countries the crisis was framed rather as foreign, something with an impact on 'someone else'. However, the reasons for and responses to the crisis were seen in their press mainly as a fiscal politics problem, and the crisis should be solved together in Europe. In central and northern countries, the European framing clearly dominated. Otherwise geopolitical framing in

Table 11.1 Geopolitical framings of the euro crisis in different country groups

Geopolitical frames	Nations/region	Reasons for the crisis	Responsible actors
European frame dominates	Germany, France, Finland, Poland, (Spain)/central and northern countries	Fiscal and social policies, starting conditions of euro	Eurozone and EU together
No frame or foreign frame dominates	UK, Belgium, Netherlands, (France, Poland)/ northern European countries	Starting conditions of euro, fiscal and social policies	Eurozone and EU together
Quite even but strong domestic frame	Greece, Italy, (Spain)/ Mediterranean countries	Starting conditions of euro, fiscal and social policies, other political roots	Eurozone and EU together – problem countries themselves

their press echoed the northern European countries' papers. Framing of the crisis differed most radically from the two other country groups in Mediterranean countries, where European, foreign, and domestic framings were quite even (except in Spain where the European frame clearly dominated). In these countries the crisis was framed relatively more often clearly as a political rather than as an economic problem, and their press promoted proportionally more the domestic approach to the responses of the crisis than was the case in other countries.

Sources behind the framing

In our content analysis, different news sources were classified: politicians, officials, economists, bankers, and society representatives. From these source groups, the politicians were the most popular group as first-mentioned sources with a share of almost one-third (31.8%) of all coded articles. After the politicians, the most popular group were bankers (all kinds of bankers together, central bankers included), economists and officials with a share of more or less one-tenth of the articles. The least popular source group was society representatives, with a less than 7% share. In all countries, Angela Merkel was by far the most cited person, except in the UK, where David Cameron was equally popular (see Chapter 5 in this book).

However, whether domestic political leaders or EU officials, the 'own boys and girls' got relatively significant publicity in all countries. The national prime ministers or ministers of finance were often at least the second most popular sources after Merkel. In Finland, the Finnish-born European Commissioner for Economic and Monetary Affairs and the euro, Olli Rehn, was the second most common international source. The same can be said about the popularity of, for example, Mariano Rajoy in the Spanish or Herman Van Rompuy in the Belgian press. Therefore, the national emphases affected the story sources significantly.

However, the sources quoted in the stories indicate that in the media coverage of the euro crisis, we are also witnessing both vertical and horizontal types of Europeanisation of national public spheres. Vertical Europeanisation consists of communicative linkages between the national and European level, and in its *top-down* mode European actors intervene in national public debates in the name of common European interests. In the euro crisis coverage, this seems evident, as the national agendas concerning the crisis are dominated by European elites and their crisis management agendas. We are also witnessing some forms of *bottom-up* integration in which national actors address European issues, as the popularity of Merkel as a primary source of euro crisis articles in almost all countries demonstrates (see Koopmans and Statham, 2010: 41).

In addition, traces of horizontal Europeanisation can be found from the crisis coverage: the euro crisis gives birth to communicative linkages as national media refer to debates and contestations in other European countries. The *weak variant* of horizontal Europeanisation occurs when media report on what happens within the national political spaces of other European countries, as has been the case with, for example, the Greek debt problem, which has become a very common topic in various national public debates. The *stronger variant* of horizontal Europeanisation is characterised by direct communicative linkages between actors in two or more European countries, which is commonly seen in our data when domestic politicians comment on statements given by leading politicians of other countries or officials of European institutions.

In general, there were no significant differences between the most popular source groups and geopolitical framings in the press coverage: European framing was the most common approach in almost every group, and foreign and domestic framings followed European in the above-mentioned order (see Figure 11.2). However, two exceptions can be found. First, bankers were less keen on geopolitical framing of the crisis – or at least, when bankers were used as the main news sources, geopolitical frames were remarkably seldom emphasised in the article. Second, in stories where society representatives – whether business people, trade union representatives, NGOs, activist groups, or just ordinary people – appeared as the main source, foreign and domestic frames were preferred to the European frame. These exceptions can be explained by the fact that bankers had a habit of approaching the crisis solely as an economic subject without any requirements for such political contextualisation as geopolitical framing. In stories with society representatives as main sources, in turn, the focus was often on particular political effects of the crisis.

Politicians were the most popular first source group in all of the studied countries. Bankers or economists were the second most common source, and together they even challenged the popularity of politicians in some countries (Belgium, Germany, Poland, and the UK). Greece was an exception, since the officials were the second most common source

Figure 11.2 Geopolitical framing and different story sources

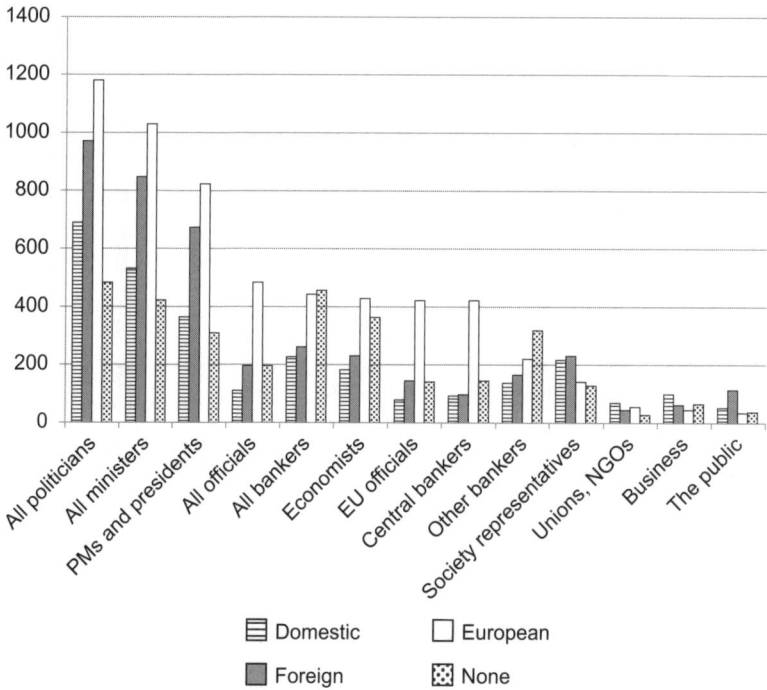

group there. It can also be mentioned that especially in the UK, but also in Germany, the bankers composed a very popular source group – both absolutely and relatively. In Britain, bankers and economists, when combined, formed a source group that was by far the most popular (see Figure 11.3). The variation of source groups also partly explains the different emphases in discussions about the reasons and responsibilities of the crisis in three different country groups defined in the previous section (see Table 11.1).

When comparing main sources with primary sufferers of the crisis, no remarkable differences occurred: within all source groups, a single country or region – mostly Greece, the EU in general, or southern EU countries – was mentioned as the principal sufferer. The second most common option was that no sufferer was mentioned. However, it seems that all source groups emphasised relatively different sufferers, groups close to their own reference group. When it comes to bankers, for example, private business and banks were mentioned as the main sufferers

Figure 11.3 Main story sources in different countries

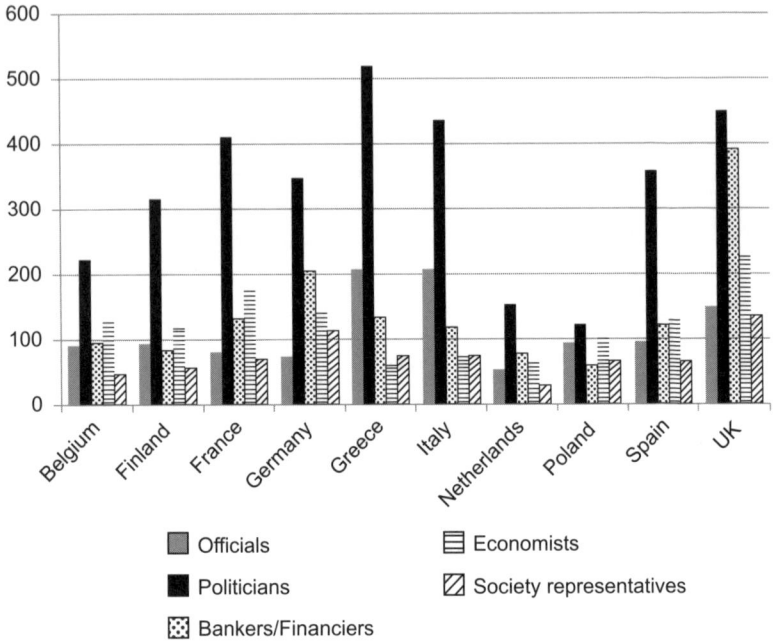

of the crisis more often than with other sources. Similarly, with society representatives, the people and private business appeared relatively often as sufferers. This emphasis is comprehensible when one acknowledges that society representatives meant in content coding precisely representatives of the people and private business.

Another interesting result was that different types of papers gave relatively more publicity to various source groups (see Chapters 8 and 9 in this book). It is not a surprise that politicians dominated the elite papers and economists were relatively the most popular sources in business papers. What is interesting is that society representatives were heard more often in popular than other papers. Combined with the results showing that the stance towards eurozone and European institutions in general was relatively critical and domestic geopolitical framing strongest in popular papers, it can be argued that these papers represented more the nationalist, Euro-sceptic voice of 'the people' than elite papers or business papers that promoted the more Europhile voice of political and economic elites (see, for example, Fiske, 1992; Sparks and Tulloch, 2000) – even if in business papers the foreign geopolitical framing was relatively popular, especially because the majority of the northern European countries' (business) papers (e.g. *Financial Times, Het Financieele Dagblad*) favoured it. One could also argue that the elite press was rather inactive in presenting options different from the elite agenda (see Chapter 8).

Discussion

The euro crisis clearly constructs a topic connecting different national public spheres to each other. Some other researches have indicated that, even before the crisis, monetary politics has been the topic most clearly Europeanising the national public debates in EU countries (see Koopmans et al., 2010: 79–81). According to our analysis, the crisis is simultaneously reported and discussed in news media all over Europe, and European institutions (the EU, the ECB) set the agenda for these discussions through their actions. In general, the geopolitical framing of the crisis emphasises the European approach instead of foreign or domestic frames: the news articles promoted overall European responsibility and solutions to the crisis and were not willing to blame any specific actors – not to mention that dropping problem countries from the eurozone was not seen as a common option.

In addition, the national press coverage seems to have been vertically Europeanised through the crisis, since European actors intervene in national public debates and European institutions penetrate national public spheres in the crisis coverage. We are also witnessing some forms of bottom-up Europeanisation in which national actors address European issues, as well as horizontal Europeanisation, where national media refer to debates and contestations in other European countries. The problems faced in Greece have been especially common topics in these kinds of Europeanised discussions of national public spheres.

However, even if the euro crisis forms a common topic for supranational discussions and Europeanises the national public spheres, there is still a long way to the pan-European public sphere in a Habermasian sense (see Chapter 9). There are at least two reasons for this. First, the European approach framed by national papers would seem to reflect mainly the views of European elites. The political and economic elites dominate the coverage, and the crisis roots and resolutions represented by the media reflect almost solely elite perspectives on the crisis. Society representatives, for example, have been strikingly under-represented in media coverage of almost all countries included.

Second, there are significant national differences in the crisis coverage, as illustrated by the differences in geopolitical framing. At least three groups of countries could be classified according to the emphases in geopolitical framings. First, in such central and northern European countries as Germany, France, Finland, and Poland, the European framing of the euro crisis was the dominant geopolitical frame. Thus, the euro crisis was in these countries dominantly framed as a pan-European crisis that demands eurozone or EU-wide solutions. Second, there were such countries as the United Kingdom, the Netherlands, and Belgium in which the crisis was not often framed geopolitically but when it was, the frame was predominantly foreign. Third, there were the Mediterranean countries, Greece and Italy – and with some exceptions Spain – in which the domestic framing had a strong foothold in the media sphere.

The differences between the countries echo previous studies on euro and EU publicity. In general, the countries with higher levels of intra-EU trade (e.g. Germany, the Netherlands) display higher levels of Europeanisation, whereas countries that have opted out of the eurozone (the UK) or countries with lower interdependence on intra-EU trade (e.g. the UK, Italy) display lower levels of Europeanisation and less favourable evaluations of European integration (Koopmans et al., 2010: 70–1, 95). To some extent, this would also be the case concerning the euro crisis coverage, as the German media – operating from the biggest economy of the eurozone – seem to frame the crisis as a European crisis. The same goes for Finland and Poland with high dependence on intra-EU trade. The British media, in turn, are not keen to frame the crisis in a geopolitical sense, and see it rather as 'someone else's problem', because the UK is not a euro country and its economy is not tied so much to intra-European trade but is rather global and connected to the financial business of the City of London.

Such countries as the Netherlands or Belgium with close intra-European trade relations with the Germans, for example, rupture the picture with their emphasis on foreign framing. However, previous studies have demonstrated that, whereas France has represented the clear case of 'Europhile' and the UK has been the explicit 'Euro-sceptic' for years, the Netherlands has represented a 'critical Europeanism' (Koopmans et al., 2010: 74, 90–1). Even if the Netherlands has marched in a front line of

European integration, support for the EU declined among Dutch citizens long before the euro crisis, because the Netherlands has been one of the largest net contributors per capita into the EU budget (see Hix 2008: 55–8). Thus, the gap between integration-positive elites and more critical masses has in many countries led to the emergence of populist movements protesting against the ruling parties and their euro policies, such as Pim Fortuyn List in the Netherlands at the beginning of the twenty-first century.

The euro crisis might prove to be a pivotal moment in the process of European integration. So far, the common European approach has been elite-driven and somewhat resisted alternative resolution options, thus causing decline in public support for European integration. It can be argued that, even if the coverage of the euro crisis in various national papers shows signs of the Europeanisation of public spheres, a clear lack of unorthodox views is still rather characteristic of European public debates constructed by the mainstream European press. The European social imaginary seems still to be rather elite-driven and exclusive. This is exactly the same problem that Simon Hix sees as the main cause for the democracy deficit in the EU. According to Hix, the EU lacks a real contest of its power and policy, which makes it more a form of 'enlightened despotism' than a democracy (Hix, 2008: 76–86).

Indeed, it is easy to see the euro crisis as European public debate resembling a domestic debate with high levels of media visibility and controversy. It is also easy to argue that these controversies concerning European economic policies should be embraced, if we are to enhance the legitimacy of European integration in the eyes of the public. Our study suggests that the coverage of the crisis – even if it has clearly echoed a European ethos amid the hardships – has somewhat failed to become a domain for combative arguments concerning the roots and resolutions of the crisis.

The big question, then, is: should we pursue some pan-European public sphere at all if the majority of European people do not long for deeper integration, and even single member states would rather promote their national than pan-European interests? Obviously, the answer depends on whether one supports or not the deeper European integration or even federative policies. As long as the solution to this big question among the EU member states remains unclear, the pan-European public sphere cannot really be formed.

12

Conclusions

Robert G. Picard

This book has asked questions about how the euro crisis was portrayed between 2010 and 2012, what readers were told across Europe, and what its implications are for Europe and European institutions. The authors have shown that the euro crisis produced a high level of media attention and that distinct national differences in the patterns of coverage existed. Overall, the euro crisis was primarily portrayed as a financial issue, with most coverage in business sections and business papers. The primary sources quoted were national government leaders and bankers/economists, and a few leaders of political parties and civil society organisations were quoted. Most reporting was market- or event-based and little coverage reflected the impact of the crisis on people, even though the majority of coverage was provided by domestic journalists rather than foreign correspondents.

Across Europe the crisis was primarily portrayed in terms of its domestic impact and domestic responses, and secondarily as a foreign and somewhat European story – except in countries with sovereign debt crisis where it was split between a domestic and foreign/European story. The roots of the crisis were primarily portrayed as national policies in affected nations, the structure of the euro system, and the actions of bankers. The primary responsibility for solving the crisis was portrayed as belonging to the eurozone members as a group, the countries with sovereign debt issues, and the EU. Although the European Union and European Central Bank were shown as central to solutions, they were portrayed as somewhat ineffectual.

In aggregate the coverage depicted all countries as suffering domestically, tended to blame foreign actors/actions for the crisis, and tended to promote European rather than domestic responses to the crisis.

The study found coverage did not explain well the European institutions involved, however, so the mechanisms and consequences of the euro system were not well explored. Economic and social consequences of the crisis and responses were also poorly covered, and thus downplayed. Overall, coverage tended to promote European rather than domestic responses to the crisis and domestic media portrayed political responsibility shifting outside their countries to European-level political and economic actors.

Political and economic events drove portrayal of roots of the crisis, responsibilities for solving the crisis, and the mechanism needed to do so and presentation was mainly driven by dominant views that pre-existed the events. Interestingly, dominant views were primarily reinforced by international rather than national sources. When there was a dominant domestic view, readers were given the impression that both national and international support existed for that perspective.

European institutions were portrayed as leading actors, but there were notable national differences in the amount of attention and trust in their effectiveness. National narratives about the crisis and Europe were based on domestic concerns, national interests and predispositions toward the EU. Citizens' trust in the effectiveness of the EU was shown to align with the press portrayals of European institutions. Nevertheless, even though trust in the EU institutions was declining or low, the press in Europe looked more to the EU rather than their national governments for answers to the euro crisis.

Perspectives on the crisis and what should be done about it varied, but the view that the primary problem of the euro was the failure of some national economic structures and policies was dominant. This book has shown that there is a considerable degree of consonance among domestic newspapers within nations. In comparing countries, the research shows there was more plural coverage in the countries with sovereign debt problems than those without debt issues, but that there were no clear southern or northern European approaches to the crisis. Coverage in countries without critical debt problems tended to reflect similar views on solutions to the crisis. The growth solution was not intensively discussed in coverage, especially in the first phase of the crisis, when most decisions on how to handle the crisis were made.

The language of news coverage was addressed using linguistic analysis of the metaphors used to describe the crisis. This book shows the crisis was primarily framed within the metaphors of war, disease, natural disaster, construction, and games, and these metaphors have significant consequences for the conceptualisation of responsibility related to the crisis, with frames related to war, construction, and games involving human agency – with some party doing something or being acted upon by another; whereas disease and natural disaster portray developments outside the control of human agency. These metaphors thus conveyed a mixed view of the responsibility for the crisis and what kinds of responses could be made.

The volume also considered whether there were differences between coverage in the business press, general press, and tabloid newspapers and found that they were not highly different in basic perspectives and approaches, leading to the conclusion that they are either influenced by the rules of journalistic production and/or are used as instruments by elite powers. The book shows coverage across business papers is more alike than that across general papers and that business paper and general paper coverage were more similar than business papers and tabloids, even though elite perspectives remained similar. The business press was more likely to view issues across borders and thus seems to play a greater role in transnationalisation of European issues than the general press and this would tend to underscore those who argue that the EU and institutions remain elite oriented and focused on financial and business interests.

Overall there tended to be more coverage of the crisis in business newspapers than those of general audiences and papers with a liberal political orientation tended to have more coverage than those with a conservative or neutral political orientation. The book also shows that larger countries devoted more attention to the crisis than smaller countries.

Given different journalistic cultures and media systems in the EU, one would expect domestic differences in stories in terms of prominence, story size, story type, sources relied upon, and geopolitical framework of stories. However, the book shows that journalist cultures and media systems do not explain patterns of coverage of the euro crisis very well. Nor do eurozone and non-eurozone membership or the degree of involvement in the crisis.

The findings align with established communication and political theories and research that show the media focus more on domestic interests than more distant issues, that blame for undesirable developments tends to be placed on factors outside of domestic control, that the media look to elites – government and financial – for leadership and solutions, and that as time passes more reflection on developments looks towards deeper explanations of what has happened and what might be done to avoid issues in the future.

The book indicates that we are still a long way from a mentally integrated Europe and that newspapers still define their identity – and that of their readers – in national terms. Nevertheless, there was strong recognition of a secondary European identity and that issues posed by the euro crisis were not only domestic but European. The portrayal of European institutions as important but not highly effective, however, did not support a case for a stronger Europe. The crisis coverage could be expected to create new expectations of the role of the EU institutions in handling the serious economic and financial issues crisis but, simultaneously, increase distrust and scepticism about the EU among those predisposed to it.

The research has underscored the impact of elite consensus on public debate, with national leaders, bankers, and economists being shown as dominant participants in discussion of and formulating responses to the crisis. This elite orientation does not enhance the public's perception of their abilities to participate in domestic and European decision-making and underscores that Europe and its institutions are still very much an elite rather than citizen construction.

Although the study revealed considerable national differences in coverage, they were often not those that would be expected given comparative media studies or the political salience of issues in the crisis. This raises the question of whether our theoretical understanding was overpowered by the magnitude and scope of the events and issues and requires adjustment when 'normal' levels of consequence are surpassed or whether they need to be fully reconsidered. Whether similar results would be found in comparative European coverage of less momentous events or issues is unknown.

Despite domestic variance in covering the crisis, explaining its consequences and responses, this book reveals the presence of a small European sphere in public consideration of the issues. Coverage clearly asserted European responsibility for dealing with the crisis and, although it accepted domestic fiscal policy as a cause of issues, also portrayed them as broader and more complex than merely the actions of individual countries. Coverage thus integrated both domestic and European issues, developments, and leaders. Although this represents a Europeanisation of the problems and solutions, it still represents dominant domestic, national public spheres but with some assimilation of a European sphere.

The results support previous research that a clear Europeanised public sphere is not evident in Europe – that national politics and culture keep discourse within national dimensions – and that media space in which

Europeans meet to discuss issues as Europeans remains underdeveloped. The study clearly shows that national media attend to developments at the EU level that affect their own nations, suggesting European discourse remains grouped in national spheres. This is closest to the kind of sphere based on 'vertical Europeanisation' that Kleinen-von Königslöw (2012) described. A small amount of coverage in national media referred to discourse taking place in other nations – indicating a limited presence of 'horizontal Europeanisation'.

These findings may represent a slight improvement on the past when Europe and its institutions, and discourse in other nations, were all but ignored in many nations. Whether the findings would apply to coverage of other issues in which Europe was not so fully engaged remains a question.

This result informs the central questions about how debate takes place and the extent to which it is possible to have European, rather than national, debates. In aggregate the results indicate the presence of public spheres at two levels: (1) strong national spheres of discussion and debate based in domestic concerns and issues, and (2) a weaker nascent European public sphere based on shared interests and common challenges. This strength of national spheres is not unexpected given domestic histories, well-established political systems, and rich national identities. The evidence of the emergent European public sphere based on broader interests and joint action indicates, however, that reliance on European institutions is accumulating and that the construction of a secondary European identity is taking place slowly and in limited ways. But the research in this volume also indicates there are different levels of expectations and different forms of participation evident for those two spheres.

Notes

1   We thank Christina Köhler and Lennart Schneider, who prepared the international data set from the data of the national teams and for their help in analysing the data for this research. Christina Köhler also provided valuable help in setting up the codebook in the first phase of this project.

2   10,492 articles were coded. Sampling in Germany, France, and Italy led to a projection of 13,718 articles (see Appendix 1 for the applied method of sampling).

3   When countries appear in tables or figures, we order them according to their interest rates for ten-year government bonds as of July 2012. These interest rates reflect the risk that the financial markets attribute to the sovereign debt of these countries and thereby indicate the exposure of the countries towards the sovereign debt crisis.

4   Please bear in mind that we are not able to control for the number of economic/political journalists employed by the respective newspapers and their resources, nor for different formats and total paginations between countries.

5   There are 837 articles in the European press that deem the structure of the euro system to be a fundamental cause of the crisis (as discussed in Chapter 3), adding to the more negative attitude of the press towards the euro.

6   The number of articles that supported growth measures increased significantly at the end of the period we studied, especially around the EU summit in May 2012 which aimed to boost growth and balance austerity.

7   This theory was first developed by Francis Bacon (1561–1626) in his *Novum Organon*.

8   As an alternative, the differences between the percentages in each country from the average percentage for the eight countries could have been calculated. For two reasons, we decided against this possibility. First, we are not primarily interested in a consensus, between different extreme positions, but in the impact of existing views on the coverage about major events. Second, the eight countries neither represent a representative sample of all relevant

countries, nor are they similar in size or economic relevance. Therefore, a mean would be an artificial construct whose value highly depends on decisions that are not relevant for the following statistical analysis.

9   We captured a broad variety of possible roots with very specialised categories, but some were rather seldom mentioned in the media coverage. Therefore, we included only statements on those roots that constitute the main bulk of coverage about roots.

10 The analysis will be restricted to articles mentioning only one source to each of the three aspects: roots, responsibility, and mechanisms. Otherwise, it would be not possible to exactly link the type of source to the content of quotes. Because of this restriction, some sources had to be neglected.

11 The chapter is the outcome of common research and mutual collaboration. Giovanni Barbieri wrote the second and third sections; Donatella Campus wrote the first, fourth, and fifth sections.

12 In this case, the percentage is calculated on the basis of the total number of articles containing a portrayal of Europe (articles with no portrayal excluded).

13 It should be stressed that the newspapers closer to the y-axis have a very small number of articles; therefore, this element must be taken into consideration in the interpretation of a possible deviancy with respect to the others of the same country or of same typology.

14 The crosstabs between newspapers and partisanship do not show any significant results in terms of quantity and quality of coverage.

15 Percentage of articles with portrayal of EU: Spain 46.7; Italy 58.5; Greece 68.3.

16 Due to space constraints, we have not included the percentages referring to the International Monetary Fund, US, and G20 since they are in most of the cases inferior to those referring to the EU.

17 See, for instance, questions A13 and A14 in the Standard Eurobarometer 77 (Spring 2012), TNS Opinion & Social.

18 Finland and Poland are missing from this analysis. Two reasons explain this absence. The first is technical: during the sampling on newspaper databases for Finnish and Polish press, it was not always easy to find out the pages of the articles; the second is empirically interesting: news on front pages in both countries are often small lines referring to the inner pages. Since there was no way to discriminate the two reasons, we decided not to include them.

19 The European Initiative for Media Pluralism is a pan-European coalition of citizens, media groups, professional bodies, and civil society organisations from across the continent created precisely to draw attention to the lack of media pluralism in Europe.

20   At the request of the European Commission, the Media Pluralism Monitor was developed in 2009 by the University of Leuven, Central European University, Jönköping International Business School, Ernst & Young Consultancy Belgium, and subcontractors in all member states. It proposes a set of indicators and a monitoring tool to 'measure' the threats to pluralism in the member states. Currently, the Centre for Media Pluralism and Media Freedom, a project co-financed by the European Union and based at the European University Institute, is developing a pilot implementation of the 'Media Pluralism Monitor'. For more information see for instance: <https://ec.Europa.eu/digital-agenda/en/independent-study-indicators-media-pluralism>.

21   D_w is calculated by 'summing the squared proportions and subtracting the sum from 1.0' (McDonald and Dimmick, 2003: 66).

22   It can be calculated by the simple average of the marginal univariate indices as explained by Agresti and Agresti (1978: 223). See also Lieberson (1969: 855).

23   D_b is calculated as 'the simple average of the between-groups diversity indices for the m pairs of marginal distributions of the m variables' (Agresti and Agresti, 1978: 226).

24   On the country level, data is aggregated in a set comprising all news stories as if only one virtual publication existed.

25   The calculation of Simpson's D_b takes only two newspapers each time, so if we are dealing with more than two newspapers (four in this case), it will be necessary to calculate the D_bs of all pairs of newspapers (six in this case) and then the average of these D_bs.

26   To analyse differences between two countries, we calculate Simpson's D_b, but if more countries are involved, we calculate the Simpson's D_b of all pairs of countries and take the averages.

27   It should be mentioned that, as the crisis unfolded, France's supposed sovereign debt problems were also addressed on some occasions, however never with the insistence noted in the other cases.

28   As far as we know, no previous research has comparatively investigated the coverage of European issues from this perspective, with the business press as the main reference for contrast. Researchers have usually compared news coverage across nations using general interest papers, ignoring the specialised press (see, for example, Koopmans and Statham, 2010).

29   Data in Figures 9.1 and 9.2 are to be understood in a comparative way: for instance, in Germany too, a 'European frame' prevails, as discussed in Chapter 12 of this book, and nevertheless the number of articles with a 'domestic' frame are above the average of the total of the considered articles.

30 These data do not take into account the different number of pages of each newspaper.

31 Under the label liberal, we included all those newspapers that, depending on the country, either are known as leftist/centre leftist newspapers or liberal ones.

32 This is true even ignoring the impact of communication and media technology, the internet, social media and so on, which increases competition between different news and advertising media. This is leading to differences in various journalist generations depending on their experience on new and older communication technologies, as well as on tightened competition and influences on journalists' careers.

33 The type of paper and whether papers are primarily home delivered or sold at news-stands can influence the extent to which front page placement is an indicator of prominence. Consequently, page placement alone should not be interpreted as an absolute indicator of prominence.

Bibliography

Adam, Silke (2007). 'Domestic adaptations of Europe: A comparative study of the debates on EU enlargement and a common constitution in the German and French quality press', *International Journal of Public Opinion Research*, 19(4): 409–33.

Agresti, Alan, and Agresti, Barbara (1978). 'Statistical analysis of qualitative variation', *Sociological Methodology*, 9: 204–37.

AIM Research Consortium (eds) (2007). *Reporting and Managing European News*. Bouchum: Project Verlag.

Arlt, Hans-Jürgen, and Storz, Wolfgang (2010). *Wirtschaftsjournalismus in der krise*. Frankfurt/Main: Otto Brenner Stiftung.

Arrese, Ángel (2000). 'El desencuentro entre periodismo y economía', *Revista Empresa y Humanismo*, 2(2): 309–35.

—— (2006). 'Simplificación y rigor en el periodismo económico', *Cuadernos de Información*, 19: 42–9.

—— (2010). 'Periodismo económico, entre el boom y el crash (1727)'. In Á. Arrese et al. (eds), *Periodismo económico: Viejos y nuevos desafíos*. Actas del XXII Congreso Internacional de Comunicación (Periodismo económico. Viejos y nuevos desafíos). Pamplona: Eunsa.

Arrese, Ángel, and Vara, Alfonso (2012). '¿Canarios en la mina? La prensa y los riesgos de la burbuja inmobiliaria en España', at Comunicación y riesgo. III Congreso Internacional de la Asociación Española de Investigación en Comunicación, AEIC, Tarragona, 20 December.

Authers, John (2012). *Europe's Financial Crisis: A Short Guide to How the Euro Fell into Crisis and the Consequences for the World*. London: FT Press.

Aydinonat, N. Emrah (2008). *The Invisible Hand in Economics: How Economists Explain Unintended Social Consequences*. London: Routledge.

Bach, Thomas, Weber, Mathias, and Quiring, Oliver (2013). 'News frames, inter-media frame transfer and the financial crisis', *Zeszyty Prasoznawcze*, 1(213): 90–110.

Badouard, Romain (2010). 'Pathways and obstacles to e-participation at the European level', *Journal of e-Democracy and Open Government*, 2(2): 99–110.

Baisnée, Olivier (2007). 'The European public sphere does not exist (At least it's worth wondering ...)', *European Journal of Communication*, 22(4): 493–503.

—— (2013). 'Reporting the European Union: A study in journalistic boredom'. In Raymond Kuhn and Rasmus Kleis Nielsen (eds), *Political Journalism in Transition: Western Europe in a Comparative Perspective*. London and New York: I.B.Tauris, 131–50.

Bastasin, Carlo (2012). *Saving Europe: How National Politics Nearly Destroyed the Euro*. Washington, DC: Brookings Institution Press.

Beblevý, Miroslav, Cobham, David, and Ódor, Ľudovít (2011). *The Euro Area and the Financial Crisis*. Cambridge: Cambridge University Press.

Bee, Cristiano, and Bozzini, Emanuela (eds) (2010). *Mapping the European Public Sphere: Institutions, Media and Civil Society*. Farnham: Ashgate.

Bellucci, Paolo, and Conti, Nicolò (eds) (2012). *Gli italiani e l'Europa: Opinione pubblica, elite politiche e media*. Rome: Carocci.

Bennett, Lance (2011). *News: The Politics of Illusion*. 9th edn. London: Longman.

Best, Heinrich, Lengyel, Gyorgy, and Verzichelli, Luca (eds) (2012). *The Europe of Elites: A Study into the Europeanness of Europe's Political and Economic Elites*. Oxford: Oxford University Press.

Beus, Jos de (2010). 'The European Union and the public sphere'. In Ruud Koopmans and Paul Statham (eds), *The Making of a European Public Sphere*. Cambridge: Cambridge University Press, 13–33.

Blumler, Jay, and Gurevitch, Michael (1975). 'Toward a comparative framework for political communication research'. In S. H. Chaffee (ed.), *Political Communication: Issues and Strategies for Research*. Beverly Hills: SAGE, 165–93.

—— (1995) *The Crisis of Public Communication*. London and New York: Routledge.

Boomgaarden, Hajo G., van Spanje, Joost, Vliegenthart, Rens, and Vreese, Claes H. de (2010). 'News on the move: Exogenous events and news coverage of the European Union', *Journal of European Public Policy*, 17(4): 506–26.

—— (2011). 'Covering the crisis: Media coverage of the economic crisis and citizens' economic expectations', *Acta Politica*, 46(4): 353–79.

Borah, Porismita (2011). 'Conceptual issues in framing theory: A systemic examination of a decade's literature', *Journal of Communication*, 61(2): 246–63.

Bounegru, Liliana, and Forceville, Charles (2011). 'Metaphors in editorial cartoons representing the global financial crisis', *Visual Communication*, 10(2): 209–29.

Breed, Warren (1955). 'Social control in the newsroom: A functional analysis', *Social Forces*, 33(4): 326–35.

Brüggemann, Michael, Hepp, Andreas, Kleinen-von-Königslöw, Katharina, and Wessler, Hartmut (2009). "'Let's talk about Europe". Why Europeanization shows a different face in different newspapers', *European Journal of Communication*, 24(1): 27–47.

Bryant, Jennings, and Oliver, Mary B. (2008). *Media Effects: Advances in Theory and Research*. London: Routledge.

Cammaerts, Bart (2012). 'The strategic use of metaphors by political and media elites: The 2007–11 Belgian constitutional crisis', *International Journal of Media and Cultural Politics*, 8 (2/3): 229–49.

Cano Jiménez, Gema (2010). 'From Spain is different to the party is over: The image of Spain through *The Economist* (2008–2009)', *Textual and Visual Media*, 3: 63–80.

Cardoso, Gustavo, and Jacobetty, Pedro (2012). 'Surfing the crisis: Cultures of belonging and networked social change'. In Manuel Castells, João Caraça, and Gustavo Cardoso (eds), *Aftermath: The Cultures of the Economic Crisis*. Oxford: Oxford University Press, 177–209.

Carragee, Kevin M., and Roefs, Wim (2004). 'The neglect of power in recent framing research', *Journal of Communication*, 54(2): 214–33.

Castells, Manuel (2009). *Communication Power*. 2nd edn. New York: Oxford University Press.

Castells, Manuel, Caraça, João, and Cardoso, Gustavo (2012). 'The cultures of the economic crisis: An introduction'. In Manuel Castells, João Caraça, and Gustavo Cardoso (eds), *Aftermath: The Cultures of the Economic Crisis*. Oxford: Oxford University Press, 1–14.

Chakravartty, Paula, and Schiller, Dan (2010). 'Neoliberal newspeak and digital capitalism in crisis', *International Journal of Communication*, 4: 670–92.

Charteris-Black, Jonathan, and Ennis, Timothy (2001). 'A comparative study of metaphor in Spanish and English financial reporting', *English for Specific Purposes*, 20(3): 249–66.

Copeland, Paul, and James, Scott (2014). 'Policy windows, ambiguity and Commission entrepreneurship: Explaining the relaunch of the European Union's economic reform agenda', *Journal of European Public Policy*, 21(1): 1–19.

Corcoran, Farrel, and Fahy, Declan (2009). 'Exploring the European elite sphere: The role of the *Financial Times*', *Journalism Studies*, 10(1): 100–13.

Cornia, Alessio (2010). 'The Europeanization of Mediterranean journalistic practices and the Italianization of Brussels: Dynamics of the interaction between EU Institutions and national journalistic cultures', *European Journal of Communication*, 25(4): 366–81.

Couldry, Nick, Livingstone, Sonia, and Markham, Tim (2007). *Media Consumption and Public Engagement: Beyond the Presumption of Attention.* Basingstoke: Palgrave Macmillan.

Crespy, Amandine (2013). 'Die eiserne lady, der weiße ritter und die schuldenkrise'. In Frank Baasner and Stefan Seidendorf (eds), *Jeder für sich oder alle gemeinsam in Europa? Die debatte über identität, wohlstand und die institutionellen grundlagen der union.* Baden-Baden: Nomos, 119–41.

Crouse, Timothy (1973). *The Boys on the Bus.* New York: Random House.

Czepek, Aandrea, Hellwig, Melanie, and Nowak, Eva (eds) (2009). *Press Freedom and Pluralism in Europe: Concepts and Conditions.* Bristol: Intellect Books.

Davis, Aeron (2000). 'Public relations, business news and the reproduction of corporate elite power', *Journalism*, 1(3): 282–304.

—— (2003). 'Whither mass media and power? Evidence for a critical elite theory alternative', *Media, Culture and Society*, 25(5): 669–90.

—— (2005). 'Media effects and the active elite audience. A study of communication in the London Stock Exchange', *European Journal of Communication*, 20(3): 303–26.

—— (2006a). 'Media effects and the question of the rational audience: Lessons from the financial markets', *Media, Culture and Society*, 28(4): 603–25.

—— (2006b). 'The role of the mass media in investor relations', *Journal of Communication Management*, 10(1): 717.

—— (2007a). 'The economic inefficiencies of market liberalization: The case of financial information in the London Stock Exchange', *Global Media and Communication*, 3(2): 157–78.

—— (2007b). *The Mediation of Power: A Critical Introduction.* London: Routledge.

—— (2011). 'News of the financial sector: Reporting on the City or to it?', *Open Democracy*, 31 May. <www.opendemocracy.net>.

De Landtsheer, Christ'l (2009). 'Collecting political meaning from the count of metaphor'. In A. Musolff and J. Zinken (eds), *Metaphors and Discourses.* London: Routledge, 59–78.

Dearing, James W. and Rogers, Everett (1996). *Agenda Setting.* Thousand Oaks: SAGE.

Diez Medrano, Juan (2003). *Framing Europe: Attitudes to European Integration in Germany, Spain, and the United Kingdom.* Princeton: Princeton University Press.

Diez Medrano, Juan, and Gray, Emily (2010). 'Framing European Union in national public spheres'. In Ruud Koopmans and Paul Statham (eds), *The Making of a European Public Sphere.* Cambridge: Cambridge University Press, 195–219.

Dinan, Desmond (2011). 'Governance and institutions: Implementing the Lisbon Treaty in the shadow of the euro crisis', *Journal of Common Market Studies*, 49: 103–21.

—— (2012). 'Governance and institutions: Impact of the escalating crisis', *Journal of Common Market Studies*, 50: 85–98.

—— (2013). 'EU governance and institutions: Stresses above and below the waterline', *Journal of Common Market Studies*, 51: 89–102.

Donsbach, Wolfgang, and Patterson, Thomas E. (2004). 'Political news journalists: Partisanship, professionalism, and political roles in five countries'. In Frank Esser and Barbara Pfetsch (eds), *Comparing Political Communication: Theories, Cases and Challenges*. Cambridge: Cambridge University Press, 251–70.

Downey, John, and Koenig, Thomas (2006). 'Is there a European public sphere? The Berlusconi-Schulz case', *European Journal of Communication*, 21(2): 165–87.

Doyle, Gillian (2002). *Media Ownership: Concentration, Convergence and Public Policy*. London: SAGE.

—— (2006). 'Financial news journalism: A postEnron analysis of approaches towards economic and financial news production in the UK', *Journalism*, 7(4): 433–52.

Duchesne, Sophie, Haegel, Florence, Frazer, Elizabeth, and Van Ingelgom, Virginie (eds) (2013). *Citizens' Reactions to European Integration Compared: Overlooking Europe*. Basingstoke: Palgrave Macmillan.

Durham, Frank D. (2007). 'Framing the state in globalization: The *Financial Times* coverage of the 1997 Thai currency crisis', *Critical Studies in Media Communication*, 24(1): 57–76.

Eilders, Christiane (2006). 'News factors and news decisions: Theoretical and methodological and advances in Germany', *Communications: The European Journal of Communication Research*, 31: 5–24.

Eley, Geoff (1992). 'Nations, publics, and political cultures: Placing Habermas in the nineteenth century'. In Craig Calhoun (ed.), *Habermas and the Public Sphere*. Cambridge, MA: MIT Press, 289–339.

Ellis, Arthur (1892). 'Influence of opinion on markets', *Economic Journal*, 2: 109–16.

Entman, Robert M. (1991). 'Framing U.S. coverage of international news: Contrasts in narratives of the KAL and Iran Air Incidents', *Journal of Communication*, 41(4): 6–27.

—— (1993). 'Framing: Toward clarification of a fractured paradigm', *Journal of Communication*, 43: 51–8.

—— (2004). *Projections of Power: Framing News, Public Opinion, and U.S. Foreign Policy*. Chicago, IL: University of Chicago Press.

Esager, Maria (2011). *Fire and Water: A Comparative Analysis of Conceptual Metaphors in English and Danish News Articles about the Credit Crisis 2008*. <http://pure.au.dk/portal/files/40317984/Fire_and_Water.pdf>.

Esser, Frank, and Strömbäck, Jesper (eds) (2014). *Mediatization of Politics: Understanding the Transformation of Western Democracies*. Basingstoke: Palgrave Macmillan.

Fabbrini, Sergio (2013). 'Intergovernmentalism and its limits: Assessing the European Union's answer to the euro crisis', *Comparative Political Studies*, 46(9): 1003–29.

Fahy, Declan, O'Brien, Mark, and Poti, Valerio (2010). 'Combative critics or captured Collaborators? Irish financial journalism and the end of the Celtic Tiger', *Irish Communications Review*, 12: 521.

Fearn-Banks, Kathleen (2010 [1996]). *Crisis Communications: A Casebook Approach*. 4th edn. New York and London: Routledge.

Fiske, John (1992). 'Popularity and the politics of information'. In Peter Dahlgren and Colin Sparks (eds), *Journalism and Popular Culture*. London: SAGE, 45–63.

Flegel, Ruth C., and Chaffee, Steven H. (1971). 'Influences of editors, readers, and personal opinions on reporters'. *Journalism Quarterly*, 48: 645–52.

Fraser, Nancy (1992). 'Rethinking the public sphere: A contribution to the critique of actually existing democracy'. In Craig Calhoun (ed.), *Habermas and the Public Sphere*. Cambridge, MA: MIT Press, 109–42.

Freedman, Des (2008). *The Politics of Media Policy*. Malden, MA: Polity Press.

Galtung, Johan, and Ruge, Mari Holmboe (1965). 'The structure of foreign news. The presentation of the Congo, Cuba and Cyprus crises in four Norwegian newspapers', *Journal of Peace Research*, 2: 64–90.

Gamson, W. A., and Modigliani, A. (1989). 'Media discourse and public opinion on nuclear power: A constructionist approach', *American Journal of Sociology*, 95(1): 1–37.

Gattermann, Katjana (2013). 'News about the European Parliament: Patterns and external drivers of broadsheet coverage', *European Union Politics*, 14(3): 436–57.

Gavin, Neil T. (ed.) (1998). *The Economy, Media and Public Knowledge*. London: Leicester University Press.

Gaxie, Daniel, and Hubé, Nicolas (2013). 'On national and ideological background of elites' attitudes toward European institutions'. In Kauppi Niilo (ed.), *A Political Sociology of Transnational Europe*. Colchester: ECPR Press, 165–90.

Gaxie, Daniel, Hubé, Nicolas, and Rowell, Jay (eds) (2011). *Perceptions of Europe: A Comparative Sociology of European Attitudes*. Colchester: ECPR Press.

Georgakakis, Didier (2004). 'Was it really just "poor communication"? Lessons from the Santer Commission's resignation'. In Andy Smith (ed.), *Politics and the European Commission: Actors, Interdependence, Legitimacy*. London: Routledge, 119–33.

Giddens, Anthony (1999). 'Risk and Responsibility'. *Modern Law Review*, 62(1): 1–10.

Gitlin, Todd (1980). *The Whole World is Watching: Mass Media in Making and Unmaking the New Left*. Berkeley, CA: University of California Press.

Gleissner, Martin, and Vreese, Claes H. de (2005). 'News about the EU constitution: Journalistic challenges and media portrayal of the European Union constitution', *Journalism*, 6(2): 221–42.

Goffman, Erving (1974). *Frame analysis: An Essay on the Organization of Experience*. Cambridge, MA: Harvard University Press.

Golding, Peter (2008). 'European journalism and European public sphere'. In Ib Bondebjerg and Peter Madsen (eds), *Media, Democracy and European Culture*. Bristol: Intellect Books, 121–34.

Gripsrud, Jostein, and Weibull, Lennart (eds) (2010). *Media, Markets and Public Spheres: European Media at the Crossroad*. Chicago, IL: University Chicago Press.

Gross, Peter (2008). 'Dances with wolves: A meditation on the media and political system in the European Union's Romania'. In Karol Jakubowicz and Miklós Sükösd (ed.), *Finding the Right Place on the Map: Central and Eastern European Media*. Bristol: Intellect Books, 125–44.

Grünberg, Jaan, and Pallas, Josef (2013). 'Beyond the news desk the embeddedness of business news', *Media, Culture and Society*, 35(2): 216–33.

Guerrara, Francesco (2009). 'Why generalists were not equipped to cover the complexities of the crisis', *Ethical Space: The International Journal of Communication Ethics*, 6(3/4): 44–9.

Guillaume, Garcia, and Le Torrec, Virginie (eds) (2003). *L'Union Européenne et les médias: Regards croisés sur l'information Européenne*. Paris: L'Harmattan.

Habermas, Jürgen (1989 [1962]). *The Structural Transformation of the Public Sphere. An Inquiry into a Category of Bourgeois Society*. Cambridge: Cambridge University Press.

—— (1996). *Between Facts and Norms: Contribution to a Discourse Theory of Law and Democracy*. Cambridge: Polity Press.

—— (2001). 'Warum braucht Europa eine Verfassung?', *Deutschland*, 6: 62–5.

—— (2006). 'Political Communication in Media Society: Does Democracy Still Enjoy an Epistemic Dimension? The Impact on Empirical Research', *Communication Theory* 16: 411–26.

———— (2009). *Europe: The Faltering Project*. Cambridge: Polity.

Hallin, Daniel, and Mancini, Paolo (2004). *Comparing Media Systems: Three Models of Media and Politics*. Cambridge: Cambridge University Press.

———— (2011). *Comparing Media Systems beyond the Western World*. Cambridge: Cambridge University Press.

Haller, Max (2008). *European Integration as an Elite Process: The Failure of a Dream?* New York: Routledge.

Halloran, James D., Elliott, Philip, and Murdock, Graham (1970). *Demonstrations and Communication: A Case Study*. London: Penguin Books.

Hanitzsch, Thomas (2007). 'Deconstructing journalism culture: Toward a universal theory', *Communication Theory*, 17(4): 367–85.

———— (2011). 'Populist disseminators, detached watchdogs, critical change agents and opportunist facilitators: Professional milieus, the journalistic field and autonomy in 18 countries', *International Communication Gazette*, 73(6): 477–94. DOI: 10.1177/1748048511412279.

Hanitzsch, Thomas, et al. (2011). 'Mapping journalism cultures across nations: A comparative study of 18 countries', *Journalism Studies*, 12(3): 273–93.

Harcup, Tony, and O'Neill, Deirdre (2001). 'What is news? Galtung and Ruge revisited', *Journalism Studies*, 2(2): 261–80.

Harrison, Jackie, and Wessels, Bridgette (eds) (2009). *Mediating Europe: New Media, Mass Communications and the European Public Sphere*. Oxford: Berghahn Books.

Hartung, Uwe (2008). 'Instrumental actualization'. In Wolfgang Donsbach (ed.), *The International Encyclopedia of Communication*, 5: 2295–7.

Heikkilä, Heikki (2007). 'Beyond "in so far as" questions: Contingent social imaginaries of the European public sphere', *European Journal of Communication*, 22(4): 427–41.

Heinrich, Mathis, and Kutter, Amelie (2013). 'A critical juncture in EU integration? The eurozone crisis and its management 2010–2012'. In F. E. Panizza and G. Philips (eds), *The Politics of Financial Crisis: Comparative Perspectives*. London: Routledge, 120–39.

Hellsten, Iina (2003). 'Focus on metaphors: The case of Frankenfood on the web', *Journal of Computer-Mediated Communication*, 8. doi: 10.1111/j.1083-6101.2003.tb00218.x.

Hellsten, Iina, and Nerlich, Brigitte (2010). 'The bird flu hype: The spread of a disease outbreak through the media and internet discussion groups', *Journal of Language and Politics*, 9(3): 393–408.

Hennessy, Alexandra (2014). 'Redesigning financial supervision in the European Union (2009–2013)', *Journal of European Public Policy*, 21(2): 151–68.

Hepp, Andreas, Lingenberg, Swantje, Elsler, Monika, Möller, Johanna; Mollen, Anne, and Hetherington, Marc (1996). 'The media's role in forming voters' national economic evaluations in 1992', *American Journal of Political Science*, 40(2): 372–95.

Hix, Simon (2008). *What's Wrong with the European Union and How to Fix it*. Cambridge: Polity Press.

Hjarvard, Stig (2013). *The Mediatization of Society and Culture*. New York: Routledge.

Hodson, Dermot (2013). 'The little engine that wouldn't: Supranational entrepreneurship and the Barroso Commission', *Journal of European Integration*, 35(3): 301–14.

Hooghe, Liesbet (2003). 'Europe divided? Elites vs. public opinion on European integration', *European Union Politics*, 4(3): 281–304.

Horner, Jennifer R. (2011). 'Clogged systems and toxic assets: News metaphors, neoliberal ideology, and the United States "Wall Street Bailout" of 2008', *Journal of Language and Politics*, 10(1): 29–49.

Hubé, Nicolas (2008). *Décrocher la Une: Le choix des titres de première page de la presse quotidienne en France et en Allemagne (1945–2005)*. Strasbourg: Presses Universitaires de Strasbourg.

Iyengar, Shanto (1991). *Is Anyone Responsible? How Television Frames Political Issues*. Chicago, IL: University of Chicago Press.

Iyengar, Shanto, and Kinder, Donald (1987). *News that Matters: Television and American Opinion*. Chicago, IL: University of Chicago Press.

Iyengar, Shanto, Peters, Mark, and Kinder, Donald (1982). 'Experimental demonstration of the "not so minimal" consequences of television news programs', *American Political Science Review*, 76(4): 848–58.

Jakubowicz, Karol (2008). 'Finding the right place on the map: Prospects for public service broadcasting in post-communist countries'. In Karol Jakubowicz and Miklós Sükösd (eds), *Finding the Right Place on the Map: Central and Eastern European Media*. Bristol: Intellect Books, 101–24.

Joris, Willem, d'Haenens, Leen, Van Gorp, Baldwin, and Vercruysse, Tom (2013). 'Eurocrisis in het nieuws: Een framinganalyse van de verslaggeving in Vlaamse kranten', *Tijdschrift voor Communicatiewetenschap*, 41(2): 162–83.

Joris, Willem, d'Haenens, Leen, and Van Gorp, Baldwin (2014). 'The euro crisis in metaphors and frames: Focus on the press in the Low Countries', *European Journal of Communication*, 29(5): 608–17. DOI: 10.1177/0267323114538852.

Kaitatzi-Whitlock, Sophia (2005). *Europe's Political Communication Deficit*. Bury St Edmunds: Abramis.

Kantola, Anu (2006). 'On the dark side of democracy: The global imaginary of financial journalism'. In Bart Cammaerts and Nico Carpentier (eds),

Reclaiming the Media: Communication, Rights and Democratic Media Roles. Bristol: Intellect Books, 192–215.

Karppinen, Kari (2013). *Rethinking Media Pluralism.* New York: Fordham University Press.

Kennedy, Gavin (2009). 'Adam Smith and the invisible hand: From metaphor to myth', *Economics Journal Watch,* 6(2): 239–63.

Kepplinger, Hans Mathias (1992). 'Artificial horizons: How the press presented and how the population received technology in Germany from 1965–1986'. In Stanley Rothman (ed.), *The Mass Media in Liberal Democratic Societies.* New York: Paragon House, 147–76.

—— (2007). 'Reciprocal effects: Towards a theory of mass media effects on decision makers', *International Journal of Press and Politics,* 12(2): 323.

—— (2011). 'Die Verdunklung des publizistischen ereignishorizontes' [The darkening of the horizon presented by the media]. In Hans Mathias Kepplinger, *Realitätskonstruktionen* [Construction of reality by the mass media]. Wiesbaden: VS-Verlag, 117–37.

Kepplinger, Hans Mathias, and Lemke, Richard (2013). 'Communication in conflicts: Instrumentalizing Fukushima'. Paper presented at ICA Conference, London.

Kepplinger, Hans Mathias, and Roth, Herbert (1979). 'Creating a crisis: German mass media and oil supply in 1973/74', *Public Opinion Quarterly,* 43: 285–96.

Kepplinger, Hans Mathias, Brosius, Hans-Bernd, and Staab, Joachim Friedrich (1991). 'Instrumental actualization: A theory of mediated conflicts', *European Journal of Communication,* 6(3): 263–90.

Kimmel, Michael (2008). 'Metaphor variation in cultural context: Perspectives from anthropology', *European Journal of English Studies,* 8(3): 275–94.

Kjaer, P., and Langer, R. (2003). *The Negotiation of Business News: A Study of Journalistic Source Interaction.* Working paper, 20035. Copenhagen: Copenhagen Business School.

Kjaer, Peter, and Slaatta, Tore (eds) (2007). *Mediating Business: The Expansion of Business Journalism.* Copenhagen: Copenhagen Business School Press.

Kleinen-von Königslöw, Katharina (2012). 'Europe in crisis? Testing the stability and explanatory factors of the Europeanization of national public spheres', *International Communication Gazette,* 74(5): 443–63.

Klimkiewicz, Beata (2009). 'Is the clash of rationalities leading nowhere? Media pluralism in European regulatory policies'. In Andrea Czepek, Melanie Hellwig, and Eva Nowak (eds), *Press Freedom and Pluralism in Europe: Concepts and Conditions.* Bristol: Intellect Books, 45–74.

——— (2010). 'Structural media pluralism', *International Journal of Communication*, 4: 906–13.

Koikkalainen, Kati (2007). 'The local and the international in Russian business journalism: Structures and practices', *Europe Asia Studies*, 59(8): 1315–29.

Koivisto, Juha, and Väliverronen, Esa (1996). 'The resurgence of the critical theories of public sphere', *Journal of Communication Inquiry*, 20(2): 18–36.

Koopmans, Ruud, and Erbe, Jessica (2004). 'Towards a European public sphere? Vertical and horizontal dimensions of Europeanized political communication', *Innovation*, 17(2): 97–118.

Koopmans, Ruud, Erbe, Jessica, and Meyer, Martin F. (2010). 'The Europeanization of public sphere: Comparisons across issues, time, and countries'. In Ruud Koopmans and Paul Statham (eds), *The Making of a European Public Sphere*. Cambridge: Cambridge University Press, 34–62.

Koopmans, Ruud, and Statham, Paul (eds) (2010). *The Making of a European Public Sphere: Media Discourse and Political Contention*. Cambridge: Cambridge University Press.

Kopper, Gerd (2007). 'Research and the meta-level of practice: Implications for training, online communicating and defining rules of European journalism'. In AIM Research Consortium (ed.), *Reporting and Managing European News: Final Report of the Project 'Adequate Information Management in Europe' 2004–2007*. Bochum and Freiburg: Projekt Verlag, 183–96.

Krosnick, Jon, and Kinder, Donald (1990). 'Altering the foundations of support for the president through priming', *American Political Science Review*, 84: 497–512.

Krzyzanowski, Michal (2009). 'Europe in crisis. Discourses on crisis events in the European press 1956–2006', *Journalism Studies*, 10(1): 18–35.

Kuhn, Raymond (2014). 'What's so French about French political journalism?' In Raymond Kuhn and Rasmus K. Nielsen (eds) (2014), *Political Journalism in Transition: Western Europe in a Comparative Perspective*. London and New York: I.B.Tauris, 27–46.

Kuhn, Raymond, and Nielsen, Rasmus K. (eds) (2014). *Political Journalism in Transition: Western Europe in a Comparative Perspective*. London and New York: I.B.Tauris.

Kunelis, Risto, and Reunanen, Esa (2012). 'Media in political power: A Parsonian view on the differentiated mediatization of Finnish decision makers', *International Journal of Press/Politics*, 17(1): 56–75.

Kutter, Amelie (2014). 'A catalytic moment: The Greek crisis in the German financial press', *Discourse and Society*, 25(4): 446–66.

Kuzyk, Pat, and McCluskey, Jill J. (2006). 'The political economy of the media: Coverage of the lumber tariff dispute', *The World Economy*, 29(5): 655–67.

Lakoff, George (1993). 'The contemporary theory of metaphor'. In A. Ortony (ed.), *Metaphor and Thought*. 2nd edn. Cambridge: Cambridge University Press.

—— (2008). *The Political Mind: Why you Can't Understand 21st Century American Politics with an 18th-Century Brain*. New York: Viking Adult.

Lakoff, George, and Johnson, Mark (1980). *Metaphors We Live By*. Chicago, IL: University of Chicago Press.

Lakoff, George, and Turner, Mark (1989). *More than Cool Reason: A Field Guide to Poetic Metaphor*. Chicago, IL: University of Chicago Press.

Lang, Kurt, and Lang, Gladys Engel (1953). 'The unique perspective of television and its effect: A pilot study', *American Sociological Review*, 18: 2–12.

Lapavitsas, Costas (2012). *Crisis in the Eurozone*. London: Verso.

Larcinese, Valentino, Puglisi, Riccardo, and Snyder Jr, James M. (2011). 'Partisan bias in economic news: Evidence on the agenda-setting behavior of U.S. newspapers', *Journal of Public Economics*, 95: 1178–89.

Lauristin, Marju (2007). 'The European public sphere and the social imaginary of the "new Europe"', *European Journal of Communication*, 22(4): 397–412.

Lewis, Justin. (2010). 'Normal viewing will be resumed shortly: News, recession and the politics of growth', *Popular Culture*, 8: 161–5.

Lieberson, Stanley (1969). 'Measuring population diversity', *American Sociological Review*, 34(6): 850–62.

Lingenberg, Swantje (2009). 'The citizen audience and European transcultural public spheres: Exploring civic engagement in European political communication', *Communications*, 34 (2009): 45–72.

Lippmann, Walter (1922). *Public Opinion*. New York: Macmillan Co.

Lloyd, John, and Marconi, Cristina (2014). *Reporting the EU: News, Media and the European Institutions*. London: I.B.Tauris.

Lundby, Knut (ed.) (2009). *Mediatization: Concept, Changes, Consequences*. New York: Peter Lang.

McAllister, Ian (2007). 'The personalization of politics'. In Russell J. Dalton and Hans-Dieter Klingemann (eds), *The Oxford Handbook of Political Behaviour*. Oxford: Oxford University Press, 571–88.

McCloskey, Donald N. (1983). 'The rhetoric of economics', *Journal of Economic Literature*, 21: 481–517.

—— (1988). *The Rhetoric of Economics*. Madison, WI: University of Wisconsin Press.

—— (1995). 'Metaphors economists live by', *Social Research*, 62(2): 215–37.

McCombs, Maxwell E. (1994). 'News influence on our picture of the world'. In J. Bryant and Dolf Zillmann (eds), *Media Effects: Advances in Theory and Research*. Hillsdale, NJ: Lawrence Erlbaum Associates, 1–16.

—— (2004). *Setting the Agenda: The Mass Media and Public Opinion*. Cambridge: Polity.

McCombs, Maxwell E., and Shaw, Donald L. (1972). 'The agenda-setting function of mass media', *Public Opinion Quarterly*, 36(2): 176.

—— (1993). 'The evolution of agenda-setting research: Twenty-five years in the marketplace of ideas', *Journal of Communication*, 43(2): 58–67.

McCombs, Maxwell E., Shaw, Donald L., and Weaver, David (eds) (1997). *Communication and Democracy: Exploring the Intellectual Frontiers in Agenda-Setting Theory*. Mahwah, NJ: Lawrence Erlbaum.

McDonald, Daniel, and Dimmick, John (2003). 'The conceptualization and measurement of diversity', *Communication Research*, 30: 60–79.

Machill, Marcel, Beiler, Markus, and Fischer, Carol (2006). 'Europe-topics in Europe's media: The debate about the European public sphere: A meta-analysis of media content analyses', *European Journal of Communication*, 21(1): 57–88.

Machin, David, and Niblock, Sarah (2011). 'The new breed of business journalism for niche global news', *Journalism Studies*, 11(6): 783–98.

McQuail, Denis (1992). *Media Performance: Mass Communication and the Public Interest*. London: SAGE.

—— (2000). *McQuail's Mass Communication Theory*. London: SAGE.

—— (2013). *Journalism and Society*. London: SAGE.

Madrick, Jeffrey (2002). 'The influence of the financial media over international economic policy'. In J. Eatwell and L. Taylor (eds), *International Capital Markets: Systems in Transition*. Oxford: Oxford University Press, 231–53.

Manning, Paul (2012). 'Financial journalism, news sources and the banking crisis', *Journalism*, 14(2): 173–89.

Marini, Rolando (eds) (2003). *Comunicare l'Europa: Campagne elettorali, informazione, comunicazione istituzionale*. Perugia: Morlacchi editore.

Mazzoleni, Gianpietro (2000). 'A return to civic and political engagement prompted by personalized political leadership?', *Political Communication*, 17: 325–8.

Menz, Georg, and Smith, Mitchell P. (2013). 'Kicking the can down the road to more Europe? Salvaging the euro and the future of European economic governance', *Journal of European Integration*, 35(3): 195–206.

Mercille, Julien (2013a). 'The role of the media in sustaining Ireland's housing bubble', *New Political Economy*, 120. Online version. DOI: 10.1080/13563467.2013.779652.

—— (2013b). 'The role of media in fiscal consolidation programmes: The case of Ireland', *Cambridge Journal of Economics*, 120. Online version. DOI: 10/1093/cje/bet068.

Merrill, Gary J. (2012). 'The revolution must wait: Economic, business and financial journalism beyond the 2008 crisis', *Ethical Space: The International Journal of Communication Ethics*, 9(1): 41–51.

Meyer, Christoph O. (2005). 'The Europeanization of media discourse: A study of quality press coverage of economic policy coordination since Amsterdam', *Journal of Mass Communication and Society*, 43(1): 121–48.

Meyer, Thomas (2002). *Media Democracy: How the Media Colonizes Politics*. Cambridge: Polity Press.

Miettinen, Timo (2010). 'Taantuma, sairaus, kriisi – talouden uusi anatomia' [Recession, illness, crisis – the new anatomy of economy], *Liiketaloudellinen Aikakauskirja*, 2: 210–14.

Millar, Frank E., and Beck, Debra B. (2004). 'Metaphors of crisis'. In D. P. Millar and R. L. Heath (eds), *Responding to Crisis: A Rhetorical Approach to Crisis Communication*. Mahwah, NJ: Lawrence Erlbaum Associates, 153–66.

Molotch, Harvey, and Lester, Marilyn (1974). 'News as purposive behavior: On the strategic use of routine events, accidents, and scandals', *American Sociological Review*, 39: 101–12.

Morgan, David (1995). 'British media and European Union news: The Brussels news beat and its problems', *European Journal of Communication*, 10(3): 321–43.

Mylonas, Yiannis (2012). 'Media and the economic crisis of the EU: The "culturalization" of a systemic crisis and Bild Zeitung's framing of Greece', *Triple C*, 10(2): 646–71.

Negrine, Ralph, Kejanlioglu, Beybin, Aissaoui, Rabah, and Papathanassopoulos, Stylianos (2008). 'Turkey and the European Union: An analysis of how the press in four countries covered Turkey's bid for accession in 2004', *European Journal of Communication*, 23(1): 47–68.

Nisbet, Matthew C. (2008). 'Agenda building'. In Wolfgang Donsbach (ed.), *The International Encyclopedia of Communication*. Oxford: John Wiley & Sons, 140–5.

Noelle-Neumann, Elizabeth, and Mathes, Ranier (1987). 'The "event as event" and the "event as news": The significance of "consonance" for media effects research', *European Journal of Communication*, 2: 391–414.

Nord, Lars (2008). 'Comparing Nordic media systems: North between West and East', *Central European Journal of Communication*, 1: 95–110.

Noord, Paul van den, and Székely, István (2011). *Economic Crisis in Europe: Causes, Consequences and Responses*. London: Routledge and European Commission.

Offerhaus, Anke (2013). *I Just Hope the Whole Thing Won't Collapse: Understanding and Overcoming the EU Financial Crisis from the Citizens' Perspective*.

TranState Working Papers from University of Bremen, 168, Collaborative Research Center, 597: Transformations of the State.

Olausson, Ulrika (2010). 'Towards a European identity? The news media and the case of climate change', *European Journal of Communication*, 25(2): 138–52.

Ondarza, Nicolai von (2013). 'Auf dem weg zur union in der Union: Institutionelle auswirkungen der differenzierten integration in der eurozone auf die EU', *Integration*, 1: 17–33.

Ornebring, Henrik (2009). 'Questioning European journalism', *Journalism Studies*, 10(1): 2–17.

Parker, Richard (1997). *Journalism and Economics: The Tangled Webs of Profession, Narrative, and Responsibility in Modern Democracy*. Discussion Paper, D-25. Cambridge, MA: Joan Shorenstein Center, Harvard University.

Parsons, Wayne (1989). *The Power of the Financial Press: Journalism and Economic Opinion in Britain and America*. Aldershot: Edward Elgar.

Peckham, Robert (2013). 'Economies of contagion: Financial crisis and pandemic', *Economic and Society*, 42(2): 226–48.

Pérez, Francisco (2013). *Political Communication in Europe: The Cultural and Structural Limits of the European Public Sphere*. New York: Palgrave Macmillan.

Peter, Jochen, Semetko, Holly A., and Vreese, Claes H. de (2003). 'EU politics on television news: A cross-national comparative study', *European Union Politics*, 4(3): 305–27.

Pfetsch, Barbara (1999). *Government News Management – Strategic Communication in Comparative Perspective*. Veröffentlichungsreihe der Abteilung Öffentlichkeit und Soziale Bewegungen des Forschungsschwerpunkts Sozialer Wandel, Institutionen und Vermittlungsprozesse des Wissenschaftszentrums Berlin für Sozialforschung, No. FS III 99–101. <www.econstor.eu/bitstream/1 0419/49821/1/30895761X.pdf> (accessed September 2013).

Pfetsch, Barbara, Adam, Silke, and Escher, Barbara (2008). 'The contribution of the press to Europeanization of public debates: A comparative study of issue salience and conflict lines of European integration', *Journalism*, 9(4): 465–92.

Porto, M. Dolores, and Romano, Manuela (2013). 'Newspaper metaphors: Reusing metaphors across media genres', *Metaphor and Symbol*, 28(1): 60–73.

Post, Senja, and Vollbracht, Matthias (2013). 'Processing crisis news: Media coverage of the economy in light of the euro-stability crisis', *Zeitschrift für Marktwirtschaft und Ethik (Journal of Market and Ethics)*, 2013(2): 116–30.

Princen, Sebastiaan (2009). *Agenda-Setting in the European Union*. London: Palgrave Macmillan.

Privitera, Walter (2012). *Gli usi della sfera pubblica*. Milan: Mimesis.

Project for Excellence in Journalism (2009). *Covering the Great Depression: How the Media have Depicted the Economic Crisis during Obama's Presidency*. Washington, DC: Pew Research Center.

Quiring, Oliver, and Weber, Mathias (2012). 'Between usefulness and legitimacy: Media coverage of governmental intervention during the financial crisis and selected effects', *International Journal of Press/Politics*, 17(3): 294–315.

Quiring, Oliver, Kepplinger, Hans Matthias, Weber, Mathias, and Geiß, Stefan (2013). *Lehman Brothers und die folgen: Berichterstattung zu wirtschaftlichen interventionen des Staates*. Wiesbaden: Springer VS.

Rajan, Raghuram. G. (2010). *Fault Lines: How Hidden Fractures Still Threaten the World Economy*. Princeton, NJ: Princeton University Press.

Ramonet, Ignatio (2002). *A rirania da comunicação*. Porto: Campo das Letras.

Rantanen, Terhi (2012). 'In nationalism we trust?' In Manuel Castells, João Caraça, and Gustavo Cardoso (eds), *Aftermath: The Cultures of the Economic Crisis*. Oxford University Press, 132–53.

Reese, Stephen D. (2010). 'Finding frames in a web of culture: The case of the war on terror'. In P. D'Angelo and J. A. Kuypers (eds), *Doing News Framing Analysis: Empirical and Theoretical Perspectives*. New York: Routledge, 84–109.

Reich, Zvi (2012). 'Different practices, similar logic: Comparing news reporting across political, financial and territorial beats', *International Journal of Press/ Politics*, 17(1): 76–99.

Reinemann, Carsten (2003). *Medienmacher als mediennutzer: Kommunikations- und einflussstrukturen im politischen journalismus der gegenwart*. Cologne: Böhlau.

Reinhart, Carmen, and Rogoff, Kenneth S. (2009). *This Time is Different: Eight Centuries of Financial Folly*. Princeton, NJ: Princeton University Press.

Richardt, Susanne (2005). *Metaphor in Languages for Special Purposes: The Function of Conceptual Metaphor in Written Expert Language and Expert- Lay Communication in the Domains of Economics, Medicine and Computing*. Frankfurt am Main: Peter Lang.

Risse, Thomas (2010). *Community of Europeans? Transnational Identities and Public Spheres*. Ithaca, NY: Cornell University Press.

Salgado, Susana (2010). *Os Candidatos Presidenciais: Construção de Imagens e Discursos nos Media* [Presidential Candidates: Construction of Images and Discourses in the Media]. Coimbra: Minerva Coimbra.

——— (2012). 'Electoral campaigns and media coverage: Theoretical approaches and contributions to the understanding of the interactions between politics and media', *Revista Brasileira de Ciência Política*, 9: 229–53. Brasília (in Portuguese).

—— (2014a). 'The media of political communication'. In Carsten Reinemann (ed.), *Political Communication Volume of the Handbook of Communication Sciences (HOCS)*, De Gruyter: Mouton.

—— (2014b). *The Internet and Democracy Building in Lusophone African Countries*. Surrey: Ashgate.

Sandvoss, Cornel (2010). 'Conceptualizing the global economic crisis in popular communication research', *Popular Communication*, 8(3): 154–61.

Scheufele, Dietram A. (1999). 'Framing as a theory of media effects', *Journal of Communication*, 49, 103–22.

Scheufele, Dietram A., and Tewksbury, David (2007). 'Framing, agenda setting, and priming: The evolution of three news media effects models', *Journal of Communication*, 57: 9–20.

Schifferes, Steve, and Coulter, Stephen (2012). 'Downloading disaster: BBC news online coverage of the global financial crisis', *Journalism*, 14(2): 228–52.

Schifferes, Steve (2011). 'The future of financial journalism in the age of austerity', Inaugural Lecture 2011, Marjorie Dean Financial Journalism Foundation, London. <https://www.city.ac.uk/_data/assets/pdf_file/0016/151063/TheFuture ofFinancialJournalismintheAgeofAusterity.pdf>.

Schiffrin, Anya (ed.) (2011). *Bad News: How America's Business Press Missed the Story of the Century*. New York: New Press.

Schiffrin, Anya, and Fagan, Ryan (2012). 'Are we all Keynesians now? The US press and the American Recovery Act of 2009', *Journalism*, 14(2): 151–72.

Schlesinger, Philip (1997). 'From cultural defence to political culture: Media, politics and collective identity in the European Union', *Media, Culture and Society*, 19(3): 369–91.

—— (1999). 'Changing space of political communication: The case of the European Union', *Political Communication*, 16: 263–79.

—— (2003). *The Babel of Europe? An Essay on Networks and Communicative Spaces*. ARENA, Working Paper 22/03. <www.arena.uio.no/publications/ working-papers2003/papers/03_22.xml>.

—— (2007). 'A cosmopolitan temptation', *European Journal of Communication*, 22(4): 413–26.

Schön, Donald (1993). 'Generative metaphor: A perspective on problem-setting in social policy'. In A. Ortony (ed.), *Metaphor and Thought*. Cambridge: Cambridge University Press, 137–63.

Schranz, Mario, and Eisenegger, Mark (2011). 'The media construction of the financial crisis in a comparative perspective: An analysis of newspapers in the

UK, USA and Switzerland between 2007 and 2009', *Swiss Journal of Sociology*, 37(2): 241–58.

Schuster, Thomas (2006). *The Markets and the Media*. Lanham, MD: Lexington Books.

Schütz, Alfred (1964). 'The well-informed citizen: An essay on the social distribution of knowledge'. In Arvid Brodersen (ed.), *Collected Papers II: Studies in Social Theory*. The Hague: Martinus Nijhoff, 120–34.

Semetko, Holli A., Claes H. de Vreese, and Jochen, Peter (2000). 'Europeanised politics – Europeanised media? European integration and political communication', *West European Politics*, 23(4): 121–41.

Shoemaker, Pamela J., and Cohen, Akiba A. (2006) *News Around the World: Content, Practitioners, and the Public*. New York: Routledge.

Shoemaker, Pamela, and Vos, Timothy (2009). *Gatekeeping Theory*. London: Routledge.

Shoemaker, Pamela J., Danielian, Lucig H., and Brendlinger, Nancy (1991). 'Deviant acts, risky business and U.S. interests: The newsworthiness of world events', *Journalism Quarterly*, 68(4): 313–27.

Simpson, E. H. (1949). 'Measurement of Diversity', *Nature* 163 (April 30): 688.

Skorczynska, Hanna, and Deignan, Alice (2006). 'Readership and purpose in the choice of economics metaphors', *Metaphor and Symbol*, 21(2): 87–104.

Sparks, Colin, and Tulloch, John (eds) (2000). *Tabloid Tales: Global Debates over Media Standards*. Lanham, MD: Rowman & Littlefield.

Splichal, Slavko (2006). 'In search of a strong European public sphere: Some critical observations on conceptualizations of publicness and the (European) public sphere', *Media, Culture and Society*, 28(5): 695–714.

Staab, Joachim Friedrich (1990). 'The role of news factors in news selection: A theoretical reconsideration', *European Journal of Communication*, 5(4): 423–43.

Starkman, Dean (2012). 'A narrowed gaze: How the business press forgot the rest of us', *Columbia Journalism Review*, Jan./Feb.: 24–30.

——— (2014). *The Watchdog that Didn't Bark: The Financial Crisis and the Disappearance of Investigative Journalism*. New York: Columbia University Press.

Strömbäck, Jesper (2008). 'Four phases of mediatization: An analysis of the mediatization of politics', *International Journal of Press/Politics*, 13(3): 228–46.

Strömbäck, Jesper, and Kaid, Lynda L. (2008). 'A framework for comparing election news coverage around the world'. In J. Strömbäck and L. L. Kaid (eds), *Handbook of Election News Coverage around the World*. New York and Abingdon: Routledge, 1–20.

Strömbäck, Jesper, Jenssen, Anders, and Aalberg, Toril (2010). 'News coverage of the financial crisis and public perception of Government regulation'. Paper presented at the American Political Science Association Annual Meeting, Washington, DC, 25 September.

Swanson, David, and Mancini, Paolo (eds) (1996). *Politics, Media and Modern Democracy: An International Study of Innovations in Electoral Campaigning and their Consequences.* Westport, CT: Praeger Publishers.

Tambini, Damian (2010). 'What are financial journalists for?', *Journalism Studies,* 11(2): 158–74.

Taylor, Charles (2008). *Modern Social Imaginaries.* Durham, NC: Duke University Press.

Terrington, Simon, and Ashworth, Matt (2008). 'Plurality: What do we Mean by it? What do we Want from it?'. In Tim Gardam and David A. L. Levy (eds), *The Price of Plurality: Choice, Diversity and Broadcasting Institutions in the Digital Age.* Oxford: Oxford Reuters Institute for the Study of Journalism/ Ofcom, 51–7.

Thompson, John B. (1995). *The Media and Modernity: A Social Theory of the Media.* Cambridge: Polity Press.

Thompson, Peter A. (2009). 'Market manipulation? Applying the propaganda model to financial media reporting', *Westminster Papers in Communication and Culture,* 6(2): 73–96.

—— (2013). 'Invested interests? Reflexivity, representation and reporting in financial markets', *Journalism,* 14(2): 208–27.

Titley, Gavan (2012). 'Budgetjam! A communications intervention in the political economic crisis in Ireland', *Journalism,* 14(2): 292–306.

Trenz, Hans-Jörg (2004). 'Media coverage on European governance: Exploring the European public sphere in national quality newspapers', *European Journal of Communication,* 19(3): 291–319.

—— (2008). 'Media: The unknown player in European integration'. In Ib Bondebjerg and Peter Madsen (eds), *Media, Democracy and European Culture.* Bristol: Intellect Books, 49–64.

Tulloch, John (2009). 'From amnesia to apocalypse: Reflections on journalism and the credit crunch', *Ethical Space: The International Journal of Communication Ethics,* 6 (3/4): 99–109.

Uchitelle, Louise (2011). 'The uses and misuses of economics in daily journalism', *History of Political Economy,* 43(2): 363–8.

Ulmer, Robert, Sellnow, Timothy, and Segger, Matthew (2014). *Effective Crisis Communication: Moving from Crisis to Opportunity.* 3rd edn. London: SAGE.

Usher, Nikki (2012). 'Ignored, uninterested, and the blame game: How the *New York Times*, marketplace and The Street distanced themselves from preventing the 2007–2008 financial crisis', *Journalism*, 14(2): 190–207.

Valcke, Peggy (2011). *Risk-Based Regulation in the Media Sector: The Way Forward to Advance the Media Pluralism Debate in Europe?* Interdisciplinary Centre for Law and ICT (ICRI) Research Paper Series. <www.law.kuleuven.be/icri> (accessed February 2014).

Van Aelst, Peter, Sheafer, Tamir, and Stanyer, James (2012). 'The personalization of mediated political communication: A review of concepts, operationalizations and key findings', *Journalism*, 13(2): 203–20.

Van Gorp, Baldwin (2007). 'The constructionist approach to framing: Bringing culture back in', *Journal of Communication*, 57: 60–78.

——— (2010). 'Strategies to take subjectivity out of framing analysis'. In P. D'Angelo and J. A. Kuypers (eds), *Doing News Framing Analysis: Empirical and Theoretical Perspectives*. New York: Routledge, 84–109.

Veltri, Guiseppe A. (2012). 'Information flows and centrality among elite European newspapers', *European Journal of Communication*, 27(4): 354–75.

Vreese, Claes H. de (2001). 'Europe in the news: A cross-national comparative study of the news coverage of key EU events', *European Union Politics*, 2(3): 283–307.

——— (2003). *Framing Europe: Television News and European Integration*. Amsterdam: Aksant.

Vreese, Claes H. de, and Boomgaarden, Hajo (2006). 'Media effects on public opinion about the enlargement of the European Union', *Journal of Mass Communication and Society*, 44(2): 419–36.

——— (2012). 'Comparing news on Europe: Elections and beyond'. In Frank Esser and Thomas Hanitzsch (eds), *Handbook of Comparative Communication Research*. London: Routledge, 327–40.

Vreese, Claes H. de, Peter, Jochen, and Semetko, Holly A. (2001). 'Framing politics at the launch of the euro: A cross-national comparative study of frames in the news', *Political Communication*, 18(2): 107–22.

Wang, Huili, Runtsova, Tamara, and Chen, Hongjun (2013). 'Economy is an organism – a comparative study of metaphor in English and Russian economic discourse', *Text and Talk*, 33(2): 259–88.

Weaver, David H. (2007). 'Thoughts on agenda setting, framing, and priming', *Journal of Communication*, 57(1): 142–7.

White, David M. (1950). 'The "gatekeeper": A case study in the selection of news', *Journalism Quarterly*, 27: 383–90.

White, Jonathan (2010). 'Europe in the political imagination', *Journal of Common Market Studies*, 48(4): 1015–38.

Williams, Ann E. (2013). 'Metaphor, media, and the market', *International Journal of Communication*, 7: 1404–17.

Williams, Ann E. (2013). 'Metaphor, media, and the market', *International Journal of Communication*, 7: 1404–17.

Williams, Ann E., Davidson, Roei and Yochim, and Chivers, Emily (2011). 'Who's to blame when a business fails? How journalistic death metaphors influence responsibility attributions', *Journalism and Mass Communication Quarterly*, 88(3): 541–61.

Yiangou, Jonathan, O'Keeffe, Mícheál, and Glöcker, Gabriel (2013). '"Tough love": How the ECB's monetary financing prohibition pushes deeper euro Area integration', *Journal of European Integration*, 35(3): 223–37.

Appendix 1: Description of Methods

'The Euro Crisis, Media Coverage, and Perceptions of Europe within the EU' project explored how the euro crisis was portrayed in media in EU countries and how differences in coverage and journalistic practices affected perceptions of the crisis and Europe. The purpose of the project was to determine how Europeans understood the challenges facing the euro and the workings of the European Union and European Central Bank through the news media of their countries. The study was designed to answer the question of how newspapers in different countries portrayed the roots of the crisis, the responses to the crisis, European institutions, and European cohesiveness and how those changed as the crisis progressed.

The project identified the major story themes and frames used by journalists about the roots and response to the crisis, the portrayal of countries intimately involved, and the portrayal of European institutions. It identified what/who is portrayed as causing the crisis, who was portrayed as having to solve the problem and how, and the broader issues the crisis unveiled regarding European integration and governance.

Hypotheses

Based on existing literature, the project started with the following hypotheses:

H1: Most articles will focus on domestic interests rather than on European interests.

H2: Most articles will place culpability for the crisis on factors outside of domestic control or on other countries.

H3: Most articles published in countries with sovereign debt problems central to the crisis (Greece, Italy, Portugal, and Spain) will place responsibility on factors other than domestic policy and economies.

H4: Most articles published in leading European economies (France, Germany, and the UK) will place fault on domestic policies and economies of countries with major sovereign debt issues.

H5: Most articles published in countries with sovereign debt problems central to the crisis (Greece, Italy, Portugal, and Spain) will portray the solution to the problem as external rather than domestic.

H6: Most articles published in leading European economies (France, Germany, and the UK) will portray the solution as domestic to countries with sovereign debt challenges rather than of other nations or institutions.

H7: As time progresses, publications' assessment of the roots of the crisis will shift from national to systemic and institutional causes.

H8: As time progresses, publications will increasingly portray European institutions as central to the roots of the problem and the solution.

H9: In early stages of the coverage, European institutions will be portrayed as peripheral to the crisis.

H10: As time progresses, European institutions will be portrayed as not having the capacity to deal with the crisis.

H11: Business papers are more likely to adopt a European identity frame, to emphasise the significance of European institutions in dealing with the crisis, and to stress the systemic roots and responses to the crisis over national policies and institutions than the broadsheets and tabloids.

H12: Tabloids are less likely to support responses to the crisis involving transfer of power to the European institutions than the broadsheets and the business papers.

Because of national differences in political stances and relations with the EU and eurozone, there were no effective bases prior to the research on which to hypothesise about what positions left of centre, centre, and right of centre papers would be expected to take, or positions papers in states with and without problematic sovereign debt might take. Consequently, no hypotheses are put forward about how they might cover the crisis.

Newspaper selection

Four newspapers in each country were selected for study: the leading financial/business newspaper, two leading papers representing conservative and liberal views, and the leading tabloid. In the absence of a tabloid, the leading centrist general circulation paper was added. This latter accommodation was included to deal with states that do not have major national tabloids, notably France, Greece, Italy, and Spain, but do have major papers representing liberal, centrist, and conservative views. The papers included in this study were:

Belgium
De Tijd
(*financial/business*)
De Standaard
(*centre-right*)
De Morgen
(*centre-left*)
Het Laatste Nieuws
(*tabloid*)

Finland
Kauppalehti
(*financial/business*)
Helsingin Sanomat
(*centre-left*)
Kaleva
(*centre-right*)
Ilta-Sanomat
(*tabloid*)

France
Les Echos
(*financial/business*)
Le Figaro
(*conservative*)
Le Monde
(*centrist*)
Le Parisien
(*liberal*)

Germany
Handelsblatt
(*financial/business*)
Frankfurter Allgemeine
Zeitung (*centre-right*)
Sueddeutsche Zeitung
(*centre-left*)
Bild
(*tabloid*)

Greece
Naftemporiki
(*financial/business*)
Kathimerini
(*centre-right*)
To Bima
(*centre-left*)
Ta Nea
(*tabloid*)

Italy
Il Sole 24 Ore
(*financial/business*)
La Repubblica
(*centre-left*)
Il Giornale
(*centre-right*)
Il Corriere della sera
(*centre*)

Netherlands
Het Financieele Dagblad
(*financial/business*)
NRC Handelsblad
(*centre-right*)
De Volkskrant
(*centre-left*)
De Telegraaf
(*tabloid*)

Poland
Puls Biznesu
(*financial/business*)
Gazeta Wyborcza
(*centre-left*)
Rzeczpospolita
(*centre-right*)
Fakt
(*tabloid*)

Spain
Expansion
(*financial/business*)
El País
(*centre-left*)
El Mundo
(*centrist*)
ABC
(*centre-right*)

United Kingdom
Financial Times
(*financial/business*)
The Times
(*centre-right*)
The Guardian
(*centre-left*)
The Sun
(*tabloid*)

Content studied

The research team identified 11 major developmental periods between 2010 and 2012 and selected coverage beginning seven days before and ending seven days after each major development as the content of the study. These inclusive dates were:

1. 4 February–18 February 2010 – EU summit (11–12 February) related to role of European governments and IMF in any intervention.
2. 25 April–9 May 2010 – eurozone members and IMF agreement for €100bn intervention for Greece (2 May).
3. 9–23 December 2010 – EU Contract change (16 December).
4. 25 July–18 August 2011 – ECB asks Italy for more austerity measures (5 August).
5. 28 September–12 October 2011 – Greek general strike against austerity measures (5 October).
6. 19 October–2 November 2011 – EU summit boosting stability fund, extending new ID, and requiring banks to raise new capital (26–27 October).
7. 5–19 November 2011 – Berlusconi resignation/Monti appointment (12–13 November), includes French austerity measures.
8. 19–30 November 2011 – EC Green Paper on stability bonds and proposal to bring national budgets under EC control (23 November).
9. 16 May–5 June 2012 – EU summit (23 May) to boost growth and balance austerity, attention on Spain, and UK governmental meetings to protect UK financial system.
10. 18 June–5 July 2012 – Spain formally requests assistance (25 June), Merkel calls the eurobonds 'economically wrong and counterproductive' (27 June), EU summit on debt crisis (28–29 June).
11. 8 July–22 July 2012 – Merkel affirmation of need for adherence to budget targets and European monitoring (15 July).

The selection focused on periods in which significant contemporary developments led to significant amounts of coverage, analysis, and evaluation involving the topics under investigation. The decision to use this structured sampling, rather than to sample the entire period of 2010–12, was made to avoid potentially missing coverage of some of the most significant events. Sampling before and after these events also captures coverage not directly related to events and ensures assessment of weekend editions that have significant and extended commentary and opinion sections in many nations.

Searching content

Database searches were made using the terms EURO and CRISIS, or their national linguistic equivalents, in order to maintain commonality. The choice of these terms has been made based on preliminary test searches made by all partners that showed they gather the largest number of articles, and desires to avoid duplication of articles that might occur if additional terms are employed. Because of linguistic and database differences, a separate coding using EURO and CRISIS and EUROPE was employed by the Spanish team.

Sampling

Based on test searches by the national research teams, universes of 2,000–2,500 articles were established for review in each country. In cases where more than 2,500 articles were present, teams employed a sample of the articles. Teams that analysed all the articles identified in their search did not need to use the sampling procedure. In order to ensure commonality in sampling methods, the following sampling method was used.

The sampling was done by day rather than by article. Thus, if the total number of articles needed to be reduced by 50%, articles appearing every other day were selected. In practice this meant:

1. All the articles on the day(s) of the central events/developments specified in the time periods above were selected.
2. All articles appearing in editions published Tuesday, Thursday, and Saturday within the +/− seven-day periods surrounding the central event were coded.
3. If the event/development happened on a day when no or not all newspapers studied appeared (e.g. Sundays, bank holidays), the articles on the next day thereafter were coded. If that next day was a Tuesday, Thursday, or Saturday, the next following day was also coded. As a result all events had the same number of coded days.

Despite the fact that probability samples were taken by some teams, the results from the sampled and unsampled dataset could be combined for comparative analysis. However, any statistical comparison among national data has to take into account the largest margin of error and lowest confidence level in the national samples.

Appendix 2: List of Variables

1. Researcher number
2. Country of article
3. Newspaper in which the article appeared

4. Date of the coverage
5. Genre (type of story)
6. Topic of the article
7. Story impetus
8. Story source
9. Page placement of the article
10. Section placement of the article
11. Size of article
12. Type of sources quoted
13. Specific sources quoted
14. What does the article indicate is the main fundamental root of the crisis?
15. Who does the article indicate should bear the main responsibility to solve the problem?
16. What does the article indicate should be the main (short-term) response to the crisis?
17a. What does the article indicate should be the primary broader (longer-term) response to the crisis?
17b. Nation that should drop the euro/carry out structural reform
18a. What does the article indicate as the main benefit from the existence of the euro currency?
18b. Country or region that is indicated as main beneficiary of the euro currency
19a. What does the article explicitly indicate as the main harmful consequence from the existence of the euro currency?
19b. Country or region that receives main harm from the euro as a currency
20a. Who does the article indicate primarily benefits or will benefit (economically or politically) from the euro crisis?
20b. What country or region is portrayed as the main beneficiary of the euro crisis?
21a. Who does the article indicate primarily suffers or will suffer (economically or politically) from the euro crisis?
21b. What country or region is depicted as primarily suffering the identified consequences of the euro crisis?
22. Identify the main geopolitical frame of the article
23. What is the main portrayal of European Commission/European Union/eurozone institutions?
24. What is the main portrayal of the European Central Bank?
25. Forecast of the consequences of the rescue measures
26. Metaphors used

Appendix 3: Codebook – Euro Crisis Project Article Analysis Collection Sheet

This codebook contains the categories and instructions for coding responses to each category. It is used in conjunction with a coding sheet on which the actual answers are recorded.

Use a separate coding sheet for each newspaper article and then transfer the data from the sheets to the project Excel data processing workbook.

If in doubt about the proper coding for a specific item, the coder should write a brief note about the doubts on the coding sheet for review by a supervisor to make the determination.

Coders should analyse only substantive articles. Do not code letters to editors, readers' comments, cartoons and illustrations or stand-alone photos. Articles that mention the euro crisis in passing – but are not specifically about it – should not be coded (examples: an article about traffic difficulties during a summit of leaders addressing the crisis or a sports article about a football match between Germany and Greece that mentions the issue).

Use of 'Other', code 98 or 980: A number of categories permit coding the answer 'Other'. Whenever the answer 'Other' is used and entered as number 98/980, the coder should also write a specifying word/brief phrase indicating what the other refers to on the code sheet.

Note about Item 1, researcher number: Each team should assign a coder number to each person doing the coding (01, 02, 03, and so on) so supervisors can identify and contact them in event of questions or issues related to articles coded.

Note about coding portrayals in articles (Items 14–21): Code only *explicit* portrayals of roots, responsibilities, responses, and so on in the article. That is, code only answers that are clearly expressed and unambiguous. The coder should not have to infer the portrayal from vague, enigmatic, or ambiguous language or article construction. If a portrayal is not clearly expressed, record number 99 (none). If more than one answer is present in the article, select the dominant (most discussed response or response given preferential coverage in the article).

Note about Item 12, sources quoted: Answers 201/202 'prime minister/ president with executive power' should include Sarkozy and Obama in France and the US. If a president *without* executive power is quoted (Germany and Italy, for example), code it as 'Other' (980) and indicate 'president (non-executive)'. Answer group 400 'bankers/financiers' does not include persons from ratings agencies. Code them as 980 'Other' and indicate 'ratings agency executive'.

Note about Item 14, root of the crisis: Because some partners wish to explore this item in greater depth, both a condensed and extended coding scheme are provided. These are compatible for comparative purposes. The coder should use the scheme specified by the national research team.

1. **Researcher number**
   Enter the number assigned to the researcher doing the coding (needed if questions arise).

2. **Country of article**
   Enter the number of the country of publication of the article being evaluated.
   Code list 2

01 Belgium	06 Italy
02 Finland	07 Netherlands
03 France	08 Poland
04 Germany	09 Spain
05 Greece	10 United Kingdom

3. **Newspaper in which the article appeared**
   Enter the publication identification number.
   Code list 3

Belgium	**Greece**	**Spain**
011 De Tijd	051 Naftemporiki	091 Expansion
012 De Standaard	052 Kathimerini	092 El País
013 De Morgen	053 To Bima	093 El Mundo
014 Het Laatste Nieuws	054 Ta Nea	094 ABC

Finland	**Italy**	**United Kingdom**
021 Kauppalehti	061 Il Sole 24 Ore	101 Financial Times
022 Helsingin Sanomat	062 La Repubblica	102 The Times
023 Kaleva	063 Il Giornale	103 The Guardian
024 Ilta-Sanomat	064 Il Corriere della Sera	104 The Sun

France	**Netherlands**
031 Les Echos	071 Het Financieele
032 Le Figaro	Dagblad
033 Le Monde	072 NRC Handelsblad

034 Le Parisien	073 De Volkskrant
	074 De Telegraaf

Germany	Poland
041 Handelsblatt	081 Puls Biznesu
042 Frankfurter	082 Gazeta Wyborcza
Allgemeine Zeitung	083 Rzeczpospolita
043 Sueddeutsche	084 Fakt
Zeitung	
044 Bild	

4. **Date of the coverage**

   Enter the date of the article publication (DD/MM/YYYY).

5. **Genre (type of story)**

   Enter the number that best describes the genre of the story being evaluated.

   Code list 5

   01 News story (description of event, decision, action)

   02 News analysis or background story (article primarily explaining the impact of an event or decision; what it means or does; explaining history of the developments; people/institutions involved; factors creating the issue)

   03 Feature story (human interest story tied to the news; describing the scene, effects on individual persons, or observations of how it came about)

   04 Editorial (the paper's opinion; written by editors)

   05 Opinion/commentary (giving authors' ideas or critique of the event or decision)

   06 Interview

   98 Other

6. **Topic of the article**

   Enter 6–10 words. Examples: Summit of European leaders; ratings agency downgrades Spanish bonds.

7. **Story impetus**

   Enter the number that best describes the impetus of the article.

   Code list 7

   01 Event-based (meeting, summit)

   02 Request-based (application, request for aid)

03   Decision-based (by government, government entity, political party/ies)

04   Statement/pronouncement-based (by official in released statement or interview)

05   Market development-based (stock prices, bond ratings, economic reports)

06   Reports in other media

98   Other

99   Not tied to a specific event or development

8. **Story source**

   Enter the number that indicates who wrote or provided the story being evaluated, as indicated in the byline.

   Code list 8

   01   Domestic-based staff writer (originated with publication)

   02   Foreign-based staff writer (originated with publication by employed correspondent)

   03   Non-staff writer (journalist freelancer/stringer, usually indicated by something like 'special to *The Times*')

   04   Newspaper itself indicated in the byline as producing the story

   05   Newspaper and news agency jointly indicated as producing the story (a localisation of agency story by newspaper staff adding information)

   06   News agency (AP, AFP, EFE, Reuters, etc.)

   07   Expert writer (academic, politician, banker, economist)

   08   Reprinted from another publication

   09   Writer's affiliation not indicated

   98   Other

   99   No writer/source indicated

9. **Page placement of the article**

   Enter the number that indicates the page on which the article begins (1 = 01, 2 = 02 ... 10 = 10).

10. **Section placement of the article**

   Enter number of the section of the paper in which the article appeared.

   Code list 10

01	Domestic/national news section	05	Editorial/opinion section
02	International news section	06	Culture/society section
03	Business or finance news section	07	Special euro crisis section
		08	Supplement or insert
04	Political section	**98**	**Other**

11. **Size of article**

    Enter the length of the article (this is a relative measure based on estimation, approximation or word counts in databases).

    Code list 11

    01 Short (fewer than 500 words; less than 1/3rd page)

    02 Medium (500–999 words; 1/3rd to 2/3rd of a page)

    03 Long (1000 words or more; more than 2/3rd of page)

12. **Type of sources quoted**

    Enter the number that indicates the main affiliation, position, or professional background of the first five persons quoted in the story (direct quotes or reference to a quote or position). If fewer than five are quoted, record only those individuals. Record each individual only *once*. If no one is quoted, enter 980. If you are not able to specify an actor using a subcategory within a category, please use the 100, 200, 300 etc. codes (Example: an article may read: '…Jim Yong Kim stated …' → please code 402 because he is the head of the World Bank. Another article may read: '…bankers agree…' → please code 400. Whenever possible use the more specific source code, thus you would not code 400 in the Jim Yong Kim case because his position can be coded more specifically to 402).

    Code list 12

    100 Officials (non-elected) [Example: EU President, Commissioner, other EU officials, appointed government minister, aide to minister, persons identified as an 'official']

       101 European Union official

       102 Unnamed European Union official

       103 Foreign government official

       104 Unnamed foreign government official

       105 Domestic government official

       106 Unnamed domestic government official

    200 National Government Leaders

       201 Foreign prime minister/president with executive power (France/US)

       202 Domestic prime minister/president with executive power (France/US)

       203 Other foreign government minister

       204 Other domestic government minister

    300 National Political Leaders (elected party head or parliamentarian, but not prime minister/minister)

       301 Foreign political leader

       302 Domestic political leader

    303 Foreign member of European Parliament

    304 Domestic member of European Parliament

400 Bankers/Financiers

    401 European Central Bank official

    402 World Bank/International Monetary Fund

    403 Foreign central bank official

    404 Domestic central bank official

    405 Foreign non-governmental banker or investment executive

    406 Domestic non-governmental banker or investment executive

500 Economists

    501 Foreign non-governmental economist (academic, organisations, banks, investment firms)

    502 Domestic non-governmental economist (academic, organisations, banks, investment firms)

600 Society representatives

    601 Foreign union leader or employee representative

    602 Domestic union leader or employee representative

    603 Foreign think tank, interest group, NGO

    604 Domestic think tank, interest group, NGO

    605 Foreign business representative (company executive, Chamber of Commerce, industry federation or association)

    606 Domestic business representative (company executive, Chamber of Commerce, industry federation or association)

    607 Foreign civil society, social movement/protester representative

    608 Domestic civil society, social movement/protester representative

    609 Foreign member of the public

    610 Domestic member of the public

980 Other

990 None (no person is quoted)

13. **Specific sources quoted**

Enter the number corresponding to specific major figures in the crisis quoted in the story (up to the first five reported).

Code list 13

01	Silvio Berlusconi	06	Jean Claude Juncker
02	José Barroso	07	Christine Lagarde
03	David Cameron	08	Angela Merkel
04	Mario Draghi	09	Mario Monti
05	François Hollande	10	Lucas Papademos

11	Georgios Papandreou	16	Dominique Strauss-Kahn
12	Mariano Rajoy	17	Jean-Claude Trichet
13	Herman Van Rompuy	18	José Zapatero
14	Olli Rehn	**98**	**Other (major players only)**
15	Nicolas Sarkozy	**99**	**Does not occur**

14. What does the article indicate is the main fundamental root or cause of the crisis? (select one)

If the article *explicitly* indicates a cause of the crisis, enter the number from the eight major categories below that best describes the portrayal of the cause. If no cause is addressed, enter number 99. If the article broadly refers to one of the major categories **(or if condensed coding is being used),** enter that category number (10, 20, 30, etc). **If extended coding is being used** and the article more specifically refers to one of the subcategories, enter the subcategory number, e.g. 34).

Code list 14

10 Starting conditions and structure of the euro system

    11 Euro was a political project not based on following economic fundamentals

    12 Incompatibility of one currency and fiscal and economic national sovereignty of nations

    13 Crisis country not ready for euro membership in economic and structural terms

20 National industrial policies and developments

    21 Countries with major sovereign debt problems' inability to build up competitive industries

    22 Countries with major sovereign debt problems' high wage increases compared to productivity gains

    23 Germany's low wage increases

    24 Germany's focus on exports

    25 Spain's construction industry bubble

30 National fiscal and social policies

    31 Overall high fiscal debt volume of all countries

    32 Countries with major sovereign debt problems' lax debt policies

    33 Countries with major sovereign debt problems grant social benefits they cannot afford

    34 Countries with major sovereign debt problems' lack of reforms of labour markets

35   Countries with major sovereign debt problems generously funded state's apparatus

36   Germany's low budget deficits/lack of expansion policies

40 Banks' and financial institutions' policies

41   (National/international) banks having financed too much of fiscal and/or private debts

42   (National/international) banks' unwillingness to further finance states debt/industries' investments

43   ECB's loose monetary policy, which helped to finance states and private debt

44   National bank supervisory authorities' inability/unwillingness to control national banks' behaviour

45   Speculation against the euro

46   Speculation against a country with sovereign debt challenges

50 Political roots

51   Unwillingness of nations to transfer power to the EU

52   Weakness of the central European institutions (European Council, European Parliament, Council of the European Union, European Commission, Court of Justice)

53   Different political cultures

54   Failure of the political class in the problem countries

60 Maastricht treaty

61   Maastricht treaty concerning budget restrictions does not match economic necessities

62   Maastricht treaty concerning fiscal restrictions and economic sanctions was softened over time leading to too high debt

70 European Central Bank (ECB)

71   ECB's restriction to avoid inflation/stable currency as the only goal does not match necessities/potential of monetary policy

72   ECB's prohibition of financing national sovereign debt not adequate in crisis situations/this crisis

73   ECB's inability to fix one interest rate fitting the needs of all euro countries (too low for some, too high for others)

80 General economic roots

81   The recession

82   Influence of globalisation and the global economy

98 Other

99 None (No cause indicated)

15. **Who does the article indicate should bear the main responsibility to solve the problem? (select one)**

If the article *explicitly* indicates responsibility to solve the crisis, enter the number corresponding to which of the following is portrayed as being mainly responsible. If no clear responsibility is indicated, answer 99.

Code list 15

01   Countries with sovereign debt problems themselves

02   Countries without sovereign debt problems

03   Eurozone members as a group

04   The European Union (Commission, Parliament, Council)

05   European Central Bank

06   International Monetary Fund (IMF)/World Bank

07   Banks, investors, and other lenders which hold debt

98   Other

99   None (no party indicated)

16. **What does the article indicate should be the main (short-term) response to the crisis? (select one)**

If the article *explicitly* indicates a response, enter the number corresponding to the main response portrayed. If no clear mechanism is indicated, answer 99.

Code list 16

01   Loans from other countries without supervision (troika, ESM, ESFS)

02   Loans from other countries with supervision

03   European Central Bank loans and bond purchases

04   Abatement of existing loan provisions (extension, reduced rates, haircut)

05   Reduction of budget deficits (tax increases, austerity measures)

06   Fiscal stimulus

07   Growth policies

98   Other

99   None (no mechanism indicated)

17a. **What does the article indicate should be the primary broader (longer-term) response to the crisis? (select one)**

If the article *explicitly* indicates a broader response, enter the number that best describes the response portrayed. If no clear mechanism is indicated, answer 99.

Code list 17

01   More EU power over national budgets

02   Nations with weak economies dropping the euro *(if selected also answer 17b)*

03 Nations with strong economies dropping the euro *(if selected also answer 17b)*

04 National structural reforms in nations with problems (labour markets, education, tax structures) *(if selected also answer 17b)*

05 Breaking up the eurozone altogether

98 Other

99 None (no broader response indicated)

17b. Nation that should drop the euro/carry out structural reform

Please select the nation or region named to drop the euro if you have chosen answer 2, 3 or 4 in category 17a.

100 Single country

101	Austria	110	Italy
102	Belgium	111	Luxembourg
103	Cyprus	112	Malta
104	Estonia	113	The Netherlands
105	Finland	114	Portugal
106	France	115	Slovakia
107	Germany	116	Slovenia
108	Greece	117	Spain
109	Ireland		

200 Country regions

210 Southern countries   220 Northern countries

980 Other

990 No specific country or region to drop the euro indicated

18a. What does the article indicate as the main benefit from the existence of the euro currency?

If the article *explicitly* indicates benefits accrue, enter the number from the major categories below that best describes the primary benefit received. Otherwise enter 99.

10 Beneficial consequences for the national economy *(if selected also answer 18b)*

11 Improves the competitiveness of national businesses *(if selected also answer 18b)*

12 Improves the stability, operation, and competitiveness of national banks *(if selected also answer 18b)*

13 Improves the position of national consumers *(if selected also answer 18b)*

14 Improves national monetary stability *(if selected also answer 18b)*

15 Lowers national interest rates *(if selected also answer 18b)*

20 Beneficial consequences for the European economy

21 Improves the competitiveness of European businesses

22 Improves the stability, operation, and competitiveness of national banks

23 Improves the position of European consumers

24 Improves European monetary stability

25 Lowers European interest rates

30 Beneficial national political consequences *(if selected also answer 18b)*

31 Clarifies principles used in monetary policy *(if selected also answer 18b)*

32 Reduces ability of governments to manipulate monetary policy *(if selected also answer 18b)*

34 Reduces pressures on government created by currency fluctuations *(if selected also answer 18b)*

40 Beneficial European political consequences

41 Advances European political integration

42 Advances the harmonisation of economic policies and taxation

43 Advances the harmonisation of regulation

44 Advances the creation of a single market

45 Strengthens the geopolitical position of Europe

50 Beneficial national social consequences *(if selected also answer 18b)*

51 Improves living standards and general well-being *(if selected also answer 18b)*

52 Reduces social inequality within the country *(if selected also answer 18b)*

60 Beneficial European social consequences

61 Improves living standards and general well-being

62 Reduces social inequality between member states

63 Makes travel easier

98 Other

99 None

18b. Country or region that is indicated as main beneficiary of the euro currency
Please select the country or region of the main beneficiary in category 18a if you answered 10–15, 30–34, or 50–52.

100 Single country

101 Austria	103 Bulgaria
102 Belgium	104 Cyprus

105 Czech Republic	117 Luxembourg
106 Denmark	118 Malta
107 Estonia	119 The Netherlands
108 Finland	120 Poland
109 France	121 Portugal
110 Germany	122 Rumania
111 Greece	123 Slovakia
112 Hungary	124 Slovenia
113 Ireland	125 Spain
114 Italy	126 Sweden
115 Latvia	127 United Kingdom
116 Lithuania	

200 Country regions

 210 Southern countries 230 EU countries in general

 220 Northern countries

980 Other

990 No main country beneficiary indicated

19a. **What does the article explicitly indicate as the main harmful consequence from the existence of the euro currency?**

If the article *explicitly* indicates harm, enter the number from the major categories below that best describes the primary harm caused. Otherwise enter 99.

10 Harmful consequences for national economy *(if selected also answer 19b)*

 11 Harms to national businesses (e.g. loss of competitiveness) *(if selected also answer 19b)*

 12 Harms to national banks (e.g. increased exposure to risks) *(if selected also answer 19b)*

 13 Harms to consumers (e.g. rising prices) *(if selected also answer 19b)*

 14 Harms to financial markets (inflow of cheap money, bubbles etc.) *(if selected also answer 19b)*

 15 Interest rates too low/too high *(if selected also answer 19b)*

20 Harmful consequences for European economy

 21 Harms to European businesses (e.g. loss of competitiveness)

 22 Harms to European banks (e.g. increased exposure to risks)

 23 Harms to consumers (e.g. rising prices)

 24 Harms to financial markets (e.g. growing instabilities, risk of bubbles)

 25 Interest rates too low/too high

30 Harmful national political consequences *(if selected also answer 19b)*

    31   Restricts national control over economic policy *(if selected also answer 19b)*

    32   Restricts ability to regulate and control financial markets *(if selected also answer 19b)*

    33   Diminishes the scope of democratic decision-making *(if selected also answer 19b)*

    34   Diminishes national sovereignty *(if selected also answer 19b)*

40 Harmful European political consequences

    41   Restricts ability to regulate and control financial markets

    42   Creates a mismatch between monetary and fiscal authority

    43   Diminishes democratic legitimacy in Europe/of the EU

50 Harmful national social consequences *(if selected also answer 19b)*

    51   Worsens living standards and general well-being *(if selected also answer 19b)*

    52   Deteriorates social services and decreases social benefits *(if selected also answer 19b)*

    53   Increases inequality *(if selected also answer 19b)*

60 Harmful Europe-wide social consequences

    61   Worsens living standards and general well-being

    62   Deteriorates social services and decreases social benefits

    63   Increases inequality

98 Other

99 None

19b. Country or region that receives main harm from the euro as a currency

Please select the country or region where the main harm in category 19a occurs, if you answered 10–15, 30–34, or 50–53.

100 Single country

101 Austria	110 Germany
102 Belgium	111 Greece
103 Bulgaria	112 Hungary
104 Cyprus	113 Ireland
105 Czech Republic	114 Italy
106 Denmark	115 Latvia
107 Estonia	116 Lithuania
108 Finland	117 Luxembourg
109 France	118 Malta

119 The Netherlands	124 Slovenia
120 Poland	125 Spain
121 Portugal	126 Sweden
122 Rumania	127 United Kingdom
123 Slovakia	

200 Country regions

210 Southern countries	230 EU countries in general
220 Northern countries	

980 Other

990 No origin of main loser indicated

20a. **Who does the article indicate primarily benefits or will benefit (economically or politically) from the euro crisis? (select one)**
If the article *explicitly* indicates a party benefits, enter the number from the major categories below that best describes the what actor, group, or country benefits according to the article. Otherwise answer 99.
Code list 20

10 One country or region in particular *(if selected also answer 20b)*

20 Political and financial authorities

21 National Parliament *(if selected also answer 20b)*

22 National Government *(if selected also answer 20b)*

23 National High Courts *(if selected also answer 20b)*

24 European Commission

25 European Parliament

26 European Court of Justice

27 European Central Bank (ECB)

28 International Monetary Fund (IMF)

30 Private economic actors

31 Commercial banks

32 Large investors/speculators/hedgefunds

33 Non-financial industries (farmers, automotive, construction)

40 Population

41 Population in general *(if selected also answer 20b)*

42 Upper class *(if selected also answer 20b)*

43 Lower/middle class (ordinary people) *(if selected also answer 20b)*

44 Younger people *(if selected also answer 20b)*

45 Elderly people *(if selected also answer 20b)*

46 Tax payers *(if selected also answer 20b)*

47 Unemployed people *(if selected also answer 20b)*

98   Other (e.g. science, arts, countries in general; other specific countries)

99   None (no group/country seen as benefitting)

20b. **What country or region is portrayed as the main beneficiary of the euro crisis?**

Please select the country or region of the main beneficiary in category 20a if you answered 10, 21, 22, 23, or 40–47.

100 Single country

101	Austria	115	Latvia
102	Belgium	116	Lithuania
103	Bulgaria	117	Luxembourg
104	Cyprus	118	Malta
105	Czech Republic	119	The Netherlands
106	Denmark	120	Poland
107	Estonia	121	Portugal
108	Finland	122	Rumania
109	France	123	Slovakia
110	Germany	124	Slovenia
111	Greece	125	Spain
112	Hungary	126	Sweden
113	Ireland	127	United Kingdom
114	Italy		

200 Country regions

210	Southern countries	230	EU countries in general
220	Northern countries		

980 Other

990 No origin of main beneficiary indicated

21a. **Who does the article indicate primarily suffers or will suffer costs (economically or politically) from the euro crisis? (select one)**

If the article *explicitly* indicates costs are incurred, enter the number from the major categories below that best describes what actor, group, or country suffers according to the article. Otherwise enter 99.

Code list 21

10   One country or region in particular *(if selected also answer 21b)*

20   Political and financial authorities

21   National Parliament *(if selected also answer 21b)*

22   National Government *(if selected also answer 21b)*

23 National High Courts *(if selected also answer 21b)*

24 European Commission

25 European Parliament

26 European Court of Justice

27 European Central Bank (ECB)

28 International Monetary Fund (IMF)

30 Private economic actors

31 Commercial banks

32 Large investors/speculators/hedgefunds

33 Non-financial industries (farmers, automotive, construction)

40 Population *(if selected and it relates to a country or region – not Europe as a whole – also answer 21b)*

41 Population in general *(if selected and it relates to a country or region – not Europe as a whole – also answer 21b)*

42 Upper class *(if selected and it relates to a country or region – not Europe as a whole – also answer 21b)*

43 Lower/middle class (ordinary people) *(if selected and it relates to a country or region – not Europe as a whole – also answer 21b)*

44 Younger people *(if selected and it relates to a country or region – not Europe as a whole – also answer 21b)*

45 Elderly people *(if selected and it relates to a country or region – not Europe as a whole – also answer 21b)*

46 Tax payers *(if selected and it relates to a country or region – not Europe as a whole – also answer 21b)*

47 Unemployed people *(if selected and it relates to a country or region – not Europe as a whole – also answer 21b)*

98 Other (e.g. science, arts, countries in general; other specific countries)

99 None (no group/country seen as losing)

21b. What country or region is depicted as primarily suffering the identified consequences of the euro crisis?

Please select the country or region of the main beneficiary in category 21a if you answered 10, 21, 22, 23, or 40–47.

100 Single country

101	Austria	106	Denmark
102	Belgium	107	Estonia
103	Bulgaria	108	Finland
104	Cyprus	109	France
105	Czech Republic	110	Germany

111 Greece	120 Poland
112 Hungary	121 Portugal
113 Ireland	122 Rumania
114 Italy	123 Slovakia
115 Latvia	124 Slovenia
116 Lithuania	125 Spain
117 Luxembourg	126 Sweden
118 Malta	127 United Kingdom
119 The Netherlands	

200 Country regions

210 Southern countries	230 EU countries in general
220 Northern countries	

980 Other

990 No origin of main loser indicated

22. **Identify the main geopolitical frame of the article (select one)**
     Enter the number that best describes the frame.
     Code list 22

     01   Domestic (addressing the crisis and developments as an internal issue
          within the publication's country; portraying the 'us/we/our' as citizens
          of the country)

     02   Foreign country (addressing the crisis and developments as an issue
          internal to another country; portraying 'they/them' as separate from
          citizens of the country in which the article was published)

     03   European (emphasising the crisis and developments as a European
          issue; approaching Europe as a collective; portraying the 'us/we/our' as
          European-wide)

     98   Other

     99   None/No clear frame

23. **What is the main portrayal of European Commission/European Union/
     eurozone institutions? (select one)**
     Enter the number that best describes the portrayal.
     Code list 23

     01   The article portrays them as insignificant in addressing the crisis

     02   The article portrays them as lacking capabilities to address the crisis
          (not having authority or property tools)

     03   The article portrays them as ineffectual or confused in addressing the crisis

     04   The article portrays them as central to addressing the crisis

05   The article portrays them as strong and determined in addressing the crisis

98   Other

99   None (no portrayal of the institutions)

24.   **What is the main portrayal of the European Central Bank? (select one)**
Enter the number that best describes the portrayal.
Code list 24

01   The article portrays it as insignificant in addressing the crisis

02   The article portrays it as lacking capabilities to address the crisis (not having authority or property tools)

03   The article portrays it as ineffectual or confused in addressing the crisis

04   The article portrays it as central to addressing the crisis

05   The article portrays it as strong and determined in addressing the crisis

06   The article portrays it as acting within its legal framework

07   The article portrays it as acting at the border or outside of its legal framework

98   Other

99   None (no ECB portrayal)

25.   **Forecast of the consequences of the rescue measures**
Enter the number that best describes the portrayal of the forecast of the consequences.
Code list 25

01   Deeper integration/transfer of national sovereignty to European institutions

02   Stronger and more stable euro

03   Success/eurozone preserved

04   Final breakup of the eurozone to more than one (north/south)

05   Failure/countries with sovereign debt problems will drop the euro finally

06   Establishment of an enduring transfer system to countries with sovereign debt problems

07   Europe-wide inflation

98   Other

99   None (no consequences indicated)

26.   **Metaphors used**
Specify up to two metaphors describing the situation or issues if they exist in the headline and the lead paragraph. Metaphors are words or phrases

that compare or apply concepts from something else (often not literally). Examples: describing the euro crisis, conditions or events as a 'battle', 'war', 'assault', 'cancer', 'hurricane', 'tsunami', 'a sinking boat', or 'under protective umbrella'. Provide an English translation unless directed otherwise by your national research team.

Appendix 4: Intercoder Reliability

The reliability of coding across countries was assessed using an intercoder reliability test of coders in each country. The results, shown on the following pages, reveal acceptable level average scores of 0.71 to 0.87 for all countries based on scores across all variables. As a general rule, coefficients scores of 0.90 or greater are nearly always acceptable, 0.80 or greater is acceptable in most situations, and 0.70 is appropriate for exploratory studies.

	B/NL	Ger	Fin	France	Gree	Ital	Pol	Spain	UK
Formal attributes									
a) Category # 5 Genre	0.92	0.75		0.89		0.75	0.69	0.83	0.89
b) Category # 7 Story impetus	0.86	0.28		0.81		0.67	0.47	0.72	0.82
c) Category # 8 Story source	1.00	0.92		0.97		0.89	0.78	0.81	0.93
d) Category # 11 size of article	1.00	1.00		1.00		0.86	0.97	1.00	1.00
Average of a–d	**0.94**	**0.74**	**0.88**	**0.92**	**0.86**	**0.79**	**0.73**	**0.84**	**0.91**
Type of sources									
a) Category # 12	0.95	0.74		0.91		0.78	0.71	0.85	0.83
b) Category # 13	0.90	0.68		0.94		0.78	0.95	0.86	0.85
Average of a–b	**0.92**	**0.71**	**0.89**	**0.92**	**0.89**	**0.78**	**0.83**	**0.86**	**0.84**
Fund. roots of the crises									
Category # 14	0.75	0.69	0.61	0.80	0.83	0.83	0.83	0.76	0.78
Main responsibility to solve									
Category # 15	0.92	0.47	0.50	0.69	0.68	0.83	0.42	0.65	0.72
Main specific mechanism									
Category # 16	0.86	0.28	0.67	0.81	0.45	0.78	0.39	0.69	0.68
Broader response									
a) Category # 17a	0.94	0.61		0.84		0.67	0.61	0.77	0.71
b) Category # 17b	0.78	0.64		0.94		0.72	0.75	0.87	0.74

	B/NL	Ger	Fin	France	Gree	Ital	Pol	Spain	UK
Average of a–b	**0.86**	**0.63**	**0.78**	**0.89**	**0.77**	**0.70**	**0.68**	**0.82**	**0.73**
Benefit from euro									
a) Category # 18a	0.97	0.89		0.94		0.97	0.97	0.74	0.94
b) Category # 18b	0.67	0.97		0.92		0.97	0.97	0.82	0.88
Average of a–b	**0.82**	**0.93**	**1.00**	**0.93**	**0.98**	**0.97**	**0.97**	**0.78**	**0.91**
Harm from euro									
a) Category # 19a	0.78	0.92		1.00		0.78	0.97	0.73	0.78
b) Category # 19b	0.78	0.97		1.00		0.83	1.00	0.79	0.94
Average of a–b	**0.78**	**0.95**	**1.00**	**1.00**	**0.96**	**0.81**	**0.99**	**0.76**	**0.86**
Benefit from euro crisis									
a) Category # 20a	0.92	0.89		0.94		0.94	0.97	0.79	0.90
b) Category # 20b	1.00	0.92		1.00		1.00	1.00	0.81	1.00
Average of a–b	**0.96**	**0.91**	**1.00**	**0.97**	**0.98**	**0.97**	**0.99**	**0.80**	**0.95**
Harm from euro crisis									
a) Category # 21a	0.72	0.39		0.89		0.72	0.42	0.65	0.68
b) Category # 21b	0.56	0.47		0.94		0.69	0.56	0.75	0.60
Average of a–b	**0.64**	**0.43**	**0.53**	**0.91**	**0.64**	**0.70**	**0.49**	**0.70**	**0.64**
Geopolitical frame									
Category # 22	0.92	0.42	0.78	0.89	0.81	0.69	0.81	0.86	0.88

	B/NL	Ger	Fin	France	Gree	Ital	Pol	Spain	UK
Portrayal of European Commission									
Category # 23	0.92	0.58	0.67	0.77	0.75	0.61	0.50	0.79	0.72
Portrayal of European Central Bank									
Category # 24	0.97	0.67	0.83	0.81	0.86	0.89	0.83	0.78	0.78
Consequences of rescue measures									
Category # 25	0.92	0.58	0.78	0.81	0.94	0.75	0.72	0.85	0.76
Average of country									
Categories # 12 to 25	**0.87**	**0.71**	**0.77**	**0.86**	**0.81**	**0.80**	**0.79**	**0.77**	**0.82**

Appendix 5: Location of Dataset and National Reports

The Euro Crisis Research Project has made its full statistical dataset available to all researchers for further analysis. The dataset can be downloaded from: <http://reutersinstitute.politics.ox.ac.uk/publication/euro-crisis-media-coverage-and-perceptions-europe-within-eu>.

Individual descriptive data reports for each of the countries studied in the research project were produced. These provide basic frequency data and findings for all the variables. The reports are available at <http://reutersinstitute.politics.ox.ac.uk/publication/euro-crisis-media-coverage-and-perceptions-europe-within-eu>.

Index

RISJ/I.B.TAURIS PUBLICATIONS

CHALLENGES

Innovators in Digital News
Lucy Küng
ISBN: 978 1 78453 416 5

Journalism and PR: News Media and Public Relations in the Digital Age
John Lloyd and Laura Toogood
ISBN: 978 1 78453 062 4

Reporting the EU: News, Media and the European Institutions
John Lloyd and Cristina Marconi
ISBN: 978 1 78453 065 5

Women and Journalism
Suzanne Franks
ISBN: 978 1 78076 585 3

Climate Change in the Media: Reporting Risk and Uncertainty
James Painter
ISBN: 978 1 78076 588 4

Transformations in Egyptian Journalism
Naomi Sakr
ISBN: 978 1 78076 589 1

EDITED VOLUMES

Media, Revolution and Politics in Egypt: The Story of an Uprising
Abdalla F. Hassan
ISBN: 978 1 78453 217 8 (HB); 978 1 78453 218 5 (PB)

The Euro Crisis in the Media: Journalistic Coverage of Economic Crisis and European Institutions
Robert G. Picard (ed.)
ISBN: 978 1 78453 059 4 (HB); 978 1 78453 060 0 (PB)